Honoring the Circle:

Ongoing Learning from American

Indians on Politics and Society,

Volume III

Honoring the Circle:

Ongoing Learning from American

Indians on Politics and Society,

Volume III

What Would Be Good to Continue Learning
from Indigenous Peoples in Politics and Economics

Stephen M. Sachs, Donna K. Dial, Christina A. Clamp, Amy Fatzinger, Phyllis M. Gagnier

Waterside Productions

Printed in the United States of America

First Printing, 2020

ISBN-13: 978-1-949001-87-7   print edition
ISBN-13: 978-1-949001-88-4   ebook edition

Honoring the Circle, Volume I
ISBN-13: 978-1-949001-83-9

Honoring the Circle, Volume II
ISBN-13: 978-1-949001-85-3

Honoring the Circle, Volume III
ISBN-13: 978-1-949001-87-7

Honoring the Circle, Volume IV
ISBN-13: 978-1-949001-89-1

Waterside Productions
2055 Oxford Ave
Cardiff, CA 92007
www.waterside.com

OVERVIEW OF *HONORING THE CIRCLE*

Four Volumes on What the West Has Learned and Still Might Learn from American Indians on Politics and Society

Volume I begins with a prelude, which includes an introduction to *Honoring the Circle* and chapter 1, "Traditional American Indian Politics and Society," a look at how inclusive participatory American Indian societies functioned well. Part I "The Impact of American Indian Tradition on Western Politics and Society," spans over two volumes. It begins in this volume with an introduction and chapters 2 and 3. Chapter 2, "The Impact of American Indians on Politics and Society in the American Colonies and the United States from Contact to 1800," covers the mixture of Indian and European influences on early American settlers, and the Indian influences on major leaders and on the development of American political institutions. Chapter 3, "The Considerable Effect of Contact on Europe," examines the impact of reports of Indians in Europe on all political philosophies.

Volume II continues part I. Chapter 4, "The Continuing Impact of American Indian Ways in North America and the World in the Nineteenth Century and Beyond," covers Native impacts on the development of the American philosophy of pragmatism, the women's movement, the 1960s youth movement, and the environmental movement. The volume closes with a conclusion to part I.

Volume III begins part II, "The Continuing Relevance of American Indian Ways and Values," which discusses learning from Indians on living well together and with the Earth. It includes an introduction on changes in Western society toward Indigenous ways of seeing and other factors that make Indigenous thinking increasingly relevant for solving major contemporary problems. Chapter 5, "Applying American Indian Principles of Harmony and Balance to Renew the Politics of the Twenty-First Century," and chapter 6, "Returning to Reciprocity: Reconceptualizing Economics and Development," cover politics and economics, including how Indigenous values of inclusive participation and mutual support can provide for well working societies today, empowering an informed active citizenry with essentially equal political and economic power to participate on an equal basis, with participatory public and private organizations.

Volume IV continues part II. Chapter 7, "Indigenizing the Greening of the World: Applying an Indigenous Approach to Environmental Issues," discusses how holistic Indigenous thinking is necessary for dealing with environmental issues. Chapter 8, "Facilitating the Unfolding of the Circle: Indigenizing Education for the Twenty-First Century," suggests how education at every level can be improved with the Indigenous approach of empowering unique people to learn experientially, as whole people, living in community. The conclusion to *Honoring the Circle* discusses how continuing to integrate Indigenous ideas into our thinking provides a path for living well together and with the planet. It shows how this approach is increasingly at the forefront of political and social discussion.

TABLE OF CONTENTS

PART II

THE CONTINUING RELEVANCE OF AMERICAN INDIAN WAYS AND VALUES

Introduction to Part II
The Growing Relevance of
American Indian Tradition and
Values for the World of the
Twenty-First Century

Stephen M. Sachs and Amy Fatzinger

Increasingly, American Indian traditional ways and values have been becoming relevant for the world of the twenty-first century, particularly in the United States and the West in general. As is developed in the following chapters, this is partly because the traditional American Indian, and indeed, more broadly, the Indigenous way of approaching life and society, offer some ways of dealing with major problems that have arisen from Western approaches. Western culture and society have many important strengths that have made, and continue to make, extremely important contributions to the world. But they also have shortcomings. Consistent with Indigenous perspectives, no person, group, or society is perfect. We all have strengths and weakness, and because of that have a great deal to offer each other—as was set out in the first chapter of this volume, and is especially clearly laid out in part II's chapter 7, "Indigenizing the Greening of the World: Applying an Indigenous Approach to Environmental Issues."

Moreover, for more than a century, there has been an increasing movement in the mainstream of US and Western culture and society toward congruence with Indigenous ways of seeing. As part 1 of this book demonstrates, some of this is a result of American Indian, and to a lesser degree, other Indigenous impacts. However, most of this development is independent, relating to a number of factors, one of which is that Indigenous approaches and thinking are increasingly appropriate in developing circumstances. Interacting with the environment is often the most obvious of the innumerable relevant areas. A number of the cases of currently emerging situations that have increasing similarities in principle to what tribal societies faced, are taken up in the politics, economics, education, and environmental chapters. For example, in a world in which people of different cultures and backgrounds are interacting at a greater and greater rate, the problem of diversity becomes more and more akin to that faced by precontact Indian peoples, so that increasingly there has been a general movement (with numerous countermovements also occurring) away from seeking unity and harmony in society through sameness, and more toward the Indigenous approach of finding unity and harmony in diversity (as is discussed in the part II politics chapter).

Section 1: Ongoing Changes in American and Western Culture toward Congruence with the Indigenous

Stephen M. Sachs

Amid the confluence of causes, US, and more broadly Western, culture in many of its aspects has for a considerable time been evolving away from some of its traditional emphases toward congruence with Indigenous ways of seeing. This has been a general overall movement, but not a uniform one. Culture is never solid or monolithic, but always amorphous at every level. It is composed of shifting interacting and mutually influencing subcultures, groups that are yet to varying degrees independent, often overlapping, and sometimes conflicting. This is especially so in an increasingly complex world.

These subcultures have their own subsystems, down to the level of the discrete interrelating individuals whose own mental processes are diverse, not entirely consistent, and to differing degrees continually evolving with inner interactions dialoguing with external interactions. Even in 1945, Gebser was able to give an overview of the ongoing shift in his intellectual history of the West, saying that from some time in the later nineteenth century on, the West had been moving from a more hierarchical three-dimensional perspective toward an integrational way of seeing.[1] It is a movement from a time when among the many ways of seeing, one tended to dominate, toward a period in which no one way of seeing dominates. It is a movement toward integrating many perspectives. This is not an easy transformation to complete. The change inspires resistance by those fearing it, and involves moving through numerous polarities, as is partially discussed in chapter 5.

The cultural shift can be understood through some examples. For instance, in terms of Carl Jung's quaternion of the human ways of perceiving and processing information used in the Myers-Briggs system of personality typing,[2] in the mid-nineteenth century the predominant culture in the United States, and most of the West, emphasized intellect or logic first. This was followed by sensing (directly perceiving through the senses), which was particularly attributed to men, who were thought generally superior to women. This is evidenced by the considerable amount of sexuality in US advertising for many years. While feeling and intuition were the bottom two modes, generally considered much less valuable than logic, in popular thought they might be exercised often by women who were thought to be generally inferior. This configuration has changed as the dominant view, at least in US society, most notably since the 1950s. A number of cultural indicators indicate this. For instance, by the 1990s one began to see advertising for workshops on how to use one's intuition in business.

What was included in major network television programming and major motion pictures began to move from valuing logic over feeling and intuition, to involving intuition as a valuable way of obtaining information or knowledge. In the late 1960s this appeared in the more avant-garde series *Star Trek*, with a star ship captain being able to use intuition as a factor in making decisions, and with various characters and species having psychic abilities. Then in 1972 the TV program *The Sixth Sense* aired in which a college professor and his assistant investigate extrasensory perception.[3]

The theme of investigating the paranormal is carried much further in *The X-Files*, which ran from 1993 to 2002 and returned in 2016. This series ends up being much more about the paranormal than about using intuition, though that is still a factor, and the episodes certainly extend beyond championing intellect, or logic, as two FBI agents, one who believes in paranormal events and one who is a skeptic, investigate such occurrences. This was one of a number of programs that get into what many people call weird phenomena. This relates to the point about TV programs being indicators of culture change, but these shows are largely tangential to considerations of moving from an emphasis upon logic or intellect, to accepting intuition as legitimate, and coming to value an integration among the ways of seeing and processing information.[5] It may be that they indicate that once one begins to accept intuition, then the door is open to the whole field of psychic phenomena and beyond.

More to the immediate point is the 1981–1987 TV show *Seeing Things*, in which a reporter's visions of past events involving murders lead him to investigate and solve the crimes.[6] This is similar to the more recent NBC television program, *Medium*, loosely based on a real-life woman's experiences; the show ran from 2005 to 2011 and was nominated for three Golden Globe awards. The program featured a psychic who used her intuition to assist the Phoenix, Arizona–area district attorney's office find clues and evidence to solve crimes.[7]

Since the meaning of the intuitive information, perhaps bolstered by feeling, was often unclear, sensing and intellect needed to be used in observing and analyzing to make sense of intuitions. This resulted in finding and using the evidence to solve the crime and to construct an adequate court case for the prosecution. A program that extended more into the occult and that likely would not have made major network prime-time drama before the 1960s was CBS's *Ghost Whisperer*. It aired from September 23, 2005, to May 21, 2010, and involved a woman who had the ability to see and communicate with ghosts.[8] By the early 2010s a number of major networks began airing programs with foci beyond conventional logic, including several involving the contemporary living out of fairy tales, among them *Grimm*.

Similarly, for more than a century, and mostly more recently, US police departments have at times used psychics in searching for clues in tough, important cases. In 1984, psychic Rennie Wiley established an agency, The Dragon's Lair, to help police officers develop their own intuitional abilities to help them solve crimes.[9] British policeman Ken Charles wrote in his autobiography that he regularly used his intuition in order to see ways criminals might leave clues that he could find and use against them in court.[10] As in Charles's case, intuition is never relied on alone by police. It is a means for helping find hard evidence that with logic can be used to solve a crime and make a case in court. This is a good example of moving toward integration of ways of sensing and processing information: intuition combines with intellect or logic.

Meanwhile, women, who historically were considered inferior to men, have been moving toward a position of equality in most social areas.[11] Where traditionally, American Indian women enjoyed a balanced reciprocity with men in their different, but fairly autonomous gender roles across different Indigenous societies as discussed in chapter 1, the gender roles in patriarchal Western societies generally kept women in dependent, subservient positions with no autonomous rights. The women's movement, begun in the nineteenth century with much American Indian inspiration, as shown in chapter 4 of this volume, has increased not only women's property and political rights and participation, but also basically moved to change gender roles generally, including in the economy. In the religious-spiritual realm, a number of authors have stated this includes "the return of the divine feminine," with the feminine principle coming to equality with male principle, or in the tradition of the psychologist Carl Jung, "the breakdown of male-female polarization in our culture, and the cultural shift towards androgyny."[12] This includes a movement toward equality of men and women in religious and spiritual practices, which has been happening in many religious and spiritual organizations. The United Methodist Church, for example, authorized full clergy rights for women in 1956, and noted in 2006 that achieving fully equal status was an ongoing process. Much has been accomplished, but much still needs to be done.

The 2000 *Book of Discipline of The United Methodist Church* does indeed affirm "women and men to be equal in every aspect of their common life." Sadly, in 2006 there are still subtle and open obstacles standing in the way and preventing women from the path leading toward God's purpose of wholeness and inclusion. Women continue to be stereotyped and encouraged to assume roles that are, by tradition, "safe" and correct for them. Although inclusive language is encouraged throughout the United Methodist Church, there continues to be a need for structural inclusiveness. This requires more than just changing our language; it requires changing our attitudes as to what roles women may serve in building the church.[13]

That this is part of a worldwide movement was exemplified in November 2014 by the Church of England for the first time approving women to become bishops.[14]

The Move toward More Holistic Spiritual and Religious Practice

The change in the spiritual status and roles of women in religion and spirituality, towards a more Indigenous way of understanding, is part of an ongoing development in the entire religious and spiritual field in the United States and the West. It is a movement away from just an intellectual, toward a broader experiential, approach, which, with variations and exceptions, has been ongoing since the nineteenth century. One aspect of this is that there has been a huge increase in the interest and participation of Americans in non-Western religions and spiritual activity that does not relate to their ethnic background or direct cultural heritage.

Among numerous others, the Hindu tradition began with a few teachers of the Vedantic philosophy active in the United States late nineteenth century, expanding by the early twenty-first century to numerous varied active groups, including The Himalayan Institute founded by Swami Rama, the Siddha Yoga global community founded by Swami Muktananada, and Ananda Marga a global spiritual and social service organization founded in 1955 by Shrii Shrii Anandamurti (Prabhat Ranjan Sarkar). Transcendental Meditation (TM), founded by Maharishi Mahesh Yogi, with a major center in Fairfield, Iowa, has become widely popular in the United States and far beyond, as a health as well as a spiritual practice.[15] The various Buddhist traditions, including those of Tibet, South East Asia, and Zen of Japan, have perhaps the largest number of adherents in the United States,[16] with a Tibetan Buddhist university, The Naropa Institute, in Boulder, CO.

Sufism was first brought to the West by Hazrat Inayat Khan and his brother and cousin, from India, first to the United States in 1910, and later to Europe, as an active universalist spiritual tradition that recognizes the underlying unity of all spiritual paths and the beauty of each. This is similar to the Baha'i religion which arose in Persia in the 1860s and is now worldwide, including in the United States. Today, Hazrat Inayat's tradition encompasses at least seven related orders or groups worldwide, including in the US, while several traditional Sufi Orders are active across the West, including in the US. Among them, centered in New York City, is a Westernized branch of the Jerrahi Dervishes, whose Grand Sheikh is in Istanbul, Turkey. The leader of the Westernized branch is a woman, Sheikha Fariha. This contrasts with the tradition in the East, where Sufi Orders have been almost universally led by men.[17]

Much of the rise of non-Western religion in the West in recent decades has been essentially "old age" in spiritual terms, though often with adaptations to the people and culture involved with it. Some of the relatively recent religious-spiritual development has involved a rise of "new age" spirituality, of many people seeking spirituality that they did not find in the tradition religious institutions.[18] However, many of traditional religious institutions have been changing also. That many Americans have been searching for something different in their spiritual life has registered in polls.

A 2006 study by the Pew Forum on Religion and Public Life found that more than a quarter of those in the US had left their childhood religion for another, or no religion, and 44 percent had switched denominations.[19] One percent identified as Buddhist, but this understates the number of people interested in or doing at least some Buddhist practice, as most of this is undertaken without a formal religious affiliation, in part because to a considerable extent Buddhism does not define itself as a religion but as a way of seeking and being.

More telling is a 2012 survey by the Pew Religion and Public Life Project in which a fifth of those polled, and a third of those under thirty years of age, said that they were not religiously affiliated (up from just over 15 percent in five years, to the highest level in the project's polling), with nearly 37 percent of that group saying they were "spiritual" but not "religious."[20] This was 7 percent of all Americans, a larger group than those who identified as Jews, Muslims, Mormons, Eastern Orthodox, Atheists, or agnostics. Of the 46 million US adults unaffiliated with any formal religion, 68 percent said they believe in God, 21 percent say they pray daily, and 58 percent said they often feel a deep connection with nature and the Earth.

The spiritual orientation that has been occurring includes not only a shift out of just intellect to encompass intuition; it has become experiential and expressive in other ways as well (depending on the individual, bringing in some degree both feeling and sensing). This can be seen in the rise of participatory spiritual dance with at least some focus on prayer and spiritual experience being in the body (not just the mind). This is the case with Dances of Universal Peace, focusing on the underlying unity of all spiritual paths and the beauty of each, which grew out of the Hazrat Inayat Khan tradition of universalist Sufism, but which has developed a broader constituency.[21] The dances are undertaken to the chants of the world's spiritual traditions. At least among their esoteric participants, these dances have practices, including movement, which engage all the ways of perceiving and processing information. Including movement and engaging the whole person is also an aspect of a number of non-Western spiritual paths that have become popular in the West. For instance, Hinduism traditionally began with hatha yoga, which involved gaining mastery of the body, including the breath, before beginning the higher spiritual practices, and some of the chanting involves movement. Many varieties of Buddhism employ walking meditations. Many of the practices of most Sufi Orders involve motion related to the meaning, including the Whirling of the Mevlevi Order, which is a way of emptying in preparation for the experience of being united with the Beloved. Thus much spiritual work is carried on in, or through, the body, which is also true of many American Indian spiritual practices, many of whom have practices involving movement, which in English is often called "dance", though that may not be a good translation of its name in the Native tradition.[22]

A contemporary spiritual practice that clearly involves the body is Five Rhythm Dance, "a dynamic movement practice—a practice of being in your body—that ignites creativity, connection, and community" (5rhythms.com/gabrielle-roths-5rhythms/). Five Rhythm Dance, which goes under various names, including "dance church," and with some sessions called "swear your prayers," is seen by many participants as a spiritual practice. Participants undertake their own dance as they are moved to move, respecting the space and wishes of others. Sometimes one dances with one or more others when mutually desired. The facilitator often indicates a theme for the session, and the community comes together in a closing circle where all are invited to share their experience.

STEPHEN M. SACHS

The Expanding Mainstream Interest in Indians

An interesting aspect of the shift in US and other Western spirituality, which is clearly an impact of American Indian tradition, has been a growing interest in American Indian ways since World War II. Some of this was inspired by John Neihardt's controversial *Black Elk Speaks: Being the Life Story of a Holy Man of the* Oglala Sioux, as told through John G. Neihardt,[23] first published in 1932, and many other sources. An indication is the publication of a huge number of popular books and recordings on American Indian culture and spirituality, as well as several very popular series of American Indian crime novels since then.[24] Though a small percentage of the US population, a significantly large number of Americans who are not Indians have become involved in American Indian ceremonies. (This has caused controversy in some American Indian communities, including concerns that some improperly trained non-Indian, "plastic shamans" are making money leading ceremonies for non-Indians and teaching Indian ways.) At least one non-Indian has been invited to lead a major Indian ceremony, while quite a number of established Indian leaders have lectured and taught Indian ways to general audiences.[25]

Academia has also evidenced a growing interest in American Indians, especially since the 1970s. Books, including this one, and courses, have abounded in many fields, including on the contributions of American Indians to Western politics and society. As author Bruce Johansen, one of the early expanders of this interest, commented in a May 8, 2016, e-mail to Stephen Sachs:

> The idea of studying Native contributions to our ideology is becoming quite popular. I think I wrote about the large conference in India last December. Now one is being organized in Brazil for September 2017. I received word last week that a similar theme is being developed this September at Notre Dame.

If I had a time machine, I would like to take a ride back to 1976, when, as a beginning doctoral student at the University of Washington in the history of communication, I broached to my dissertation committee the idea of studying the influence of the Haudenosaunee (Iroquois) Confederacy on the ideology of democracy through Benjamin Franklin. The idea came to me from the Choctaw filmmaker Phil Lucas, who recommended I read a 1952 essay by Felix Cohen in The American Scholar. Most of my committee members thought I was crazy.

The growth in mainstream interest in the Indigenous of the Americas has been strongly reflected in literature and popular culture, to which Indians have increasingly contributed.

Section 2: American Indians and Literature, Cinema, and Popular Culture

Amy Fatzinger

As Betty Booth Donohue's opening to part I, "The Indianization of American Literature," details, evidence of Native influences in American literature is indisputable. American Indians were an almost unavoidable subject in early works of American literature, although most writers—including Herman Melville, Nathaniel Hawthorne, and Henry David Thoreau—portrayed American Indian characters as having the limited options of civilization or extinction.[26] American Indians are similarly linked to the origins of American cinema, as images of Native people were among the first moving images Thomas Edison recorded on film.[27] American Indians have continued to remain a popular subject in literature, cinema, and scholarship; by 1997 they were the subject of at least 30,000 books and they have appeared in several thousand films.

Until recently, the vast majority of media representations of American Indians were created by non-Indians; of the thirty thousand books, about 90 percent are authored by non-Indians, and on screen they are most often stereotypically portrayed as savages or noble savages in Westerns.[28]

Although there were a few early American Indian writers and filmmakers who helped shape America's print and visual narrative cultures, contemporary literature and cinema produced by American Indian authors and filmmakers is redefining Native participation in, and resistance to, American culture by first and foremost shifting toward self-representation, which is both an act of sovereignty[29] and key to positioning Native knowledge and experiences in broader American contexts.

N. Scott Momaday's 1969 Pulitzer Prize for *House Made of Dawn*[30] marked a significant turning point in American Indian literature. While texts by non-Native authors that objectify, stereotype, and exploit American Indian people and cultures still abound, *House Made of Dawn* proved to be a gateway for other Native writers. Along with Momaday, writers such as Leslie Marmon Silko, James Welch, Gerald Vizenor, and Simon Ortiz firmly established a place for Native voices in the canon of American literature. Others soon followed, including Louise Erdrich, Joy Harjo, Linda Hogan, and Sherman Alexie among many others. Momaday has argued that "the native voice in American literature is indispensable. There is no true literary history of the United States without it,"[31] and Susan Power concurs:

Native peoples, and their stories and histories are not a social studies unit of an interesting sub-category of American Literature to be haphazardly included in courses such as "Literatures of the Outsider in America," if at all. We are American history, we are American literature. Every track and trace of the American experience runs through our communities, our cultures.[32]

Indeed major anthologies of American literature, including the Norton and the Bedford,[33] now include examples of American Indian oratory and works by contemporary writers such as Momaday, Silko, and Erdrich. American Indian writers have continued to gain recognition in both Native and mainstream literary circles; Erdrich's *The Round House*,[34] for example won several awards, including the 2012 National Book Award, and Alexie's *The Absolutely True Diary of a Part-Time Indian*[35] won numerous awards including the 2007 National Book Award for Young People's Literature, and the 2008 Boston Globe-Horn Book Award.

America's fascination with American Indians as narrative subjects is even more evident in its cinematic history. American Indians appeared in the majority of some 7,000 Westerns;[36] such representations reveal far more about America's imaginary interpretations[37] of Native people than about Native people themselves. Although revisionist Westerns such as *Little Big Man*[38] (dir. Arthur Penn, 1970) portrayed Native people more sympathetically, they most often continued to tell stories about Native people from an outsider's point of view (in terms of both the films' directors and protagonists) and most Native characters were played by non-Native actors.

American Indians and their histories continued to be appropriated and romanticized well into the 1990s, particularly in the popular historical films produced in and around America's Quincentenary celebration in 1992, including *Dances With Wolves*[39] (dir. Kevin Costner, 1990); a new adaptation of James Fenimore Cooper's *Last of the Mohicans*[40] (dir. Michael Mann, 1992); and Disney's *Pocahontas*[41] (dir. Mike Gabriel and Eric Goldberg, 1995).

In 1998, two feature films revolutionized Native cinema in the United States, *Smoke Signals*[42] (dir. Chris Eyre) and *Naturally Native*[43] (dir. Valerie Red-Horse). *Smoke Signals* is celebrated as the first feature film written, directed, acted, and produced by Native people, and *Naturally Native* was written, co-directed, acted, produced, and funded by Native people. *Smoke Signals* and *Naturally Native* both focus on Native protagonists and communities, and all Native roles are acted by Native actors. They precipitated additional films[44] acted and directed by Native directors, and set new standards even for non-Native directors who work in American Indian cinema. According to Sherman Alexie, "Movies have never allowed us to be fully functioning members of the national consciousness and society" but *Smoke Signals* marks a departure from this problem and, as Amanda J. Cobb suggests, "challenge[s] pop culture by creating pop culture."[45]

Some noteworthy examples of expressions of cultural sovereignty through cinema since 1998 include *Atanarjuat: The Fast Runner*,[46] a cinematic interpretation of an Inuit oral narrative told entirely in the Inuit language (dir. Zacharias Kunuk, 2001) and *Milepost 398*,[47] the first film created by an all Navajo cast and crew (dir. Shonie De La Rosa and Andee De La Rosa, 2007). To date, however, *Smoke Signals* remains the Native film with the widest release and is the subject of extensive critical scholarship.

Despite these significant developments American Indians' self-representation in both literature and cinema, representations of Native people in American popular culture remain a mix of lingering stereotypes and sovereign expressions of cultural identity. Caricatures of American Indians are still present in Thanksgiving decorations, Halloween costumes, and mascots for sports teams, and films that recycle old stereotypes—such as *Avatar*[48] (dir. James Cameron, 2009) and *The Lone Ranger*[49] (dir. Gore Verbinski, 2013)—draw far bigger crowds than Native-produced media.

On television, too, American Indians remain a recurring topic, but despite some positive developments such as Adam Beach's role on *Law and Order: Special Victims Unit* from 2007–2008, American Indians have had few opportunities for self-representation;[50] Elaine Mile's role on *Northern Exposure* from 1990–1995, for example, was the "only prominent female Native television character of the twentieth century in the United States."[51] Indigenous-controlled media outlets in other countries, however, including Canada, Australia, and New Zealand, offer hope that more opportunities will be forthcoming in the United States. The first American Indian television station in the United States, First Nations Experience (FNX) launched in San Bernardino in 2011, and Native Nations disseminate information within their communities and beyond through social media and numerous Native-owned radio stations and newspapers, including the prominent online news source *Indian Country Today*. FNX began to be more available nationwide, in 2014 through PBS channels.

Meanwhile, American Indian innovators continue to develop media that is culturally relevant as well as more broadly impactful, such as the internationally recognized Iñupiaq video game *Never Alone (Kisima Inŋitchuŋa)*.[52] Thus American Indians in literature, film, and TV, since the mid-twentieth century, have had a growing, yet still limited, role in assisting in moving many strands of American, and wider, culture toward more Indigenous ways of seeing and being.

In Europe, there has been a huge interest in American Indian ways stemming in part from Indians coming to Europe to perform in wild west shows from the 1800s to 1935. This interest and perception of Indians was greatly augmented by the novels giving favorable treatment to Indians of Karl May, who lived from 1842 to 1912.[53] So popular were May's Indian novels that he has sold more books than any other German author. In Germany alone, in the mid-1990s there were an estimated one and a half million Indian hobbyists, making Indian regalia and taking part in ceremonies.

When author Stephen Sachs gave a lecture in Prague, Czech Republic at the Naprstovo Muzeum—the beyond Europe ethnographic museum—on the Lakota tradition of the Pipe, some fifty people attended. As a result he was invited by Czech Indian hobbyists to the house of "our chief." The walls were covered by very well beaded regalia and other items they had made. He was shown a photograph of one of two Indian summer camps in the Czech Republic, with a circle of twenty-four teepees. At the many ceremonies he had attended he had never seen so many teepees. At those ceremonies, he has observed numerous people watching and participating from Holland, France, Germany, Switzerland, and

Finland. Indeed, at one Lakota Sun Dance in New Mexico, most of the singers on that occasion were French.

Going the other way, every summer a number of American Indian spiritual leaders go to Europe to lecture, teach, and lead ceremonies. This is an interesting impact of American Indian tradition in Europe, with likely cultural effects beyond itself. But it also is indicative of cultural needs and changes in the West.

Section 3: At the Heart of Western Culture, the Cutting Edge of Physics: Western Science Is Finally Catching Up with American Indian Tradition

Stephen M. Sachs

A major aspect of Western culture is science. Science is both reflective of it as a whole and a major influence on its other aspects. Since the nineteenth century, Western science, and especially physics has moved from a mechanical model of the universe to seeing reality more as a thought. Increasingly in recent years, Western science, as well as Western culture as a whole, is coming closer to viewing reality as American Indians traditionally have perceived it.[54] This is particularly true of contemporary physics. The connection was enunciated early, when it was said that Einstein's theory of relativity, including the application of the Lorenz Transformation showing that the rate of passage of time varies according to (or is relative to) the speed of an object, was understood by only a few of the world's physicists, and the Hopi Indians.[55]

Prior to Einstein, Western physics looked at time as a constant flow—a medium of linear measurement. Traditionally, the Hopi, and other Native people, see time more relatively, "not as a liner measurement, but as a relationship between events. These events reflect the intensity of the observer, for time varies with each observer."[56] This is very close to the popular explanation given, early on, for the new scientific view of time in relativity. When one enjoys oneself, time appears to move much faster than when one does not enjoy an experience.

Another aspect of current scientific thought about time which has come to approach Indigenous American conceptions is the idea that the measurement of time in terms of natural cycles is relevant to place. A January 23, 2007 article in *The New York Times* science section, Natalie Angier, "Making Sense Of Time, Earthbound and Otherwise,"[57] discussed the various ways of measuring time in terms of natural cycles, from the very smallest particles (such as the 10^{-22} of a second that it takes an electron to orbit a proton) to the very long cycles of the cosmos as a whole. Angier noted that in between were the cycles of rotation of the planet around its star, in our case the sun, and of the planet on its axis, which with their relative constancy on Earth for the past four billion years:

> have set the dials and counters of virtually all of life. Elsewhere in the solar system are other worlds taking care of their business, working their quirky times. Saturn, for example, spins as snappily as it accessorizes, completing a day in 10 1/2 hours; but being almost ten times farther than the sun, it needs 30 years to finish its own. Mercury, by contrast, orbits the Sun in just 88 days, but rotates at a miserly one and a half times during an entire mercurial "year," which means that the side facing the sun has a chance to bake at 700 degrees Fahrenheit, while the half staring out into space turns as cold and miserable as that poor little demotee from the planetary pantheon, Pluto.

The Native relativity of time and place is more detailed than the emerging Western view. For instance, the Hopi year is marked by a series of nine precisely astronomically timed ceremonies[58] that would have a different timing in a different location—or totally other ceremonies would be held—because of differences of place.

Moreover, place is sacred, which Western science is, at most, barely coming to approach. As scholar Gregory Cajete states:

Particular places are endowed with special energy that may be used but must be protected. This sentiment extends from the notion of sacred space and the understanding that that the Earth itself is sacred. The role of people is to respect and maintain the inherent order and harmony of the land.[59]

The relativity of place, and the relation of place (and time) to the observer, that is fundamental in Native views, has been an emerging element of post Newtonian physics. Two observers, traveling at different speeds, may see the same event differently, and simultaneously correctly—without contradicting each other—from their separate locations.[60] In the Indigenous way of seeing, each place has its own quality and perspective. But it is critical that each of the separate places only have meaning in their relation to the whole, composed of all the other places. That everything is related is central to Native cultures. The Lakota, for example, say, *Mitakue Oyasun:* "all my relations—amen!" when completing a prayer or passing a sacred object. This agrees with Indigenous views from around the world, as *Mitakue Oyasun*, like the Hindu Om (representing the prime sound in the universe, in which everything is vibration), when fully stated, contains all the vowels,[61] as does the Muskogee word for the creator, "iyabileyuppe."[62]

For Indigenous people, there is an overarching unity, founded in interdependent diversity. Everything is alive, even the rocks,[63] though different kinds of beings have different energies. We are all relatives, and need to treat each other as such. Every being, human or otherwise, has its place in each of the various circles of life. For human beings, these circles of relationship extend from the family, through the band or tribe, to the land in which they live ... and ultimately to the Earth as a whole. This has social and behavioral implications for people, as is developed in chapter 1, and applied to contemporary society in the chapters that follow this introduction. The core value is that of respect. Each person, each being, has a perspective to offer on the larger whole that cannot be understood from just a single view point, or even several limited perspectives. In this way of seeing, everyone needs to have a say and have their concerns included on any question that effects them.[64] The synergy of this inclusiveness leads to better decisions and greater harmony.

Harmony, balance in life within and without, is the goal of the individual and the community, for Native peoples. But in a dynamic and evolving world, life continually falls out of balance, and harmony in inner and outer relationships needs to be restored. For the Diné (Navajo), for instance, there are many healing ceremonies for different circumstances all of which involve a restoring of living according to the prime value, *hozo*,[65] most often translated as beauty, encompassing harmony and balance. When interpersonal relationships fall out of balance, then a facilitation is needed among the concerned parties to restore a balanced relationship. This process continues today on the Navajo Nation in its Peacemaking Courts.[66] This is not only an internal personal, and interpersonal social concern. Attaining, restoring, and maintaining harmony are physical concerns as well. The physical is just a different aspect of an integrated, interrelated whole. For example, "In the Muscogee Creek cosmos, all things consist of particular combinations of body, mind and spirit. When these are not in harmony, one is truly lost and healing becomes necessary for the entity to continue."[67]

In a more limited way, the interconnectedness of everything is now a major element of contemporary physics. Since Einstein wrote with Nathan and Podolsky in 1935,[68] it has been noted that quantum mechanics, on its face, indicates that there can be instantaneous linkage between two widely separated events with subatomic particles. More recently, it has been shown in the laboratory that intervening space does not isolate particles from each other, so that even extremely widely separated particles can act simultaneously as if they were in direct contact.[69] Even over tremendously long distances, Greene, *The Fabric of the Cosmos* says:

Something that happens over here, can be entwined with something that happens over there even if nothing travels from here to there—and even if there isn't enough time for anything, even light [which travels at a constant speed of 186,000 miles per second], to travel between the events.[70]

Moreover, in contemporary physics, Greene says:

The weirdness of relativity arises because of our personal experience of space and time differs from the experience of others. It is a weirdness born of comparison. We are forced to concede that our view of reality is but one among many— an infinite number, in fact—which all fit together in the seamless whole of spacetime.[71]

... the central principle of special relativity is that no observational vantage point is singled out over any other... [just as for American Indians all of the places in the circle must be given equal respect].[72]

The extent to which the interconnectedness exhibited among particles, together with the "seamless whole of spacetime" of contemporary physics approach the wholeness and interrelatedness of Native views, is arguable. But there are at least three additional points that increase the extent of convergence. First, in recent years the view of Western physics that most of space is empty has been in the process of being replaced with a conception, somewhat reminiscent of the older Western idea that space is composed of ether, that space is filled with an ocean of energy fields, called Higgs fields, forming a Higgs ocean. Thus if all of space, all matter and energy, are within an all pervading Higgs ocean (which is standard current physics theory, but has yet to be supported experimentally), then there is a unifying container of all that is.[73]

A key part of the theoretical reason for believing that there is a Higgs ocean, stems from the second point of the increasing Native worldview—contemporary physics convergence, that it appears necessary to complete the symmetry of the universe suggested by the set of symmetries for which there is solid experimental evidence. Symmetry has been becoming increasingly important in physics.[74] A symmetry exists when an object can be subject to a manipulation with no effect on its appearance (such as rotating a sphere does not change how it looks to an observer), or when a law of physics operates equally in different places (the equality of perspectives is such a symmetry). "The reason that these symmetry operations are so useful lies in the fact that they are closely related to 'conservation laws.' Whenever a process in the particle world displays a certain symmetry, there is a measurable quantity which is 'conserved;' a quantity that remains constant during the process. These quantities provide elements of consistency in the complex dance of subatomic matter and are thus ideal to describe the particle interactions."[75] Symmetry has now become so prominent, that, "From our modern perspective symmetries are the foundation from which laws spring."[76] The growth of the importance of symmetry in physics then begins to touch Indigenous American concepts of balance, harmony, and beauty.

Particles, Fields, and Current Physics— Traditional Native Convergence

The third, and very much related point of the increasing physics—Native view connection, involves the current understanding in physics of the nature of particles. A subatomic particle, such as a photon, is in fact both a particle and a wave.[77] The wave aspect of a particle in motion is such that the location of the particle can be in a multitude of places, with a probability of its location being in any one position (which, shortly, will bring us to the next point). The wave itself extends everywhere. Everything concrete that we know of either is a particle, or is composed of particles, all of whose waves extend everywhere. Hence, without getting into the speculative question of just what that involves, for which Western science does not yet have any firm answer, it is clear, that at a minimum, all the waves overlap. This implies an interconnection: a relationship. To what extent this agrees with what a Lakota means in saying *Mitakue Oyasun* (all my relations) is not yet discernable. But there is now at least some minimum point of congruence that did not exist prior to the rise of quantum mechanics.

In contemporary physics, the location of a subatomic particle is variable in principle, and can only be said to be fixed through a measurement that cannot simultaneously measure the particle's momentum (Heisenberg's uncertainty principle). Indeed, the defined location is the result of the observer's interaction with the particle in the process of measurement (which means that we are in a relationship with everything we observe!). As Werner Heisenberg states, "What we observe is not nature itself, but nature exposed to our method of questioning."[78] In this view, the center of the universe is nowhere, which means that it is everywhere in a universe in which everything is interrelated with everything else. This is the resulting principle of "nonlocality."[79]

Nonlocality and the Seventh Direction

Nonlocality has a correspondence in American Indian ways of seeing, with the Lakota, for example, in the "seventh direction." Speaking two dimensionally, there are the Four Directions, the four cardinal points in the Western compass, though the term is sometimes used to refer to all the directions. One needs to add above and below, Sky and Earth, to make the "big six." Then there is the seventh direction, which is within everything, and surrounds everything—it is everywhere. It is the center of the circle, the center of the world, or universe or all that is. Thus, wherever a Sun Dance may be held, the circle of the world is recreated in the ceremonial circle with the Tree of Life in the focal point, the center of the world, where spiritual energy made present by the ceremony enters the world. Arthur Amiotte states, that when the four sacred leaders of the Sun Dance come to that moment in the preparation for the ceremony where they sanctify the center of the ceremonial circle where the Sun Dance Tree of Life will be placed:

> They have arrived at that potential place that will become the center of the world. First sanctifying the knife over burning sage to dispel evil, then resanctifying it in the smoke of sweetgrass to bring in the good influence, the earth is cut in a sacred mandala. This is the first of the "mellow earth alters" that release the potential of the earth. For this is where the axis mundi will be placed. The tree of life, the connection between the masculine powers of the zenith and the feminine powers of the nadir; that means that principle, that pipe, that body, that avenue through which the sacredness of the world will be connected, and to which man in awesome sacrifice will be connected so that he, too, may participate in the bringing down and bringing up and the sharing of the sacred power of the *wakan* [sacred]. In a cross formation, the lines are cut in the four cardinal directions to reestablish this place as indeed the center of the world. Sacred tobacco and sacred paint are placed in these cuts.[80]

Similarly, in a Lakota Pipe ceremony or talking circle, wherever it may be held, whoever holds the Pipe or the talking stick is the center of the circle. Joseph Campbell reports that, in what was recorded in *Black Elk Speaks*, Black Elk states, "In my vision, I saw myself on the central mountain of the world, Mount Harmon, [Harney Peak]." But he added, "The center of the world is everywhere."[81]

The Sun Dance Ceremony is held annually because in the interactions of life the world gets out of balance, and so there must be a return to the center, a renewal of the world, a renewal of harmony and balance. As the Chaudhuris tell us of the Muskogee tradition, harmony, balance, beauty, peace is not automatic, one has to work continually to attain and maintain it at every level.

Given the unpredictable elements of nature and the quirks of human nature, the search for harmony takes sustained effort in all social institutions.[82]

Hence, in personal inner work and in all relationships, including with the natural environment and all its life forms, one continually participates in processes for returning to harmony. Each Native culture did this in a different manner, but almost all followed the same general principles, at least until they became too large or events put them sufficiently out of balance.[83]

The Indigenous View of Uncertainty and Chaos or Complexity Theory

For Native people the world was seen as exceedingly complex, with many uncertainties. The Ojibwa, for instance, saw reality as fluid and circumstantial.

The successful hunter and power seeker kept his options open. An aspect of one's environment could shift form at any moment, act unusually, reach out for one's attention and reveal its hidden identity. Stones might speak, lightning could strike from a cloudless sky and winds might kick up from a weird direction. Through this force field of subjective actions, one maneuvered with caution.[84]

Though, perhaps strongly stated to make its point concerning a Native view of uncertainty, this comment is not just about relations with the other than human environment, but involves human interaction as well. In a complex world with many uncertainties, it is wise to have available a number of strategies and tactics. One should begin, however, with hospitality and peace building diplomacy when interacting with strangers, or with those who may be powerful, and hence dangerous. And if one is to be in conflict with one party, it is a good idea to keep peaceful relations with others, not only to avoid having to fight on multiple fronts, but because one never knows who may become an ally or a peacemaker, when needed. Scott Pratt writes that this was precisely the view of the Narragansett, and one that greatly influenced the development of Roger Williams's ideas on tolerance.[85] It is a pragmatic, experiential basis for the principle of respect, and the inclusiveness that follows from it.

In a complex and changing world, one never knows from where resources, such as ideas and information, useful assistance, or tangible goods may come from. Thus facilitating good, inclusive relations is advantageous. This can be seen in the career of a very successful contemporary Indian activist, LaDonna Harris (Comanche). Harris was the founder and first president of Oklahomans for Indian Opportunity in 1965, and of Americans for Indian Opportunity in 1970. As the wife and political ally of Democratic senator from Oklahoma Fred Harris, she was in a position to facilitate among and for Indians on many issues in the federal government. Position merely provided the potential for opportunity. Personal stature and ability transformed that potential into success. Harris, acting with traditional Indian inclusiveness, was able to bring all but the most extreme people together on Indigenous issues, to develop mutual understanding and find common ground. In addition, when she met people of ability who supported her goals, she would make note of them. Later, when their perspective or talents were useful for the task at hand, she would involve them in the work. For about a decade, she and a few other Natives, mostly women, were the prime catalysts in gaining Indian advances in Congress and the national executive branch, so that in 1979 the *Ladies Home Journal* declared her the Woman of the Year and the Decade.[86]

In a complex world, major developments often begin with a small action. Relatively weak actors may have the power to initiate change if the conditions are right for it at a particular moment. Traditional knowledge of that has guided some Indigenous activists to make connections, which might eventually provide important opportunities, and to remain conscious of the need to act when leverage moments occur.

For example, Vine Deloria Jr., a former president of the National Congress of the American Indians, reported that there were a few occasions on which he could suggest to a member of Congress, and get put into a bill, as high paid lobbyists are often able to do, a small change such as adding "and Indian Tribes" after, "authorizing States," when there was no opposition to the proposal.[87] He also stated that it was not a bad thing being a "token Indian," if one remembered who one was. As the sole Native on the board of what later became the National Museum of the American Indian, Deloria saw a leverage moment in a board meeting just before a press conference launching an important exhibit opening. This enabled him to force the appointment of more Indians to the board, under threat of his embarrassing the board with a statement at the press conference. This began the turnover of board members that soon brought Native people into the majority, setting the stage for the eventual development of the National Museum. Deloria was always careful in choosing his battles. While criticizing many anthropologists' actions involving Native people, he did not simultaneously complain about historians, though he had similar concerns about many historians' treatment of Indians.

The Indian approach to complexity and uncertainty is very close to chaos theory, and related complexity theory, which have arisen in the last 30 years in physics and other fields. The social science versions of it have developed at the same time that traditional Western categories and academic field boundaries have been becoming more permeable, and Western thinking has moved toward the holism that characterizes traditional Native American understanding.[88]

Indeed, chaos theory itself is an interdisciplinary development. That development, however, was slowed in its early stages because one of its key developers, meteorologist Edward Lorenz, was only able to publish his findings in meteorological journals.[89] Chaos or complexity theory, in physics often called quantum chaos, is a methodology for studying complex systems with dynamics that are non-linear and too great to measure. It is a method for holistically looking at a system when it is not practical to reduce it to its component parts, which is the traditional main thrust of Western science, including physics. At first such systems appear to be in chaos, or beyond description, including mathematical description. But further analysis shows the system to be explained more simply, often by finding fractals (the term derived from fractional): any image that displays the attribute of self-similarity. This often means that a simpler equation or explanation may duplicate the complex relations of a larger system.

In addition, complex systems in chaos and complexity theory often involve "the butterfly effect." This is the long term significant impact on atmospheric conditions that might be caused by such a minute action as a butterfly flapping its wings, at that tipping point when conditions are open to major change from an extremely small action. It is where a seemingly insignificantly small action or variation can result in very large impacts, ultimately changing the state of a system, as occurred in the appointment of Vine Deloria to a museum board, ultimately transforming that institution.

String Theory, Grand Unified Theory, and Indigenous Views of a Unified Universe: The Song of the Creator

One of the applications in physics of chaos theory has been to deal with the rough and seemingly random quantum jitters that appear in the smallest of known subatomic levels. Working at that level has recently given rise to super string theory, according to which the smallest particles are actually vibrating strings of energy.[90] This would seem to be an extension of Einstein's realization, with $E=MC^2$, that energy and matter are interchangeable, and it is consistent with the ancient Hindu belief, long widely held in the east, that everything is energy, and everything is vibration. It also resonates with the view of many American Indians that singing is a sacred expression of being.[91] Perhaps, one could say that the world—the cosmos—is the song of the creator.

Out of string theory has come a debated development in physics, of grand unified theory (GUT), in which a unified explanation of the universe, working with what is currently accepted about its subatomic levels, is possible, if one posits that reality exists in a number of dimensions beyond the three, and four if one includes time, that we are normally aware of in everyday life.[92] This set of theories, and proposed theories, which would include the possibility of phenomena such as teleportation and worm holes, allowing travel or transportation across space (and conceivably time) through a dimension beyond the normal four, would be consistent with, and provide a necessary condition for (though other such conditions are conceivable) the kinds of spirit phenomena and reported powers of Indian medicine (or holy) people presented in Vine Deloria Jr., *The World We Used to Live In: Remembering the Powers of the Medicine Men.*[93]

Is Everything Living, Including the Earth? Some in Biology Converge on the Indigenous View

Perhaps more important, grand unified theory does provide a deeper basis in physics for viewing all that is as a unified whole, in which everything is related. Current GUT theories do not yet encompass the hypothesis that everything is alive according to traditional biological definitions, though GUT does see the universe as a self-sustaining system, composed of other self-sustaining systems—for example the Earth—which in some scientific views is the essence of life. Moreover, unlike the nineteenth-century view of the universe as a more or less static machine, contemporary physics understands the universe as dynamic and evolving, through a number of stages (which is also the case with living organisms).[94] This has very rough parallels in the view of some Native peoples, such as the Hopi, who say that life has been developing through a number of worlds.[95]

For the idea that everything, including the earth, is alive, to approach being considered seriously in Western science, one needs to look to biology. There, one can find that for the last few decades, some mainstream biologists have been discussing the idea that the living matter on the earth functions as an interacting system, as if the planet were a living organism: the Gaia hypothesis.[96] Others on the edge of biology are beginning to propose related theories. For example, Rupert Sheldrake, presented a very controversial hypothesis that natural morphogenetic fields which help the coming into being and ordering of embryos and other systems, among their effects is "formative causation." According to this hypothesis, that if a member of a species of animals learns to do something, other, even unrelated, members of that species will have an easier time learning to that same thing, and will do so more quickly. Sheldrake stated in 1981 that there was preliminary evidence supporting the hypothesis but not yet a proof of it.[97]

Going a step further with morphogenetic fields, and increasing links among biology, physics, medicine, and psychology, psychologist Gary E. R. Schwartz, PhD, and assistant professor of medicine Linda G. S. Russek, PhD, argue in *The Living Energy Universe*:

Not just animals and plants, but rivers and clouds, planets and stars, electrons and protons, waves and particles, even light and energy itself. That every system, in some essential way, contains eternal, living, remembering and evolving memories. That the whole universe is a living, remembering, self-revising process—a living energy universe. And therefore, in a deep sense, all things—great and small—visible and invisible, material and spiritual, past and future—are in an energetic state of creative "becoming," a universal revising process of dynamic perpetual bloom.[98]

Parallel to Sheldrake, Schwartz, and Russek, physicist David Bohm, in a different interpretation of the mainstream of quantum mechanical field theory, argues that the "enfolding and unfolding universe," with its "implicate orders", is essentially alive. Each of the orders has meaning, and while people are usually not aware of it, human nervous, sense experience, and brains are coterminous with the material environment.[99] Further:

the explicit and manifest order of consciousness is not ultimately distinct from that of matter in general. Fundamentally, these are essentially different aspects of the one overall order.[100]

It would suggest that everything, including ourselves, is a generalized kind of meaning. Now I am not thereby attributing consciousness to nature. You see, the meaning of the word "consciousness" is not terribly clear. In fact, without meaning I think there would be no consciousness. The most essential feature of consciousness is consciousness of meaning. Consciousness is the content; its content is the meaning. Therefore it might be better to focus on meaning rather than consciousness. So I am not attributing consciousness as we know it to nature, but you might say that everything has a kind of mental side, rather like the magnetic poles. In inanimate matter the mental side is very small, but as we go deeper into things, the mental side becomes more and more significant.[101]

This same view is the conclusion of some fairly mainstream cutting edge biology research by Almo Farina and his research group of the *Istituto di Biomatematica* at the University of Urbino, in Italy. In studying eco-fields relating to local habitats, they found that local landscapes had underlying fields, linked together non-locally in overlapping exchanges. Messages were being exchanged between species, and also with relevant inanimate objects. Thus it appeared that the birds and the trees were talking to each other, as were the grass, soil, and rocks.[102] The Farina led research does not consider human participation in this communication, but psychologist Will Taegel in discussing the Urbino research explicitly states that an implication is that if human beings will listen, they can participate in this communication, and that indeed, this provides an explanation for the experiences of some people foreseeing natural events such as earthquakes.[103]

These findings in physics, biology, medicine, and psychology closely parallel the traditional view of many American Indian and other Indigenous cultures, including in their oral traditions, of plants telling medicine people which parts of certain plants to use to treat illness and other physical conditions. But while this view is still beyond the mainstream of Western science, bit by bit, the mainstream has been inching toward a similar position.

For example, there is the report in *Science*, during December 2006, of the discovery of a far smaller microbe than previously known, living in very inhospitable conditions in water as caustic as battery acid, containing high concentrations of toxic metals, including arsenic:

> Scientists say the discovery could bear on estimates of the pervasiveness of exotic microbial life, which some experts suspect forms a hidden biosphere extending down miles whose total mass may exceed that of all surface life. It may also influence the search for microscopic life elsewhere in the solar system, a discovery that would prove that life in the universe is not unique to Earth but an inherent property of matter.[104]

It has not happened yet, but the convergence between the mainstream of Western science and Native worldview has advanced so far in a little over a century, that it is now possible to imagine a mainstream scientist being comfortable with the idea of, "all my relations," *Mitakue Oyasun*, even as some on the edges of Western science already are. Indeed, in spring of 2019, science writer Ferris Jabr reported, "The Earth Is Just as Alive as You Are: Scientists Once Ridiculed the Idea of a Living Planet. Not Anymore," *The New York Times*, April 20, 2019, https://www.nytimes.com/2019/04/20/opinion/sunday/amazon-earth-rain-forest-environment.html.

Related Developments to Biology and Physics in Medicine and Psychology

The changes that have occurred in experimental and theoretical science in the West, as already hinted at, have been mirrored in the applied sciences, including in medicine and psychology. The traditional Western view in the early nineteenth century (which can be traced back to Plato's *The Republic,* including Books VIII and IX) was that human beings were superior in kind to animals because of the higher quality of human intellect, and that intellect, located in the brain, should rule the body and be superior to the emotions which were sense related. Thus, thinking, both in the narrow and broad senses was located in the top of the head.

While human beings needed their whole bodies, what made them human was just a small part of their body, at its highest part both physically and morally. This was part of the hierarchical Western way of seeing, which Gebser calls three-dimensional consciousness. That began to change in the late nineteenth and early twentieth centuries.

One of the major change agents was Edmund Jacobson, MD, who was sent in 1905 by Northwestern University president, psychologist Walter Scott Dill, to study at Harvard with three leading thinkers of the day, William James, Josiah Royce, and Hugo Munsterberg.[105] James told Jacobson to study "the whole man." Jacobson studied the startle reaction to unexpected loud noises, finding there was no obvious startle reaction in more relaxed patients. This was the first systematic study of relaxation, and the beginnings of progressive relaxation (PR) in the West.

After graduating from Harvard, Jacobson worked with Edward Bradford Tichner, who likely influenced Jacobson with his context theory. This theory asserted that the meaning of words originates, in part, in body postures involving the skeletal muscle system, and in his expertise at introspection. This led to Jacobson to make detailed observation ("introspection") of minute kinesthetic sensations and accompanying mental processes. That allowed clinical interpretation of localized body tensions to be correlated with meanings of acts that occur in one's imagination.

A later influence came not from American Indians, but from India, where he studied various yogas and relaxation techniques related to them. This likely included the use of relaxation techniques in raja yoga as an important aid in reaching higher levels of consciousness. Later Dr. Jacobson collaborated with A. J. Carlson to find ways to measure tension. All this and other studies and experience led Jacobson to develop methods to help patients relax, both for physical health, and, as an alternative to Freudian psychology, to undertake introspection. Jacobson's work with relaxation was quite prominent, and his patients included President Franklin Roosevelt.

This work was an important step in moving to an understanding that the entire body—muscles, various glands and chemical systems, and the entire nervous system, etc. are involved in thinking. It showed that thought is not just the result of intellect, but as Jung contributed, sensing, feeling, and intuition are involved as well. Later studies of biofeedback contributed significantly to this knowledge (again including input from the ancient—formerly Indigenous—traditions of India),[106] along with considerable other work in medicine and psychology.

By the 1970s and 1980s a number of doctors and other medical people began noticing that the mind body connection could be accessed in treating diseases and making medication more effective through the use of visualization exercises, particularized for the way particular diseases and specific medications functioned. This impacted the public consciousness through a number of mostly popular books, among them: Mike Samuels, M.D. and Nancy Samuels, *Seeing Through the Mind's Eye: The History, Techniques and Uses of Visualization* (1975); Stephanie Mathews Simonton, O. Carl Simonton, MD, and James L. Creighton, *Getting Well Again: A Step by Step, Self Help Guide to Overcoming Cancer for Patients and their Families* (1978); Shakti Gawain, *Creative Visualization* (1978); Jean Achterberg, Co-Director of the Professional School of Biofeedback, in Dallas, Texas, and associate professor and Director of Research in Rehabilitation Science at the University of Texas Health Center in

Dallas, *Imagery and Healing: Shamanism and Modern Medicine* (1985); and Bernie S. Siegel, MD, *Love, Medicine and Minerals: Lessons About Self-Healing from a Surgeon's Experience with Exceptional Patients* (1986).

That the mind's ability to impact the body has entered the mainstream culture is made clear by Kate Pickert, "The Art of Being Mindful," the cover story of *Time* magazine, February 3, 2014, which discussed how to undertake meditation and use it for health and well-being, particularly by reducing stress, as Jacobson had pioneered.[107] The article discusses the growing popularity, including in business, of meditation to reduce stress and help people focus and keep their attention on a topic amid multitasking and numerous distractions. It also reports considerable research in progress on the health benefits of meditation, including findings published in *Proceedings of the National Academy* of Sciences in 2004, and research funded by the National Institutes of Health (NIH).

Going further, but not yet in the mainstream of medicine, cell biologist and medical school professor and researcher, Bruce H. Lipton, PhDM, wrote in *The Biology of Belief* of "the new biology" in 2005 that the genes are the blueprint and the environment is the contractor: "a cell's life is controlled by the physical and energetic environment and not by the genes."[108] Thus, it has been accepted widely in the West that our thoughts and beliefs very much impact our bodies, and who and how we are, along with the body's role in affecting the mind, in what is now a more equalitarian, dialectical than the previous hierarchical relationship: a move toward an Indigenous way of seeing, as developed in chapter 1.

Section 4: Other Aspects of Western-Indigenous Convergence

Stephen M. Sachs

The coming together of various fields in the pure and applied sciences is part of a more general move away from the fragmented specialization of Western separate categories of knowledge reflected in academic structures divided into separate fields and departments that often have little awareness of each other. It is a move toward a more holistic interdisciplinary approach to knowledge and academics, moving in the direction of traditional Native holistic ways of thinking and viewing problems. In earlier times, when in many ways life was less complex, and there was less specialized knowledge, the Western division of knowledge and of academia into diverse fields was quite practical. Philosophy then provided a general overview, and contained accessible knowledge of many fields. Today, the tremendous growth in extent of knowledge and the proliferation of specialist fields and subfields has caused a fragmentation that is no longer viable, requiring the development of interdisciplinary studies, and teamwork among specialists, along with other efforts to restore a holistic understanding and appropriate application of knowledge.

Moreover, as is developed in chapter 7 below, "Indigenizing the Greening of the World: Applying an Indigenous Approach to Environmental Issues," one of the strengths of Western science, giving it significant power, has been its narrowing the focus of endeavors by reducing what is considered to only what is immediately understood as relevant. The weakness is that this approach fails to consider broader and longer term factors and impacts, producing a range of problems. The most notable is the entire set of environmental crises afflicting the world, as well as individual areas, communities, and people. Fortunately, the reality of broader complexities has been increasingly intruding upon the West and its science. Western science and other fields increasingly have been moving toward more holistic perspectives and methods more in keeping with the more passively experimental approach of Indigenous science.[109] This can be seen in the rise of complexity theory and of ecological studies and their application.

Related, changes in Western culture have also been underway for some time, several of which are discussed in the next chapter, "Applying American Indian Principles of Harmony and Balance to

Renew the Politics of the Twenty-First Century." For example, the combination of the Western emphases on power as control and on hierarchy in public and private affairs, including in organizations, has produced growing inefficiencies and other problems as the scope and size of organizations and human activities have grown. This has led to a movement away from hierarchy toward more democratic and equalitarian organizations and ways of carrying out all kinds of undertakings.

Just one aspect of this is that with growing complexity and increasing specialization fragmenting knowledge and work, unitary control has been becoming increasingly ineffective. To counter these difficulties, participatory teams of doctors, scientists, and other experts have become more and more common for carrying out complex enterprises. Similarly, Western court systems and other adversarial conflict resolution processes that focus only on narrowly construed relevant facts and issues, have more and more been found to have inadequacies. In response, with direct influence from traditional Indigenous ways, broader and more cooperative problem solving, dispute resolution methods and processes have enjoyed a growing popularity in the United States, elsewhere in the West, and in the broader world. All of this, including a number of other relevant trends and developments in culture and society in the West are considered in the next chapter and those that follow.

In the course of briefly considering a complex set of broad and multifaceted changes in culture and practice in the United States and elsewhere, in this introduction, setting a context for part II of this volume, it has only been possible to touch the surface of those developments. Only a few examples could be briefly mentioned, without developing them to any extent, or considering issues that are involved with each of them.

New developments to meet ongoing problems often continue some of the difficulties they are intended to meet, or create new problems. If they are advances, they may only be partially so. To take just one example of those considered in the next chapters, the rise of "new age" spirituality, while moving to bring in needed dimensions that many people found missing from traditional religious institutions, has been criticized by numerous members of traditional non-Western spiritual traditions that have been sources for new age development. A major complaint is that many new agers rush to try to apply practices that usually take considerable time to understand and master. As a result, the methods are too frequently misunderstood and misused, often making them ineffective and sometimes harmful. Similarly, there are complaints that in a society with a strong emphasis on making money and advancement in the market, some involved in both the older religions and the newer spiritual enterprises contradict their supposed work with an excess of spiritual materialism.[110]

It is important to keep in mind that the trends discussed here are not uniform, have not been proceeding uniformly, and are constantly undergoing greater and lesser modifications. As is clear from the discussion in the next and following chapters, the authors find many of the trends tending to move forward as potentially, and often actually beneficial, when they are appropriately brought into practice. But there are also cross and counter trends, some driven by wealthy individuals and groups at a time of increasing concentration of wealth in a few hands. Amid a complex interaction of shifting forces, it is impossible to accurately predict the outcome. The intention of the authors is to encourage trends which appear socially and individually beneficial, amid a convergence between developing Western thought and American Indian and other Indigenous traditional ways of seeing and acting.

Notes to Part II Introduction

1. Jean Gebser, *The Ever-Present Origin* (Athens: University of Ohio Press, 1986).
2. Carl Jung, *Psychological Types* (New York: Harcourt Brace, 1923). Application of Jung's understanding in Western culture can be seen in Isabel Meyers, *Gifts Differing* (Palo Alto, CA: Consulting Psychologists, 1980); David Keirsey and Marilyn Bates, *Please Understand Me: Character*

and Temperament Types (Delmar, CA: Permethius Nemesis, 1984); Eduardo Duran and Bonnie Duran, *Native American Postcolonial Psychology* (Albany: State of New York University Press, 1995), which holds that while Jung's perspective is essentially correct, his model needs to be adjusted for different cultures, and a Native American model is posited by the authors (particularly 65–83).

3. "The Sixth Sense," [TV Series, 1972], IMDb, http://www.imdb.com/title/tt0068132/.

4. "The X-Files," [TV Series, 1993–2002], IMDb, http://www.imdb.com/title/tt0106179/.

5. Among the television programs that exemplify this development are *The Twilight Zone* (1959–1964), which may have been a modest beginning; *Night Gallery* (1960–1973); and *The Outer Limits* (1963–1965 and 1995–2002).

6. "Seeing Things," [TV Series, 1981–1987], IMDb, http://www.imdb.com/title/tt0078685/.

7. "Medium," [TV Series, 2005–2011], IMDb, http://www.imdb.com/title/tt0412175/.

8. "Ghost Whisperer," Wikipedia, http://en.wikipedia.org/wiki/Ghost_Whisperer; "Ghost Whisperer," [TV Series, 2005–2010], IMDb, http://www.imdb.com/title/tt0460644/. Note that leading forms of media in the West, including television, have long included a "horror stories" genre. But previously this was largely restricted to a limited place in the media and would almost never have broken into prime time (or its equivalent).

9. Katherine Ramsland, "Psychic Detectives," Crime Library, http://www.crimelibrary.com/criminal_mind/forensics/psychics/11.html (unfortunately this webpage no longer works). Wiley's agency also put together a network of psychics and police officers to assist local police, whose specialty was helping locate stolen property. See Vernon J. Geberth, *Practical Homicide Investigation: Tactics, Procedures, and Forensic Techniques*, 4th ed. (London: CRC, 2006).

10. Ken Charles, *Psychic Cop*, with Derek Schuff (London: Blake, 1995).

11. See "The Changing Role of Women in American Society," Indiana University Lilly Family School of Philanthropy, http://www.philanthropy.iupui.edu/files/file/thechangingroleofwomeninamericansociety.pdf; "Sex Roles: A Journal of Research; All Volumes and Issues," SpringerLink, http://link.springer.com/journal/volumesAndIssues/11199, a publication which carries extensive research on the changing roles and status of women; Rick Nauert, "Change in Pronoun Use Reflects Women's

Role in Society," PsychCentral, August 10, 2012, http://psychcentral. com/news/2012/08/10/change-in-pronoun-use-reflects-women's-role-in-society/42945.html, which reported: "New research suggests progress in gender equality can be traced by the language found in published literature over the past 50 years. In a new study led by San Diego State University researchers, investigators explored how the language in the full text of more than one million books reflected cultural change in US women's status. Findings are published in the journal *Sex Roles.*"

12. On the return of the divine feminine, see Llewellyn Vaughn-Lee, *The Return of the Feminine and the World Soul* (Point Reyes, CA: The Golden Sufi Center, 2009); Andrew Harvey, *The Return of the Mother* (New York: Putnam, 2001); Barbara Threecrow, *Return of the Sacred Feminine and Teachings of the Grandmothers* (Kingston, NY: Spirit Stone, 2009). In one expression of this, "2013 Dawn of a New Era: Year of the Woman, Return of the Feminine; Sacred Energy of Number 13," Mystic Mamma, http://www.mysticmamma.com/2013-dawn-of-a-new-era-year-of-the-woman-return-of-the-feminine-sacred-energy-of-number-13/, which stated:

2013 marks the dawn of a new era. The Mayan long count calendar culminated its 13th B'ak'tun cycle, and now a new one begins! The potential of what we create is in our hands. As the Maya and many Indigenous elders say, it is a time to re-establish our connection with the Earth and to open our hearts to the wisdom of the feminine in order to restore a balance between the male and female energies. This year of 2013 is symbolic in that the number 13 has always been associated with the Goddess and the Divine Feminine. After a very transformational 2012, we are ready to step forward with our hearts and forge new pathways for ourselves and future generations. Here is some inspiration I gathered about the symbolism of the number 13, and the energy supporting the Feminine to come forth and bring her healing hands upon the planet.

On Jung: Gary Toub, "Jung and Gender: Masculine and Feminine Revisited," Jung Page, http://www.cgjungpage.org/learn/articles/ analytical-psychology/147-jung-and-gender-masculine-and-feminine-revisited, which states: "identities. The process also mirrors and furthers 'the breakdown of male-female polarization in our culture, and the cultural shift towards androgyny.' By recognizing an inner image of female in men."

13. "Status and Role of Women: Home," Florida Conference of the United MethodistChurch,https://www.flumc.org/statusandroleofwomenhome.

14. Katrin Benhold, "Church of England Approves Plan Allowing Female Bishops," *New York Times*, November 17, 2014, http://www.nytimes.com/2014/11/18/world/europe/church-of-england-approves-plan-allowing-female-bishops.html?ref=todayspaper.

15. For the Hindu related groups, see Himalayan Institute, http://www.himalayaninstitute.org; "Welcome to the Siddha Yoga Path," SYDA Foundation, www.siddhayoga.org; "Ananda Marga: Self-Realization Service To All,"Ananda Marga, www.anandamarga.org; "Transcendental Meditation: The Technique For Inner Peace and Wellness," Maharishi Foundation, www.tm.org.

16. See Richard Hughes Seager, *Buddhism in America* (New York: Columbia University Press, 1999); David W. Chappell, *Engaged Buddhism in the West* (Boston: Wisdom, 2000). A directory of Buddhist centers is "Buddhanet's World Buddhist Directory," Buddha Dharma Education Association/BuddhaNet, http://www.buddhanet.info/wbd/country.php?country_id=2. Naropa University (www.naropa.edu/) is in Boulder, CO.

17. The Sufi Order International, more recently named the Inayati Sufi Order ("The Inayati Order: A Sufi Path of Spiritual Liberty," http://inayatiorder.org), was, as of 2016, one of six federated orders or groups following in the tradition of Hazrat Inayat Khan; "The Baha'i Faith," Bahá'í International Community, http://www.bahai.org; Nur Ashki Jerrahi Community, http://www.nurashkijerrahi.org.

18. See Wouter J. Hanegraaff, *New Age Religion and Western Culture: Esotericism in the Mirror of Secular Thought* (Albany: State of New York University Press, 1998).

19. Nela Banerjee, "Poll Finds a Fluid Religious Life in U.S.," *New York Times*, February 26, 2008, https://www.nytimes.com/2008/02/26/us/26religion.html.

20. Mark Oppenheimer, "Examining the Growth of the 'Spiritual but Not Religious,'" *New York Times*, July 18, 2014, https://www.nytimes.com/2014/07/19/us/examining-the-growth-of-the-spiritual-but-not-religious.html; "'Nones' on the Rise," Pew Research Religion

and Public Life, October 9, 2012, http://www.pewforum.org/2012/ 10/09/nones-on-the-rise/.

21. "Dances of Universal Peace," Dances of Universal Peace International, www.dancesofuniversalpeace.org.

22. For example, the Ute ceremony popularly known as the "Sun Dance" has a name in Ute that translates as "Thirsty Stand" (personal communication from a number of Utes to Stephen Sachs while attending the Southern Ute Sun Dance from 1986 to 2016). The discussions of spiritual practices in this paragraph comes from the observations and experiences of Sachs, a senior teacher in the universalist Sufi Order International, who has attended meetings of various spiritual groups. In addition, on the use of walks in Southeast Asian Buddhist practice, see Joseph Goldstein, *Insight Meditation: The Practice of Freedom* (Boston: Shambhala, 1987).

23. Black Elk, *Black Elk Speaks: Being the Life Story of a Holy Man of the Oglala Sioux*, as told through John G. Neihardt [1932] (New York: Pocket, 1959).

24. The number of popular books published in the United States on American Indian culture and spirituality is far too large to list here. A few examples are the controversial novel by Hyemeyohsts Storm, *Seven Arrows* (New York: Ballantine, 1972), which however one feels about it sold over 300,000 copies and impacted numerous people by inspiring interest in Native American spirituality; Joseph Epes Brown, *The Sacred Pipe: Black Elk's Account of the Seven Rites of the Oglala Sioux* (Norman: University of Oklahoma Press, 1953); John (Fire) Lame Deer and Richard Erdoes, *Lame Deer: Seeker of Visions* (New York: Washington Square, 1972); Wallace Black Elk and William S. Lyon, *Black Elk: The Sacred Ways of a Lakota* (New York: Harper and Row, 1990); Charles A. Eastman (Ohiyesa), *The Soul of the Indian: An Interpretation* [1911] (Lincoln: University of Nebraska Press, 1980); Mari Sandoz, *Crazy Horse: The Strange Man of the Oglalas* [novel] (Lincoln: University of Nebraska Press, 1942); Lee Irwin, *The Dream Seekers: Native American Visionary Traditions of the Great Plains* (Norman: University of Oklahoma Press, 1994); Gerald Mohatt and Joseph Eagle Elk, *The Price of a Gift: A Lakota Healer's Story* (Lincoln: University of Nebraska Press, 2000); Joseph M. Marshall III, *The Lakota Way: Stories and Lessons of Living* (New York: Viking Compass, 2001); Doug Boyd, *Rolling Thunder* (New York: Dell, 1974); George Bird Grinnell, *By Cheyenne Campfires* [1922] (New Haven: Yale University Press, 1971); J. T. Garrett and Michael Garrett, *Medicine of the Cherokee: The Way of Right Relationship* (Santa Fe,

NM: Bear, 1996); Ruben Snake, *Ruben Snake: Your Humble Serpent*, as told to Jay Fikes (Santa Fe, NM: Clear Light, 1996); Frank Waters, *The Book of the Hopi: The First Revelation of the Hopi's Historical and Religious World-View of Life* (New York: Random House, 1963); Paula Gunn Allen, *The Sacred Hoop: Recovering the Feminine in American Indian Traditions* (Boston: Beacon, 1986); D. M. Dooling and Paul Jordan-Smith, eds., *I Become Part of It: Sacred Dimensions in Native American Life* (New York: HarperCollins, 1989); Peter Nabokov, *Where the Lightning Strikes: The Lives of American Indian Sacred Places* (New York: Viking, 2006), and hundreds of other more specialized books.

Among the many popular mystery novels of American Indians are those of Tony Hillerman that center on Navajo policemen, including: *Listening Woman, The Blessing Way, Skin Walkers, The Ghost Way, The Dark Winds, Dance Hall of the Dead, People of Darkness, The Fallen Man*, and *A Thief of Time* (many of these are Avon paperbacks); Margaret Cole's novels set on the Wind River Reservation in Wyoming; and the novels of Mardi Oakley Medawar, including *Death at Rainy Mountain, The Witch of Palo Duro*, and *Murder at Medicine Lodge*.

25. Author Stephen Sachs has observed, and spoken to, numerous individuals about the considerable non-Indian participation at many different Native ceremonies and gatherings since 1984, some involving well-known medicine like Wallace Black Elk, Leonard Crow Dog, and Rolling Thunder. The major ceremony led by a non-Indian is the Texas Sun Dance, whose leader, having danced for a number of years in Leonard Crow Dog's annual Sun Dance on the Rosebud Reservation, was asked by Crow Dog to establish and lead that ceremony according to Michael Hull, *Sun Dancing: A Spiritual Journey on the Red Road* (Rochester, VT: Inner Traditions International, 2000).

26. Lucy Maddox, *Removals: Nineteenth Century American Literature and the Politics of Indian Affairs* (New York: Oxford University Press, 1991).

27. Neil Diamond, dir., *Reel Injun: On the Trail of Hollywood's Indian* (New York: Lorber Films, 2009), DVD.

28. Philip J. Deloria, "Historiography," in *A Companion to American Indian History*, ed. Philip Deloria and Neil Salisbury (New York: Oxford University Press, 2004).

29. For more on Native cinema, especially as an act of cultural or visual sovereignty, see Michelle Raheja, *Reservation Reelism: Redfacing, Visual Sovereignty, and Representations of Native Americans in Film* (Lincoln: University of Nebraska Press, 2010); Dean Radner, *Engaged Resistance:*

American Indian Art, Literature, and Film; From Alcatraz to the NMAI (Austin: University of Texas Press, 2011).

30. N. Scott Momaday, *House Made of Dawn* [1968] (New York: Perennial, 1999).

31. N. Scott Momaday, *Man Made of Words* (New York: St. Martin's Griffin, 1997), 14.

32. LeAnne Howe, "The Story of America: A Tribalography," in *Clearing a Path: Theorizing the Past in Native American Studies*, ed. Nancy Shoemaker (New York: Routledge, 2002), 45.

33. See Nina Baym, et al., *The Norton Anthology of American Literature*, vol. 2 (New York: W. W. Norton, 1994); Sandra M. Gilbert and Susan Gubar, *The Norton Anthology of Literature by Women: Traditions in English*, vol. 1 (New York: W. W. Norton, 2007); Michael Myer, *The Compact Bedford Introduction to Literature* (Boston: Bedford, 1997).

34. Louise Erdrich, *The Round House* (New York: HarperCollins, 2012).

35. Sherman Alexie, *The Absolutely True Diary of a Part-Time Indian* (New York: Little, Brown, 2007).

36. Edward Buscombe, *'Injuns!': Native Americans in the Movies* (Bodmin, Cornwall, UK: Reaktion, 2006), 24.

37. See Robert F. Berkhofer Jr., *The White Man's Indian: Images of the American Indian from Columbus to the Present* (New York: Alfred A. Knopf, 1978).

38. Arthur Penn, dir. *Little Big Man* [1970] (Hollywood, CA: Paramount, 2003), DVD.

39. Kevin Costner, dir. *Dances with Wolves* [1990] (Santa Monica, CA: MGM Home Entertainment, 2015), DVD.

40. Michael Mann, dir. *Last of the Mohicans* (Beverly Hills, CA: Twentieth-Century Home Entertainment Fox, 1992), DVD.

41. Mike Gabriel and Eric Goldberg, dirs. *Pocahontas* [1995] (Burbank, CA: Buena Vista Home Entertainment, 2012), DVD.

42. Chris Eyre, dir., *Smoke Signals* (Burbank, CA: Buena Vista Home Entertainment, 1998), DVD.

43. Valerie Red-Horse and Jennifer Wynn Farmer, dirs., *Naturally Native* (Red-Horse Productions, 1998), VHS.

44. Alexie and Cobb, quoted in Dustin Tahmahkera, *Tribal Television: Viewing Native People in Sitcoms* (Chapel Hill: University of North Carolina Press, 2014).

45. See Chris Eyre, dir., *Skins* (Century City, CA: First Look Media, 2002); Sherman Alexie, dir., *The Business of Fancydancing* (New York: Wellspring Media, 2003); Sterlin Harjo, dir., *Barking Water* (New York:

Kino Lorber, 2010); Sterlin Harjo, dir., *Four Sheets to the Wind* (Century City, CA: First Look Studios, 2007); Timothy Ramos, dir., *California Indian* (Against the Wind Films, 2011); Georgina Lightning, dir., *Older Than America* (New York: IFC Films, 2007); Randy Red Road, dir., *The Doe Boy* (New York: Wellspring Media, 2001); Sydney Freeland, dir., *Drunktown's Finest* (Indion Entertainment Group, 2014); Keo Woolford, dir., *The Haumāna* (Hula Nation Filmworks, 2013); Shelley Niro, dir., *Kissed by Lightning* (Kissed By Lightning Productions, 2009); Andrew Okpeaha MacLean, dir., *On the Ice* (On the Ice Productions, 2011).

46. Zacharis Kunuk, dir., *Atanarjuat: The Fast Runner* (Culver City, CA: Sony, 2001), DVD.

47. Shonie De La Rosa and Andee De La Rosa, dirs., *Milepost 398* (Sheephead Films, 2007), web video.

48. James Cameron, dir., *Avatar* (Beverly Hills, CA: Twentieth Century Fox, 2009), DVD.

49. Gore Verbinski, dir., *Lone Ranger* (Burbank, CA: Buena Vista Entertainment, 2013), DVD.

50. Dustin Tahmahkera, *Tribal Television: Viewing Native People in Sitcoms* (Chapel Hill: University of North Carolina Press, 2014).

51. Raheja, *Reservation Reelism*, 62.

52. Sean Vesce, dir., *Never Alone* (Upper One Games, E-Line Media, 2014).

53. On the Wild West shows, see Steve Friesen, *Lakota Performance in Europe: Their Culture and the Artifacts They Left Behind*, with Francois Chladiuk, forward by Walter Littlemoon (Norman: University of Oklahoma Press, 2017); Robert W. Rydell and Rob Kroes, *Buffalo Bill in Bologna: The Americanization of the World, 1869–1922* (Chicago: University of Chicago Press, 2005). On Karl May, see Ruben Snake, *Ruben Snake: Your Humble Serpent*, as told to Jay Fikes (Santa Fe, NM: Clear Light, 1996), 77, 169–71; Karl May USA, http://www.karlmayusa.com. On Indian leaders going to Europe, this was reported to Stephen Sachs directly by Indian leaders and their associates (and by Europeans who attended the events they led in Europe).

54. Reflecting Indigenous views more broadly, it can be said that contemporary physics is coming closer to traditional views from cultures outside the West, as exemplified by the relationship developing between Western physics and traditional Eastern thought as set forth in Fritjof Capra, *The Tao of Physics* (Toronto: Bantam, 1984). As to American Indian views—as indicated in the discussion of place below—they are in principle, and in fact, quite varied. But there is an underlying, and generally agreed on, set of values and ways of seeing and doing. This

is indicated, for example, in A. Timas and R. Reedy, "Implementation of Cultural-Specific Intervention for a Native American Community," *Journal of Clinical Psychology* 5, no. 3 (1998): 382–93; James A. Moran, "Preventing Alcohol Use Among Urban American Youth: The Seventh Generation Program," in *Voices of First Nation People: Human Service Considerations*, ed. Hilary N. Weaver (New York: Haworth, 1999), 51–68; Maria Yellow Horse Brave Heart, *"Oyate Ptayela*: Rebuilding the Lakota Nation Through Addressing Historical Trauma Among Lakota Parents," *Voices of First Nations People*, 106–26. That there is generally a set of common values in Indigenous worldviews, referred to in relation to Capra's writing, and shown specifically in the collaboration of Americans for Indian Opportunity (AIO) of the United States with Advancement for Maori Opportunity of New Zealand (founded with collaboration with AIO) that is based on a common set of principles can be seen by looking at the AMO website (http://www.amo.co.nz/) and by frequent statements made to that effect by members of both organizations (as has been witnessed frequently by the author).

The shifts towards Indigenous thinking in Western physical sciences have also been occurring in the social sciences since the nineteenth century. A good example is in anthropology, where earlier European ethnocentric views of human evolution, often supported by insufficient good information, were at first countered around the beginning of the twentieth century by Franz Boaz's empirical approach, which focused on gaining good data on individual societies and subgroups as a precursor to developing theory. Many of the next generation of anthropologists in Boaz's tradition began to develop theory, or apply existing theory from other fields, to anthropology. In this empirically based tradition, the attempt was always to understand as accurately as possible the examined societies and cultures on the basis of observation and informant interview (or expression by members of the culture). But, in the Western science tradition, this was primarily undertaken by the anthropologist as outside observer—although it included participant observation and inclusion of views expressed by members of the studied group. By the early twenty-first century, a movement was developing in anthropology that emphasized understanding a culture from its own point of view as much as possible, at times including a culture's perspective within—or coexistent with—the anthropologist's way of seeing. This last development can be seen David C. Posthumus, *All My Relatives: Exploring Lakota Ontology, Belief, and Ritual* (Lincoln: University of Nebraska Press, 2018). The earlier pre-history and history of anthropology is partially outlined in "History of Anthropology," Wikipedia, https://en.wikipedia.org/wiki/ History_of_anthropology. Also see Sol Tax, "Franz Boas: German-American Anthropologist," *Encyclopedia Britannica*, https://www.britannica.com/biography/Franz-Boas.

55. On relativity, see Capra, *The Tao of Physics*, 50–53, also 5, 28, 43, 66–71, 134, 136, 147, 150–173, 178, 185, 188–91, 193–96, 249, 252, 264, 278, 288; Brian Greene, *The Fabric of the Cosmos: Space Time and the Texture of Reality* (New York: Alfred Knopf, 2004), particularly chap. 3.

56. Frank Waters, *Pumpkin Seed Point: Being with the Hopi* (Athens, OH: Swallow, 1969), 104. For a broader discussion of time for the Hopi, with some comparison to the modern view of time in the West, see chap. 9, "Time."

57. Natalie Angier, "Making Sense Of Time, Earthbound and Otherwise," *New York Times*, January 23, 2007, D1, D3.

58. Waters, *Pumpkin Seed Point*, 105–7.

59. Gregory Cajete, *Native Science: Natural Laws of Interdependence* (Santa Fe, NM: Clear Light, 2000), 70, also 74, 77, 89, 91, 93–95. See also Nabokov, *Where the Lightning Strikes*; Vine Deloria Jr. and Daniel R. Wildcat, *Power and Place: Indian Education in America* (Golden, CO: Fulcrum, 2001), 2–3, 13, 36–37, 75–76.

60. Greene, *The Fabric of the Cosmos*, chap. 3, particularly 55–56, 58–61, 65, 67.

61. See Gerald Mohatt and Joseph Eagle Elk, *The Price of a Gift: A Lakota Healer's Story* (Lincoln: University of Nebraska Press, 2000), 3, 35, 145–46, 298–99; Joseph M. Marshall III, *The Lakota Way: Stories and Lessons of Living* (New York: Viking Compass, 2001), 211, 227.

62. Jean Chaudhuri and Joyotpaul Chaudhuri, *A Sacred Path: The Way of the Muscogee Creeks* (Los Angeles: UCLA American Indian Center, 2001), 26.

63. Raymond A. Bucko, *The Lakota Ritual of the Sweat Lodge: History and Contemporary Practice* (Lincoln: University of Nebraska Press, 1998), 38–39, 77, 82, 136, 236 n32. Bucko provides a large number of references to other sources. Particularly interesting is the version of the Lakota creation story, recorded in James R. Walker, Raymond J. DeMallie, and Elaine A. Jahner, eds., *Lakota Belief and Ritual* (Lincoln, University of Nebraska Press, 1991), 50–51. This is further developed in Albert White Hat Sr., *Life's Journey: Zuya; Oral Teachings from Rosebud* (Salt Lake City: University of Utah Press, 2012), in which appears: "Before there was any other thing, or any time, there was *Inyan* [Rock]

and his spirit was *Wankan Tanka* [Great Mystery]." To have a companion, *Inyan* created *Maka* [Earth] out of himself (but note, in relation to chaos and complexity theory, to be discussed below, the process did not proceed exactly as *Inyan* had intended), and "he shrank and became hard and powerless." Nabakov, *Where the Lightning Strikes*, 28–29, reports that in the complexity of Ojibwa views, not all stones are alive, but some are. That many Indigenous peoples find rocks to be alive is shown though the book.

64. As discussed in chapter 1 of this book. For a longer discussion of this in general terms, with examples from several tribes, see LaDonna Harris, Stephen M. Sachs, and Barbara Morris, *Re-Creating the Circle: The Renewal of American Indian Self-Determination* (Albuquerque: University of New Mexico Press, 2011), chaps. 1, 4. This general pattern is also discussed briefly in Sharon O'Brien, *American Indian Tribal Governments* (Norman: University of Oklahoma Press, 1989), chap. 2. For discussion of how some particular traditional Native nations were participatory, see Lewis Henry Morgan, *League of the Iroquois* (Secaucus, NJ: Citadel, 1996); Bruce G. Trigger, *The Huron: Farmers of the North* (Fort Worth, TX: Holt, Rinehart, and Winston, 1990), especially chap. 6, "Government and Law"; Morris Edward Opler, *An Apache Way of Life: The Economic, Social, and Religious Institutions of the Chiricahua Indians* (Lincoln: University of Nebraska Press, 1996), particularly 460–71 on politics; Clyde Kluckhohn and Dorethea Leighton, *The Navaho* (Cambridge, MA: Harvard University Press, 1974), 111–23; Robert W. Young, *A Political History of the Navajo Tribe* (Tsaille, Navajo Nation, AZ: Navajo Community College Press, 1978), 15–16, 25–27; Alfred W. Bowers, *Hidatsa Social and Ceremonial Organization* (Lincoln: University of Nebraska Press, 1992), particularly 26–64; Catherine Price, *The Oglala People, 1841–1879: A Political History* (Lincoln: University of Nebraska Press, 1996), particularly 7–21, 33–34, 60–62, 98–99, 156, 168, 172–73, and which drew on many sources, including the Walker papers; James R. Walker, *Lakota Society*, ed. Raymond DeMallie (Lincoln: University of Nebraska Press, 1982), pt. 1, particularly documents 6–16 (this is the second of three edited volumes of the James R. Walker papers published by the University of Nebraska Press:); Ruth Landes, "The Ojibwa of Canada," in *Cooperation and Competition Among Primitive Peoples*, ed. Margaret Mead (New York: McGraw-Hill, 1937), chap. 3; Jannette Mirsky, "The Dakota" in *Cooperation and Competition Among Primitive Peoples*; Chaudhuri and Chaudhuri, *A Sacred Path*, particularly chap.

9, but throughout the rest of the work, including in the creation myth discussed in chap. 3.

65. See Kluckhohn and Leighton, *The Navaho*; James F. Downes, *The Navajo* (New York: Holt Reinhart, and Winston, 1972), particularly chap. 2, 3, 8; Young, *A Political History of the Navajo Tribe*; Alice Reichard, *Navaho Religion* (New York: Pantheon, 1950).

The similar Muskogee view is set out in Chaudhuri and Chaudhuri, *A Sacred Path*, who write:

The beautiful astronomical legends give us a picture of the balance of male and female energies, thereby showing the patch of darkness in light and light in darkness, all circling in the search for harmony in motion. The legends provide a humanities parallel of the science of the Creeks which also sees the search for balance between the four elements and the synergy linking the cycles of dynamic energies of the earth, the water, the sun (fire), and the sky (air). This is no romantic pipe dream, but the vision of an earth-centered culture with sacred trust responsibilities. The Earth centered physics involves exchanges between and transformations of various forms of energy and the cycles of energy among soil, water, nutrients, animals, sunlight, air and rain in an environmentally balanced manner. (19)

66. Harris, Sachs, and Morris, *Re-Creating the Circle*, chap. 4, pt. 2.
67. Chaudhuri and Chaudhuri, *A Sacred Path*, 23. This theme pervades chap. 4.
68. Greene, *The Fabric of the Cosmos*, 254–71, but particularly 268–71, "The Return of the Aether." A. Einstein, N. Rosen, and B. Podolsky, "Can Quantum-Mechanical Description of Physical Reality Be Considered Complete?" *Physics Review* 47 (1935): 777, reported in Greene, *The Fabric of the Cosmos*, 11.
69. Greene, *The Fabric of the Cosmos*, 11–12, 84.
70. Ibid., 80.
71. Ibid., 78, also 75.
72. Ibid., 118.
73. Ibid., 254–71, most particularly 268–72, "The Return of the Aether."

74. On symmetry, see Capra, *The Tao of Physics*, chap. 16. For a more current view, Greene, *The Fabric of the Cosmos*, chap. 8, particularly 219–25.

75. Capra, *The Tao of Physics*, 239.

76. Greene, *The Fabric of the Cosmos*, 225.

77. Ibid., chap. 4, 6, 7. See particularly 90.

78. Capra, *The Tao of Physics*, 127, quoting Werner Heisenberg, *Physics and Philosophy* (New York: Harper, 1958), 58. For more on this point, see chap. 10, 11.

79. See David Bohm and B. J. Hiley, *The Undivided Universe: An Ontological Interpretation of Quantum Theory* (London: Routledge, 1993), especially chap. 7, "Nonlocality." This is true both for American Indian and a variety of traditional Eastern ways of seeing. For a discussion of the uncertainty principle in the course of a consideration of the parallels between contemporary physics and ancient Eastern metaphysics, see Capra, *The Tao of Physics*, 125–29, 143–46, 178–79, 207–9, 251–53.

80. Arthur Amioette, "The Lakota Sun Dance," in *Sioux Indian Religion*, ed. by Raymond J. DeMallie and Joseph R. Parks (Norman: University of Oklahoma Press, 1987), 79.

81. As stated by Campbell in an interview with New Dimensions Radio with Michael Toms in the spring of 1970, which is reproduced in Joseph Campbell and Michael Toms, *The Wisdom of Joseph Campbell: In Conversation with Michael Toms* (Carlsbad, CA: New Dimensions/Hay House, 1997), tape 1, side 2. The reference is to Black Elk, *Black Elk Speaks*.

82. Chaudhuri and Chaudhuri, *A Sacred Path*, chap. 9, especially where quoted 68.

83. Native North Americans understood that in a complex interactive world, harmony will constantly be lost, individually and collectively (in agreement with the concept of entropy in physics), and that steps must be undertaken to regain it. Hence, on the spiritual-psychological level, Indian cultures had ceremonies for reestablishing balance. For the Navajo (Diné), for example, virtually all ceremonies are healing rituals to return people to beauty; see Kluckhohn and Leighton, *The Navaho*; Downes, *The Navajo*, particularly chap. 2, 3, 8; Young, *A Political History of the Navajo Tribe*; Reichard, *Navaho Religion*.

In addition to healing rituals for rebalancing individuals and/or groups, many tribes had major rituals for the "renewal of the earth and the people," such as the Sun Dance of the Lakota and other

Plains, Rocky Mountain, and Great Basin tribes. On the Lakota Sun dance, see Thomas E. Mails, *Sun Dancing at Rosebud and Pine Ridge* (Sioux Falls, SD: College of Western Studies, 1978); J. R. Walker, *The Sun Dance of the Oglala and Other Ceremonies of the Oglala Division of the Teton Dakota*, Anthropological Papers of the American Museum of Natural History 16, pt. 2 (New York: American Museum of Natural History, 1917); Walker, *Lakota Belief and Ritual*. On the Cheyenne Sun Dance, see E. Adamson Hoebel, *The Cheyennes: Indians of the Great Plains* (New York: Holt, Rinehart, and Winston, 1960). On the Shoshone, Ute, and Crow Sun Dances, see Joseph G. Jorgensen, *The Sun Dance Religion: Power to The Powerless* (Chicago: University of Chicago Press, 1972). See how this worked in Muskogee terms in Chaudhuri and Chaudhuri, *A Sacred Path*.

84. Nabokov, *Where the Lightning Strikes*, 33.

85. Scott L. Pratt, *Native Pragmatism: Rethinking the Roots of American Philosophy* (Bloomington: Indiana University Press, 1997), chap. 5, particularly after 84 and chap. 6, particularly 130–34.

86. See Stephen M. Sachs, "LaDonna Harris, Founder of Americans for Indian Opportunity: Leadership in the Tradition of Native American Women's Voices," *A Leadership Journal: Women In Leadership; Sharing the Vision* 3, no. 1 (1998); Stephen M. Sachs, "Working in the Circle: American Indian Leadership and Collaboration through Applying Traditional Values in the Context of the Twenty-First Century," *Proceedings of the 2004 American Political Science Association Meeting* (Washington, DC: American Political Science Association, 2004); Harris, Sachs, and Morris, *Re-Creating the Circle*, chap. 6. Some of this information comes from the author working with Ms. Harris and AIO for over a quarter of a century, beginning in 1990.

87. Stated by Vine Deloria in a panel discussion at the 2005 Western Social Science Association Meeting, attended by the author. The incident concerning the expansion of the museum board was confirmed in a discussion of Vine Deloria's career at the 2006 Western Social Science Association Meeting (attended by the author) by Suzanne Harjo, president of the Morningstar Foundation and a longtime proponent of the development of the National Museum of the American Indian. She stated that she was one of a number of people whom Deloria had contacted to be prepared to speak publicly if the board did not agree to appoint more Indigenous members.

88. A large collection of articles on complexity theory and chaos theory is available at Ben Ramalingam and Harry Jones (with Toussaint Reba and John Young), "Exploring the New Science of Chaos and Complexity: Ideas and Implications for Development and Humanitarian Efforts," Overseas Development Institute, October 2008, https://www.odi.org/sites/odi.org.uk/files/odi-assets/publications-opinion-files/833.pdf. For a social science application of complexity theory in Indian affairs, see Nicholas C. Peroff, *Menominee Drums, Tribal Termination, and Restoration* (Norman: University of Oklahoma Press, 1982). On chaos theory in general, also see "Chaos Theory," Wikipedia, https://en.wikipedia.org/wiki/Chaos_theory; "Chaos Theory," TechTarget, WhatIs.com, https://whatis.techtarget.com/definition/chaos-theory; "Chaos Introduction," www.zeuscat.com/andrew/chaos/; Matthew A. Trump, "What is Chaos? An Interactive Online Course for Everyone," Ilya Prigogine Center for Studies in Statistical Mechanics and Complex Systems, University of Texas at Austin, order.ph.utexas.edu/chaos/.

89. "Chaos Theory, a Brief Introduction," IMHO: In My Humble Opinion, https://www.scribd.com/document/223409613/Chaos-Theory-a-Brief-Introduction-IMHO.

90. Greene, *The Fabric of the Cosmos*, chap. 12.

91. To begin with, wind is life, living spirit. When wind blows through a human being, as with a song through a whistle or a flute, it is a sacred expression of being.

92. Greene, *The Fabric of the Cosmos*, pt. 4, 5. See also the recent experiment stopping a pulse of light, then restarting it in another place, in Kenneth Chang, "Wizardry at Harvard: Halt Light and Then Move It," *New York Times*, February 8, 2007, A11.

93. Vine Deloria Jr., *The World We Used to Live In: Remembering the Powers of the Medicine Men* (Golden, CO: Fulcrum, 2006).

94. Greene, *The Fabric of the Cosmos*, pt. 3, mostly in chap 9–11. See particularly 254, 320–21.

95. See Thomas E. Mails and Dan Evehema, *Hotevilla: Hopi Shrine of the Covenant, Microcosm of the World* (New York: Marlowe, 1995), chap. 2; Waters, *Book of the Hopi*, chap. 1–5; Elise Clews Parsons, *Pueblo Indian Religion* (Lincoln: University of Nebraska Press, 1966), chap. 3.

96. "Gaia Hypothesis," Wikipedia, https://en.wikipedia.org/wiki/Gaia_hypothesis; Stephen Miller, "Gaia Hypothesis," UCD Energy Research Group, University College Dublin, 1989, http://erg.ucd.ie/arupa/references/gaia.html; M. Pidwirny, "Chapter 5: The Universe,

Earth, Natural Spheres, and Gaia; (d). The Gaia Hypothesis." PhysicalGeography.net (reproduced from *Fundamentals of Physical Geography*, 2nd ed., 2006), http://www.physicalgeography.net/fundamentals/5d.html; "Gaia Hypothesis: Proposed By Dr. James Lovelock and Dr. Lynn Margulis," Inter-Disciplinary Publications of Peace and Of Great Souls, http://www.mountainman.com.au/gaia.html.

97. Rupert Sheldrake, *A New Science of Life: A Hypothesis of Formative Causation* (Los Angeles: J. P. Tarcher, 1981).

98. Garry E. R. Schwartz and Linda G. S. Russek, *The Living Energy Universe* (Charlottesville, VA: Hampton Roads, 1999), xv.

99. Lee Nichol, ed., *The Essential David Bohm* (London: Routledge, 2003), through much of the book, but especially 171–82 and chap. 3.

100. Ibid., 115.

101. Ibid., 171.

102. Almo Farina, "The Eco-Field: A New Paradigm for Landscape Ecology," *Ecological Research* 19 (2004): 107–10; Almo Farina, *Principles of Landscape Ecology: Toward a Science of Landscape* (Dordrecht, the Netherlands: Springer, 2007); Almo Farina, *Ecology, Cognition, and Landscape: Linking Natural and Social Systems* (Berlin: Springer-Verlag, 2010); Will Taegel, *The Mother Tongue: Intimacy in the Eco-Field* (Wimberley, TX: 2nd Tier, 2012), particularly chap. 7.

103. Taegel, *The Mother Tongue*, chap. 7 in particular, relating to the theme and discussion of the entire work.

104. William J. Broad, "From Scum, Perhaps the Tiniest Form of Life," *New York Times*, December 23, 2008, 1.

105. Author Stephen Sachs, while at graduate school in Chicago from 1960 to 1965, knew Edmund Jacobson, visiting with him and his wife on a number of occasions during which they discussed Dr. Jacobson's work with progressive relaxation (PR) and related views about psychology. On a few occasions Jacobson treated Sachs with his progressive relaxation techniques as a method not only for promoting physical health, but also for developing self-consciousness as an alternative to Freudian psychology. In addition, F. J. McGuigan and Paul M. Lehrer, "Progressive Relaxation: Origins, Principles, and Clinical Applications," in *Principles and Practice of Stress Management*, eds. Paul M. Lehrer, Robert L. Woolfolk, and Wesley E. Sime (New York: Guilford, 2009).

106. In the early 1990s Stephen Sachs spoke with a biofeedback researcher who had worked with Swami Rama, head of the Himalayan Institute,

which had a school of hatha yoga, and one of whose emphases was working with American medical doctors and psychologists on applying the Hindu tradition for improving health. The researcher said that after Swami Rama had quite aptly demonstrated biofeedback techniques that were measured on the research group's equipment, he began producing readings on the instruments that were so much beyond what scientific theory of the day accepted that they dared not make those results public. Sachs visited the Himalayan institute in Honesdale, PA, a number of times (as well as attending one Himalayan Institute annual conference in Chicago) and had several interactions with Swami Rama, as well as undertaking individual meditations with leading Himalayan Institute teacher Dr. Arya and having considerable contact with a student of Swami Rama's who headed the Deer Path Yoga Center in Bloomington, IN.

107. On the cover of *Time*, February 3, 2014, it reads, "The Mindful Revolution: The Science of Finding Focus In a Stressed-Out, Multitasking Culture by Kate Pickert." The table of contents lists the short description of the article on 40–46 as "Head Space," while the title, under the heading of "Health," on 40–41 is "The Art of Being Mindful."

108. Bruce H. Lipton, *The Biology of Belief* (Santa Rosa, CA: Mountain Love/Elite, 2005), quote on 15.

109. Cajete, *Native Science*. Native science—or since there is no word for "science" in Native languages, the Indigenous equivalent of science—is more passively experimental than Western science. This is because, while Western science identifies hypotheses to test and then creates experiments to test those hypothesis (some of which are extremely intrusive into the subject being tested, particularly in biology where living people, animals, and plants are often put through injurious procedures, which Natives would not undertake out of respect for the living beings). In contrast, Native science is accomplished largely by careful long-term observation, with experimental learning applying the hypothesized conclusions in practice and then making adjustments according to what does and does not work. In some instances, Native science may be slightly more actively experimental, as for example in aspects of the development of most of the world's plant food via selectively choosing seeds and, possibly, some crossbreeding. This, however, is nothing like the more aggressive experimentation that Western science uses, and moreover is undertaken with a holistic concern for all the effects and side effects

that may be involved. Thus Native science is usually much slower in developing knowledge, but the traditional knowledge that is developed is quite sound, and often is more accurate in its findings about what works well in particular locations. Western science tends to put more emphasis on general principles and therefore often pays much less attention to the needs to adapt those principles to the realities of particular places—too often with disastrous results—than do Native approaches, which emphasize the importance of place, as is discussed with examples in the next chapter on politics and in the environmental chapter.

110. Chogyam Trungpa, *Cutting Through Spiritual Materialism* (Boulder, CO: Shambhala, 1973).

Chapter 5: Applying American Indian Principles of Harmony and Balance to Renew the Politics of the Twenty-First Century

Stephen M. Sachs and Phyllis M. Gagnier

Section 1: Inclusive Participatory Democracy

Stephen M. Sachs

The public affairs of the world are greatly out of balance at this writing in the fall of 2019. In the United States, and many places across the globe, people are deeply divided, with massive peaceful demonstrations in numerous nations, violence at varying levels in others. Relations among people, and with the Earth, are often out of harmony. From an Indigenous point of view, there is too much emphasis on, and struggle for, power as control, and not enough on empowerment. The causes are many. Some have to do with overly narrow view of economics and development, which are taken up directly in the next two chapters on economics and ecology. Others have to do with how we come to view the world and guide our actions in it. These are considered in the chapter on education. All of these are interrelated with the political, which is where we begin.

STEPHEN M. SACHS

Applying the Principle of Diversity or Place

American Indians and Indigenous societies, while still organized as bands and tribes before they began to expand into states, while not perfect, did relatively well in providing good lives for almost all their citizens, as was shown in the section on traditional Native American societies, in the opening chapter of these volumes. At the center of virtually all Indigenous political and social relations has been a respect for all people, all beings, with the Earth seen as a living being. All people, and indeed all beings, are considered relatives. Thus, one's community is to be thought of as a family in which everyone has a responsibility toward everyone else. As the Comanche say, individuals and societies need to live and function according to four basic values, the "Four Rs": Relationship, Responsibility, Reciprocity, and Redistribution.[1] It follows from the nature of relationship that community members have responsibilities for one another. This responsibility requires reciprocity in relationships to maintain, and at times recreate the harmony and balance of the community. Thus, reciprocity involves a redistribution to achieve and maintain a dynamic balance. This is not just a redistribution of concrete things, but of all that is valued, including actions.

To keep the community in harmony and balance, everyone's welfare needs to be provided for. Since the autonomy of each individual, and her/his ability to contribute to the community are highly valued, so far as possible, assistance ought to be given to others in ways that are empowering, rather than in ways that cause dependence. Indeed, empowerment is critical to maintaining a well-balanced community of harmonious relationships. This balance rests on a continuing reciprocity creating and preserving interdependence. Interdependence is undermined by an excess of dependence.

All of the basic principles of Indigenous relationships have been part of an all pervading spirituality and general worldview, without dogma, that each society has held in its own way. Diversity has been honored so that respect has not been limited to members of the same society, or holders of the same worldview. It has been understood that in a complex world no one or group can have a full understanding of the world, or even major issues. Everyone benefits from an exchange of views, and dialoguing on the issues. Everyone concerned has something of value to contribute to the broader understanding.

We need to return to this kind of valuing of diversity, differences in place. To a degree, movement in that direction has been occurring in the West and elsewhere. This has been occurring behind the more reported, often angry exclusiveisms as has been seen, including in the United States. In the advancing struggle for gaining equality, the concept of equality has largely moved from assimilation with everyone becoming a member of the dominant group, or essentially the same, to multicultural diversity with people becoming accepted for who they are in their own personal or group culture. It has involved a shift from undertaking a melting pot process, to taking a tossed salad approach. This has been seen in the ongoing struggles for racial, women's, gender, economic, religious, and ethnic equality.[2] It is also at the heart of the rise of multiculturalism in numerous nations. As Natalia Simanovsky noted:

> In Canada, multiculturalism is deemed by the majority of society to be a successful government policy precisely because it promotes, among other things, national unity. For the most part, multiculturalism in Canada fosters social cohesion by placing all cultures on an equal footing. It creates common values, such as tolerance, that can be shared by the many different members of society, despite the fact that many citizens originate from a variety places with disparate religious backgrounds. In other words, multiculturalism can be defined as an approach that aims to assist with the integration of immigrants and minorities, remove barriers to their participation in Canadian life and make them feel more welcome in Canadian society, leading to a stronger sense of belonging and national pride.[3]

But while in the US, Canada, and elsewhere there have been uneven and inconsistent gains in this direction, the world, and almost all nations will only function well today, if all move much further from feeling the necessity of unity through sameness and conformity, to unity through diversity. This can produce great synergy, as shown in the discussion of work teams below.

The principle of diversity, with respect for all members of the community encompasses everyone having an equal say in all decisions that affect them. This is essential for people to actually be full and equal members of the community, and also to feel that they are honored members of the community. This is a necessity for their own wellbeing, as well as for encouraging their continued participation and support for the community and the way it functions.

Applying Traditional Principles of Inclusive Participatory Democracy in the Twenty-First Century

Some form of inclusive participatory democracy is necessary in the best society. This requires a full and equal vote by all competent, of age, citizens, in all relevant decisions—something that is still being struggled for in the United States. But voting is the tip of the ice berg of participation. It is only meaningful if it is supported by a much larger base.

For everyone to have an equal say in huge post-industrial societies the means of expression have to be equal and equally accessible to all, while the media needs to be equally expressive of all points of view and opinions. It must also report accurately the full range of relevant information in a balanced manner. There are a variety of vehicles that can be used in a post-industrial society to attain the open access and broad representation of views necessary for a participatory society. One route is to require, in a fully private, or mixed private-public media system, broad and diverse ownership of electronic and print media, supported by equal access requirements.

The "fairness doctrine," for example, developed by the US Federal Communications Commission (FCC), in 1949, required broadcasters to cover public issues and provide each side with equal coverage, or opportunity to respond.[4] As issues often have multiple aspects and sides, the full range of views ought to have the opportunity to be heard. As time, or space, for such discussion might be limited, it would be legitimate for less time to be given to views well outside the mainstream. Such equal time regulations might apply to print, or other media, as well.

This was argued for, but rejected by a majority of the US Supreme Court in *Miami Herald Publishing Co. v. Tornillo*.[5] The same openness can be achieved in a fully public media system, if diversity of control and opinion are built into it. The system would have to be truly common, and not dominated by or operated with advantage for any governmental or private interests, or combination of interests. Similarly, an open and neutral internet, without censorship or favoritism of one opinion or group over another is essential in the information age, as is the right and ability of people to freely form social, economic, and political interest groups, with broad freedom of expression and petition in practice. In addition, information relevant to public affairs needs to be broadly and equally readily available and accessible, with secrecy limited to an appropriate minimum, if citizens are to have the knowledge necessary to make good decisions.

Election campaigns for public office, or for citizen voting on issues, ought to be carried out with equal time provisions for all candidates and issues on the ballot, as they are in many European countries.[6] This has been proposed for US presidential elections, as exemplified by the Fair Elections Act in the Maine House of Representatives proposed by Diane Russell in fall 2013, and the proposal of US senator Bernie Sanders, in 2013.[7] Under this arrangement, during the period leading up to the voting (often six weeks), a series of debate formats (though each candidate or position can decide if they wish to debate or present) are provided with equal time for each candidate or position during prime time on radio and television. No candidate or position can run radio or television advertising during the run up to the election period. Usually, the "debates" take place more frequently as the time of voting approaches. The system only functions fairly if sufficient television and radio time is provided, so that the public has opportunity to get to know the candidates and positions on issues adequately, and lesser known candidates do not have a disadvantage in the election.

In addition, it may be useful to apply a device used in one US presidential debate, to have a trustworthy neutral non-partisan organization select a representative sample of undecided voters (or of voters generally) to ask questions of the candidates in the debate.[8]

Another necessity is to make the opportunities to vote easily accessible by providing convenient polling locations for all, at appropriate and sufficient times, perhaps including lengthy periods of early voting and voting by mail.[9] In addition, adequate safeguards need to be in place to ensure the voting and the counting of votes is fair and honest, with sufficient reviews available to correct errors, cheating, and other malfeasance.

Increasing Citizen Participation and Input with Electronic Democracy

The development of the internet with websites, social media, E-mails, Skype, video-conferencing, etc., provides new possibilities for communicating, bridging geographical and social distances. It offers possibilities for citizen participation and building community that were not previously available. Barber, and Becker and Slaton, suggest that electronic technology can be used to strengthen participatory democracy by such means as televising town meetings, establishing a national civic communications cooperative, and providing an extensive and up to date online library. With equal access to the internet, his would equalize access to information and promote full civic education of all citizens. Democracy can also be enhanced via the internet through extensive, balanced, electronic journalism and publishing. It can provide convenient means for citizens to petition government and non-governmental entities, and it can be used to undertake scientific polling.[10]

Some municipalities in the United States regularly televise city council and other important meetings. For example, the City of Stockton, California operates Channel 97 in Stockton as a Government Access Cable Television channel devoted to Stockton City Government, including live broadcasts of Stockton City Council Meetings on Tuesday at 5:30 pm, rebroadcast daily at 11:30 a.m. and 7:00 pm. Channel 97 also carries a City Informational Bulletin that gives information about City services, upcoming meetings and special city events when no other programs are scheduled.[11]

Barber is among those who propose developing electronic balloting so that citizens could quickly and often be involved in making a large number of decisions that currently are made by representatives, with voters logging on to computers at home or in easily accessible public places. Some limited use of electronic voting may eventually become possible. At least for the moment, there is the technical problem of being able to ensure secure and unhackable or otherwise incorruptible electronic voting. As of fall 2019, secure web voting appears to be beyond the capability of technology for at least the near future. More important is the difficulty of busy citizens to keep up with the details of numerous complex issues in order to be frequently and regularly involved in making competent legislative or administrative decisions.

More promising is the use of electronic means to assist enhancement of public dialogue, for example by regularly establishing focus groups of representative citizens to research, in a holistic participatory manner. Assisted by experts, and with access to relevant information, these groups could consider the full range of approaches to, and views on, sets of important issues. The deliberations as a whole, and summary discussions and recommendations, could be readily available to anyone on the internet. This could be followed up with televised sessions in live time, available for replay on the internet, telephone and/or Skype (or equivalent) public forums in which anyone could participate in the concerned jurisdiction (from village or city ward to the nation). Some experiments have been done with this approach.[12] James S. Fishkin proposes the implementation of deliberative opinion polls among a statistically representative sample of citizens that are not too large to preclude meaningful discussion, These polls would attempt to model what the general public would think if, hypothetically, it could be immersed in deliberative processes.[13] In September 2019 Fishkin and Larry Diamond used polling to find 526 people constituting a representative sample of all American voters to come together for four days, supported by neutral experts, to discuss major public policy issues in small groups and in all participant sessions. By discussing issues pragmatically, avoiding charged and ideological terms, participants were able to dialogue easily, often sharing from their own experience. In the process people with widely different views who have been on opposite sides of political divides were able to understand and appreciate each other in the course of becoming more informed. Many participants said that the discussions did not change their views on issues, but did get them to understand and respect divergent perspectives. A review of participants early expressions, and what they later stated, did indicate that many did develop new positions on concrete questions, even if their general philosophies remained essentially unchanged.

These approaches, while quite useful, in many instances abstract from everyday life experience when they are used beyond actual local or internet communities that regularly interact on pragmatic issues.[14] Perhaps the most promising teledemocratic vehicles are those that help to build community and trust. This is extremely important, because from an Indigenous point of view, shared by many contemporary commentators, many current societies suffer from an atomization and alienation that has seriously diminished the quality of human relations, and hence the quality of life, within society. Much of the web of good relations that were the hallmark of the family, like the functioning of well working Indigenous communities, today has become fractured and skewed. Consequently, it has become necessary to rebuild community, and to reestablish trustful, reciprocal, relationships among citizens and social groups. Applying Fishkin and Diamond's 2019 representative meeting approach to regularly meeting groups might be a very fine method of community building.

One development moving in this direction since the 1980s is a shift by government and nonprofit organizations dealing with welfare issues and programs to take social capital and community assets-based approaches to target communities.

"Social capital" describes the durable networks that form social resources through which individuals and groups strive for mutual recognition.[15] As such, social capital is the necessary infrastructure of civic and community life that generates 'norms of reciprocity and civic engagement.'[16] Assets-based development stresses locally generated knowledge that permits communities to mobilize their assets, broadly conceived, to address problems.[17] An increasing number of local projects, as well as funding programs in foundations and federal agencies, have begun to incorporate these insights. By treating communities as social capital networks, rather than strictly as discourse communities, we can begin to ground the connective elements of new information technologies in social life and social structure.[18]

For the increasing rise of social networks, the internet, especially social media, as well as e-mail and other electronic communications, have been extremely empowering. This has been an important factor in enabling participatory democracy by democratizing organizations of all kinds, as is discussed below. It is significant that across much of the Middle East, the Arab Spring, which began in Tunisia in 2011, was largely organized and participatively coordinated through social media and networking.[19]

The emergence of internet networks by advocacy groups for the purposes of sharing information and ideas and engaging in mutual problem solving could already be seen in California in the mid-1980s. This was the case with the Institute for Global Communications (IGC), serving individuals and groups engaged in advocacy for social justice, human rights and the environment, and HandsNet, which expanded from a set of California-based community organizations working locally in the areas of hunger and nutrition, homelessness and housing, and community economic development, to serve as a national communication vehicle.[20] Fredland reports:

> Both have organized new models that generate information out of the needs of their members. Both draw their information, at least in part, directly from their members and represent: few forms of what I call "distributed responsibility," which makes widely decentralized nodes of the network primary information gatherers. Finally, they address specific organizing problems (in very different ways) and have been driven by this practical problem focus.

Such networks can build community by linking and empowering members, whom they serve, around common problem solving needs and efforts, and representing their members in political arenas, with the speed, volume of information capacity, and breadth of coverage to keep their lobbying and petition functions quite representative.

The number and range of issues and actions that representatives of local groups, and people at the grassroots level, become involved in are greater than the constituents themselves can decide upon, or even monitor in detail. But they can monitor representative samples, establish monitoring personnel and systems, and can require that new policies, and major questions which arise in the course of operation be deliberated inclusively and participatively. Any number of means can be employed, depending on the circumstances, from face to face meetings, e-mail exchanges and voting, to teleconferences. As Mansbridge shows from working with such groups, as trust is established and maintained in the network, it is not necessary for everyone involved to participate in every instrumental decision, or review every action, once basic policy is established by participatory process. The entire group can be involved again whenever specific decisions or the general policy come into question, or the need to make new policy or action guidelines arises.[21] This is quite similar in principle, but using contemporary means, to how the Wendot and other Indian federations conducted business participatively and inclusively beyond the local community (as discussed in chapter 1).

It is important to note that such networks can function for their own and their members' independent information, guidance, and decision making; for planning and advocacy, often to government, but also to nongovernmental organizations (whether business or nonprofit); and as direct inputs to government.

This occurred in the state of Vermont, beginning in the 1980s, when the city of Burlington, under the leadership of socialist mayor Bernie Sanders, made economic development a major focus of his administration. The city established neighborhood planning assemblies, along with a local government access channel, Town Meeting Television. The channel began as a vehicle for citizens to air deliberative and access concerns, and then moved quickly toward an emphasis on planning for sustainable development.[22] In 1992 Vermont launched a statewide telecommunications planning process. Then, in 1994, with the assistance of a grant from the US Department of Housing and Urban Development (HUD), which had come to place increasing emphasis in its community development grants on assets-based strategies, the City of Burlington, "established a public access telecomputing center as a model of how to move disenfranchised communities from a focus on housing development issues to ones of sustainable community economic development."[23] This is somewhat similar to the non-electronic (but computer assisted) democratic process that the Comanche Nation of Oklahoma established in the 1990s to build community consensus on proposals to the tribes government council, the Comanche Business committee, discussed below.

Beyond Electronic Democracy

Electronic communications for building community and inclusive participatory democracy are extremely important in the twenty-first century. But like all vehicles they have costs and limitations as well as advantages. One issue is that the internet has been used by hate, terrorist, and criminal groups for clearly socially destructive purposes. As with all expression, public and private regulation should be aimed at maintaining openness and equal access. But at the point where expression is significantly damaging or dangerous, appropriate regulation is necessary to protect individuals and society. Recently in the US, politicians lying and people spreading false information on the internet have become serious problems. Some regulation is needed against misuse of the internet. But in a fully inclusive and balanced society, a diverse and aggressive press and an engaged and well educated public are the best defense against misuse of electronic media. These issues are discussed below, and in chapter 8 on education. A broader problem is that interactions by electronic means lose important substantive aspects that are essential parts of face to face relationships. Moreover, staring at a computer and television screens for too many hours for virtual experience, not only denies direct experience, but creates physical problems for people, especially young people, for whom it is important to limit the time they spend in electronic activity. The very young ought not to be exposed to computer and television screens at all.[24]

We need to engage in direct activity and interactions, to be socialized to fully meaningful life as whole people living within society, to build and maintain healthy, rewarding relationships with one another, and with our environment, including nature. As Indigenous people say, it is a question of balance. This author, for example, works with the internet and e-mail to produce issues of two online journals, and worked to develop several books and many papers, including this one, word processing on a computer and exchanging chapter files for comment and editing by e-mail with people at a distance, some of whom he had not yet met in person. But he also spends time in personal and community interactions in the concrete world, engages in enjoyable physical activity in dance and hiking, which provides much beauty in the course of renewing his relationship to nature, while taking time for inner reflection and meditation. All of the time, activity and interchange spent off-line, is critical for maintaining the dynamic balance and perspective to function well online.

To achieve social harmony, people have to achieve inner harmony. Treating each other (and being treated) respectfully is a major help with that. But we also have to do our own inner work. At a minimum, we need to reflect regularly to clear the psychological complexes, impacts of trauma, guilt, etc., and to clear our consciences by asking for and acting to seek forgiveness for inevitable transgressions, while giving thanks for what we have received. Ultimately, we need to take responsibility for doing this, but we also have to have the humility to ask for appropriate help, when needed.

In addition, as Native people recognize, there is a spiritual (not necessarily religious) side of life that needs the opportunity to unfold. This can be just recognizing human spirit, in ourselves and others, or it can be something more. We each find it differently, but we need to give it space to be whole people and be able to relate well with others. Some find it in meditation or spiritual practice, others in music, in dance, in nature, in the space between steps while walking, or just in quiet moments. To be whole people, and empower ourselves to be good citizens, we have to give ourselves the inner space to be who we really are.

Direct Ways of Building Community

Community building for individual, group, organization, and political empowerment can, and must, take place in non-electronic ways, as important as the tools of electronic communication, linking, and interaction are. An interesting example has been the development of time dollars (a form of co-production) by Edgar Cahn.[25] Time dollars build and maintain relationships among people through a non-money (or by creating a special non-currency money) system of creating reciprocity, returning people to the kinds of relationships that were the hallmark of well-functioning Indigenous societies. The time dollar system is very simple, and operates effectively through time banks functioning with a very simple computer accounting program.[26] The principle is that for one hour of work, that the organization or community in question wishes to designate as eligible, a person doing that work receives credit for one time dollar that can be spent for any good or service identified by the organization or community. Thus people are empowered by earning services or goods, rather than being given them, and reciprocal relationships are established. As a result, people deal better with each other. Indeed, some people who have been engaged in criminal activity do not do so with people they are now related to by time dollar networks, because they need each other.

This has many other applications, but has been extremely useful in low income areas. For example, Sarah spends time as a companion four hours in a week for elderly and disabled Margie. In return, the neighborhood organization time bank provides her with one time dollar with a collaborating attorney for legal work, that she could not otherwise afford, and three hours of plastering and painting work by unemployed George, who in turn is able to buy with time dollars a used computer from the neighborhood organization time dollar store, that he needs to start his own business.

Time dollars have as many applications as the creativity of people can come up with. They have been used to help young people stay in school and do well. For example Tom has had trouble doing the work in his sixth grade math class, but he knows enough to tutor fourth graders in math so he can earn enough time dollars to buy sporting goods (or a computer) that he wants. Seeing that he can help the younger students in math gives him confidence, and an interest in succeeding in his own studies, in which his performance greatly improves. The Time Dollar Institute (renamed Time Banks USA) reported, "In January 2006, *The Chronicle of Philanthropy* reported that about 25,000 people in the United States and 60,000 internationally participate in Time Banks, strengthening the bonds among participants and increasing their effective purchasing power by the equivalent of millions of dollars. There are more than one hundred Time Bank programs in the United States, including two operated by Making Connections sites. Twenty-six other countries also have Time Banks. In November 2007, the International Time Banking Conference drew 238 leaders from thirty-one states and twelve countries. Other ideas developed by Cahn to allow clients of formal service systems to play a more active role in service provision are being adopted by organizations ranging from the National Legal Aid and Defender Association to England's [sic] National Health Service."[27]

Appropriate Decision Making Structures and Processes

Traditionally, American Indian and other Indigenous societies benefited greatly by deciding by consensus, talking issues through, taking everyone's concerns and interests into account, until everyone agreed, or acquiesced (having had their say and seeing no point in continuing to push a position that lacked support). Deciding in this way often is more time consuming than making decisions by majority vote, but it has several advantages. First, there is an emphasis on creating holistic decisions, as best as possible including and balancing everyone's concerns. That often leads to better decisions than are achieved in a majority vote process. There one side may simply overpower the other. Further, compromises that are attained to achieve a majority, may be more about giving bits and pieces to the involved parties that do not fit well together, than creating a well-balanced set of actions. Second, the inclusiveness, has a stronger tendency to create actual unity, and a sense of identity with the group, encouraging continued participation, than does a majority vote system of deciding, which may more easily promote divisiveness and faction.

Traditional Native societies operated in a context that was of smaller scale than the broader, more widely interconnected world, of the twenty-first century. Deciding by consensus often works very well in relatively small groups and communities, but the application of its principles are more complex in today's larger scale societies.

Traditional Indian federations give some clues as to how modern mass societies can use their communications technology to become far more participatory. The Wendot, Haudenosaunee, and Muskogee, for example, as shown in chapter 1, after first discussing issues, sent representatives to tribal, and in turn to federation councils. Decisions at higher levels had to be ratified at lower levels, so discussion often went back and forth between levels. Representatives to higher levels, were thus actually more representative of their constituents than is generally the case in current legislatures.

In a limited way, that device can be, and indeed has been, applied in different settings in recent years. For instance, Yugoslavia included this method in moving to a participatory form of government and economy, though a number of flaws made the system as a whole less democratic in practice than theory. Beginning around 1950, until the step by step demise of its liberal period starting in the mid-1970s, Yugoslavia operated its government and all but the smallest businesses using participatory principles.[28] This included requiring legislators at every level to discuss annual budgets and major proposals with voters at meetings across their districts between the time of proposal and final voting, while economic enterprises functioned as cooperatives under worker self-management. In the larger cooperatives ("self-managed enterprises") issues relating to the entire workplace had to be decided by the central workers council, and by employees in each of the businesses units, often with back and forth dialogue between the center and the parts, until a decision was finalized. The successes, despite the limitations, of the Yugoslav social and workers' self-management system for a number of years shows the possibility of such arrangements functioning on a considerably larger scale, and in a much more diverse and complex socio-economic-political system, than that of traditional American Indian nations, if they are applied appropriately for the situation in question.[29] Further evidence is the success of numerous organizations in the United States and around the world in operating participatively in this manner, as is discussed below.

The Example of Participatory Budgeting

A more recent set of developments in citizen participation are suggestive of what might be accomplished in a fully democratic society. One example is participatory budgeting at the local level to directly involve people in the budgeting process.[30.] Good budgeting requires expertise. This can be included in popular participation in budgeting by having neutral experts act as resource people to the participants to point out the consequences of alternative proposals, and to show technically how desired goals might be met, at what costs, and with what benefits. The current move toward participatory budgeting at the local level began in Porto Alegre, Brazil in 1989 and has since spread in various forms to over 1200 municipalities worldwide, including more recently to New York City, Vallejo, California, and Chicago, Illinois. Local citizens participating in setting budgets in the United States extends back to continuing participatory decision making on all local issues by New England town meetings (an Indigenous influenced development). Other previous instances include participants having a say in how funds were spent in local Community Action Programs (CAP) in the War on Poverty under the Equal Opportunity Program of the Economic Opportunity Act of 1964. Just what participatory budgeting means has varied widely in the post 1989 cases. In some Canadian instances, it has taken place at the organization level, with concerned people involved in setting school and housing budgets, and hence the actual priorities of the organizations. In Chicago's 49th Ward, residents took part in meetings to determine spending choices for capital improvements. The result was that the included projects expanded from the usually funded "high priorities" list, such as fixing potholes in streets, to also include such usually not funded "lower priority" projects, as dog parks, community gardens, decorative bike racks, and murals.

In Porto Alegre all of the city's residents were invited to take part in meetings to establish the municipal budgeting priorities. This is a city of more than one million people, with widespread poverty and income disparity. A third of the population lived in isolated slums with little access to city utility and social services, In the first years less than 1,000 people participated, but after a decade the number had grown to some 1,400, as people saw the resulting change in city priorities. The results included an increase in sewer and water connections from 75 percent of households in 1988 to 98 percent in 1997. The revised budgeting brought extensive increases in the number of schools, public housing projects, and health services.

The outcomes of participatory budgeting vary according to the range of issues to be publicly decided, and according to the breadth and quality of the participatory process. The results indicate that participatory budgeting, appropriately applied, can be an effective means of public participation. The process tends to diversify and equalize power, as it empowers people in the course of encouraging their participation. At the same time, there is an equalizing effect on the distribution of public goods in the course of building and strengthening human relations in the community, which enhances the communities commonness (and *communitas*). In the fully participatory society, participatory budgeting can be used as part of broader participation at every level, using processes appropriate to the given situation.

The Use of Citizens' Assemblies

A recent pair of examples of applying citizen participation to dealing with substantive issues is the utilization at the provincial level of citizen assemblies in British Columbia and Ontario to develop electoral reform proposals.[31] Similar citizen participation processes were later applied internationally, as well as by the City of Jackson, Mississippi, that was ongoing in 2017. The citizens' assembly process was first applied in British Columbia. In the 1996 provincial legislative election, under a first-past-the-post electoral system, the New Democratic Party had gained a majority of seats in the Assembly, despite the Liberal Party winning a majority of the popular vote. On regaining power in 2001, the Liberal party instituted a "Citizens' Assembly on Electoral Reform to assess all possible models of electing MLAs [(members of the legislative assembly)], including preferential ballots, proportional representation, and our current system," and to "Give the Citizens' Assembly a mandate to hold hearings throughout BC, and if it recommends changes to the current electoral system, that opinion will be put to a province wide referendum."[32]

The BC Citizens' Assembly began work in fall 2003, with the goal of analyzing alternative electoral systems in terms of their ability to conform to the democratic values of fair election results through proportionality, effective local representation, and greater voter choice. The assembly members were chosen through a process that began by mailing information about the project to two hundred randomly selected voters in each of the province's electoral districts. Interested recipients attended selection meetings. A random selection was then made from those who volunteered at the meetings to participate in the Assembly, balancing age and gender, with one man and one woman being chosen from each electoral district, plus two Aboriginal members. This produced a Citizens' Assembly of 160 people.[33]

The Assembly began with a four-month learning period, assisted by staff, designed to meet the members learning needs. It took place every other weekend in six sessions, with material sent to participants in advance.

> Learning sessions opened with a plenary session for all Assembly members. The plenary generally consisted of a lecture (with PowerPoint presentation) that lasted 45 to 50 minutes. Following the presentation, members could raise questions of clarification.
>
> Each presentation ended with a set of questions for discussion by the members. These questions were addressed in 12 discussion groups that varied in number from 10 to 15 members—the size of each group was, in part, decided by

the size of the available rooms. The discussion groups typically lasted 45 to 60 minutes.

Members were assigned to discussion groups on a random basis, staying with their group for the weekend. The groups changed each weekend, which helped members get to know one another better while exposing them to a variety of perspectives.

Following the discussion groups, members reconvened in plenary and a spokesperson for each group reported back the results of their discussions to the Assembly. The afternoon session followed the same pattern as the morning session. The sessions were usually separated by 30–45 minute breaks. This allowed members to talk informally with one another and with staff, and provided ample time for movement between the various rooms of the Centre for Dialogue complex.

Facilitators were appointed to help discussion groups and to provide information on the topic under discussion. Prior to each weekend, the facilitators and the Assembly's research staff met to review and discuss the weekend agenda and review the learning materials. In a number of instances, suggestions from the facilitators were used to modify the presentations and discussion group plans.

Following each session, the facilitators and staff met again for a debriefing. These meetings gave the facilitators an opportunity to share experiences on best practices, and to identify process problems and any specific content issues that members found challenging.

All of the plenary learning sessions were open to the public (the discussion groups were for members only). As well, all of the learning materials (including lecture notes and PowerPoint presentations) prepared for the members were available to the public through the Assembly's website, once they had been distributed to the members.[34]

A discussion forum website was established for members only, while all the plenary sessions were videotaped and broadcast to the public several times. The process also included team building and opportunities for members to learn computer and website skills. At the end of the learning session a planning meeting was undertaken to prepare for the public consultation stage of the project.

Public consultation took place through a series of 50 well-advertised public hearings around British Columbia from May to June that were located so that any interested citizen would not have to drive more than 30 minutes to attend a hearing. In large urban centers, multiple hearings were held on different days of the week, two or three weeks apart, to try to maximize the opportunity for people to attend. The hearing format varied according to the number of people attending.

Each hearing started with introductions from the local Assembly member. The introduction outlined the process to be followed during the evening.

A short video presentation was then given. This provided an overview of the Assembly, how it was created and the different phases of its processes, and a brief introduction to the five main families of electoral systems. The video concluded with an invitation to get involved through public hearings, submissions and watching the Assembly's website.

The primary role of the Assembly members on the panel was to listen to the presenters and ask for clarification and further information. The intention was to create an atmosphere where the public—presenters and audience—felt they could speak freely and openly.

After the Assembly members had finished questioning a presenter, audience members were invited to question the presenters. Members of the public were free also to express their opinions on what they considered to be appropriate electoral models for the Assembly to consider.

In some of the smaller communities, few members of the public attended and only one or two people made presentations. In these instances, chairs were rearranged in a circle (see *Appendix: Informal Meetings*) and the hearings became an informal dialogue on the attendees' opinions on different aspects of electoral systems and their thoughts on what would be the best electoral system for British Columbia. The moderator managed the discussion.

An information table was set up at all of the hearings to distribute materials prepared by the Assembly's communications staff. These materials included a number of Fact Sheets, which provided a written overview of the work of the Assembly, and summarized information on electoral and voting systems.[35]

Close to 3,000 people attended the hearings, at which more than 350 citizens made presentations. Members of the public sent in 1,603 substantive written submissions on the issue of electoral reform. Almost all of these were submitted electronically, and were posted on the assembly website. A few of the submissions provided links to other websites that provided information and discussion cornering electoral reform. Surveys on the question were circulated at hearings, with almost 2,500 distributed and 1,066 returned. The surveys were collated by staff and analyzed by an external consultant, to provide the assembly members with overall views of the survey results and specific comments.

The deliberation phase of the BC Citizens' Assembly took place from September to November 2004. Part of the discussion proceeded over the members-only section of the Assembly website. The main deliberations unfolded across several meetings in Vancouver, whose formal sessions were open to the public. Over the span of six general meetings, with continued breakouts for small group discussion and time for informal discussions, the assembly developed a consensus to recommend an alternative electoral system. The assembly's proposal was then made public for consideration by the BC voters to further discuss the issue and then decide on it in a referendum on May 17, 2005. Voters in the 2005 referendum voted against the alternate electoral proposal, leaving the existing system in place.

Ontario undertook a similar Citizens' Assembly on Electoral Reform process from April to June 2006. In this instance 103 randomly chosen citizens, one from each Ontario constituency, participated in the Assembly. The Ontario assembly also recommended changing the electoral system, but the public voted to retain the existing process. Many participatory democrats argue that the fact that Assembly's recommendations failed to pass in the two Canadian provinces is not an indication of failure, but simply the results of specific applications of a broad public deliberation process. Interest has continued in holding such assemblies, and as of October 2016, at least two additional applications of the process had been undertaken in Europe.

A Citizens' Assembly on Electoral Reform, The Burgerforum, was instituted by the government of Holland.[36] The Dutch assembly recommended some small changes in the country's election process, which were adopted by the Parliament. In Ireland in 2011, following the financial crisis that began in 2008, a series of political developments were begun which included citizens' assemblies that considered a number of major issues.[37]

The first stage was the 2012–14 Constitutional Convention composed of a chairperson nominated by the government, thirty-three representatives chosen by political parties, and sixty-six randomly chosen citizens. The convention made eighteen recommendations for constitutional amendments and twenty for other changes to laws or parliamentary standing orders. Some of the proposals were accepted by the government, some were rejected, and others were referred to committees for further consultation. In the prelude to the next national election, in 2016, there were a number of proposals for citizen discussions of major issues. Following the election, the newly formed Fine Gael–independent minority government made a commitment to citizen participation:

We will establish a Citizens' Assembly, within six months, and without participation by politicians, and with a mandate to look at a limited number of key issues over an extended time period. These issues will not be limited to those directly pertaining to the constitution and may include issues such as, for example how we, as a nation, best respond to the challenges and opportunities of an ageing population. That said, we will ask the Citizens' Assembly to make recommendations to the Dáil on further constitutional changes, including on the Eighth Amendment [which guarantees a fetal right to life], on fixed term parliaments and on the manner in which referenda are held (e.g. should "super referendum days," whereby a significant number of referenda take place on the same day, be held).

The two houses of the Irish Parliament, in July 2016, approved the establishment of a citizens' assembly to consider the four issues raised by the government, a Green Party amendment, "how the State can make Ireland a leader in tackling climate change," and "such other matters as may be referred to it". The Citizens' Assembly of ninety-nine randomly chosen eligible voters and alternates, chaired by a judge of the Supreme Court of Ireland, was formed in September 2016, and was to hold its first meeting on October 15.

The ILIS Process: A Contemporary Indigenous Example

A contemporary Native American case demonstrates that governance can be made more representative and effective, and the political system more participatory through interaction between consensus decision making bodies at different levels. From 1990 to 1992, the Comanche Nation of Oklahoma applied the Indigenous Leadership Interactive System (ILIS) to overcome serious problems with the culturally inappropriate form of government that had been imposed on many Indian nations by the US government.[38] The

Comanches traditionally lived in small bands governed in a participatory manner with leaders acting as facilitators, who, as respected wise elders, provided guidance to public opinion and discussion. In 1990, the tribal business council elected at large from the four Oklahoma Comanche communities was established to make decisions for the community. Tribal members felt alienated at not being directly involved in tribal affairs, and, in fact, often were not even represented. This resulted in low turnout in elections and at annual general tribal meetings. The council had difficulty in passing any measures, no matter how appropriate and well framed they might be, for lack of consensus. This was accompanied by a great deal of infighting in the community—especially on political issues—by people who, no longer able to participate directly in community affairs, felt unable to fulfill the basic tribal value of contributing to the wellbeing of the community.

To improve this situation, ILIS, an inclusive participatory strategic planning process, was applied to the specifics of the Comanche situation and culture. ILIS was designed according to traditional Indigenous North American values, using contemporary consensus decision making techniques and technology. The process was established to provide public input to the Business Committee, with meetings at the tribal level and in the four Comanche Communities. The tribal level meetings were composed of representatives of every relevant group in the Comanche Nation, while the four communities held general meetings of their Comanche citizens. Discussion of issues concerning the tribe as a whole went back and forth between the tribal and community meetings until consensus was established, while individual communities made decisions on their local issues. The result was that, so long as the ILIS process was used, measures upon which Comanche consensus had been built were easily passed by the Business Committee. Proposals for which no consensus had been established, continued not to pass, while the local committees developed and carried out a number of projects. Meanwhile, the atmosphere and relations across the Comanche Nation improved, participation increased at annual tribal general meetings and in elections, and for the first time in a decade a tribal chair was reelected.

Increasing Use of Participatory Process in the United States

Since the 1970s, the United States and the West have been experiencing a considerable growth in the application of consensus and other participatory decision making processes in many types of organizations,[39] This has occurred partly as a result of American Indian influence, as discussed in part I of this volume, but largely through independent development arising from the needs and changing culture of the contemporary era. Thus, a number of organizations working to have input into public decision making have been operating participatively. MoveOn.org, focusing on "Democracy and Action", regularly polls its members about what its positions and priorities should be, empowers its members to initiate their own petitions at local, state and national levels, and only accepts small monetary donations from individuals in order to keep power diffused internally.[40] Similarly, Occupy Wall Street, a protest and political action movement, also has worked to function as democratically as possible, particularly within local groups.[41] Organizations such as the National Coalition for Dialogue and Deliberation,[42] the Network for Peace Through Dialogue,[43] and Search for Common Ground[44] attempt to expand thoughtful participatory citizen discussion of important issues, helping people to come together in solving issues and overcoming differences.

In 2017 there are only a small number of highly participatory political groups in the United States and in numerous other countries. But with the rise of protest and action movements worldwide, including Occupy, Arab Spring (regardless of its ultimate success in bringing change),[45] and mass movements in Brazil and numerous other countries, the number, generally has been increasing, regardless of ups and downs over time.[46] Ultimately, for a society to reach its participatory potential, virtually all groups need to function inclusively democratically.

Section 2: Democracy within Organizations and between Organizations and the Community

Stephen M. Sachs

The Movement for Organizational Democracy

A worldwide movement for organizational democracy has been underway, since the end of World War II, that has the potential for playing a major role in democratizing societies around the world. In its most developed form, it is a full contemporary application of traditional Indigenous inclusive democratic principles. Indigenous institutions are largely very flat, equalitarian people-based structures, with basically equal status of participants. They have largely equalitarian rewards in concrete terms, but with a limited hierarchy of reward in terms of honor, according to one's achievements in contributing to the wellbeing of the community or group.

These organizations are based on trust. But the trust did not automatically arise. It had to be built, maintained, and renewed, partly in the court of public opinion, but also through ceremony, such as mutual gifting, or holding a pipe or other spiritual ritual.[47] In some situations, Native societies did function with limited hierarchy, such as in battle where the war leader had a limited authority to command largely autonomous warriors[48] because it was critical to act quickly in a coordinated manner, and there was not time for lengthy discussion. The US Army has mirrored this aspect of Indigenous practice in continuing to operate using its traditional chain of command during operations and training for operations, while using participatory teams for planning and evaluation.[49]

By contrast, with some notable exceptions, after the Middle Ages, European, and later European American, organizations, functioned largely hierarchically, on the basis of control. They functioned with differential status and rewards based largely on position in the hierarchy, as well as on the basis of loyalty and service to the hierarchy and the standards it passed down the organization.[50]

Hierarchical organizations do have a great deal of power. When operating properly they have the ability to make quick, unified decisions to coordinate action, as was discussed by Alexander Hamilton in *Federalist*, 81. There, Hamilton stressed the need for a unitary, hierarchical executive branch for the US government to administer policy and command the armed forces. But there are also shortcomings of hierarchical organizations, which in business led to movements to modify hierarchical structures. This eventually developed into a currently ongoing movement to transform them into participatory organizations.

In the mid-nineteenth century, businesses in the West were generally rather small, hierarchically organized, and managed by their owners. Production took place in what were essentially workshops. The employee was motivated largely by pleasing the employer to keep her or his employment, and to receive either a wage or piece work payment for work done. There was little relation between the employee and market forces of supply and demand. In that circumstance, however, the separation of the employee from the market was fairly small and not essential, and the dysfunctional aspects of hierarchy were minimal.[51]

By the early twentieth century, the leading capitalist enterprises had become quite large and technologically more complex, with production taking place in factories. Generally, these "corporate" firms were hierarchically managed by non-owners. Generally, the stockholder owners elected the board of directors who chose the management. At this stage two major problems began to have obvious effects.

First, hierarchical organizations suffer from inefficiencies that are compounded by the fact that employees who are paid fixed wages or salaries have no direct connection to the market and thus are only very slightly and indirectly motivated by it.[52]

Second, developments in the production process presented new questions of how work could best be organized and undertaken. This gave rise to the scientific management movement and business consulting in this period. In general, consultants like Frederick Taylor[53] developed important reforms, many of which are still useful if they are properly applied in their proper and limited context. As applied in the early twentieth century, scientific management tended to reinforce the main principles of the dominant form of organization: a system of hierarchical control in a structure of many levels based upon differential status and reward and utilizing top down decision making.[54] As there were basic problems with this model that accelerated as organizations grew in size and technology became more complex, as early as the 1920s some experiments began with forms which were based upon different principles. These innovations were grafted on to the hierarchical model.[55] This included some generally limited use of participation and introduction of some economic incentives, primarily individual piecework bonuses for production workers, commissions for sales personnel and stock options for some managers.

By the 1930s, with the development of the human relations movement,[56] it began to be recognized that there was a human side of management that needed to be taken into account. At a minimum, superiors needed to make subordinates feel valued. Some thought that subordinates might have useful suggestions and information to pass up the organization. During the late '40s, this blended with the emergent cybernetics approach to organization, stressing the need for feedback as part of improved organization communications.[57]

By the 1960s, organizations in the mainstream of business began to modify the hierarchical model grafting onto it a variety of arrangements. These included quality circles and other group suggestion processes,[58] quality of worklife programs that included at least some labor-management decision making, autonomous work teams on the shop floor and in the office;[59] and in some places in Europe, limited Co-determination with some employees or their union representative on the top management board—the equivalent of the board of directors.[60]

Outside of the mainstream, some examples of a different model of organization began to appear based upon employee participation that were forerunners of a new model for organizing and rewarding work. Often they produced some spectacular successes. However, as precursors, they often suffered from defects in structure and/or culture, or were pressured by the differently functioning environment, to take on such imperfections.

The most notable of these were the cooperatives at Mondragon, in the Basque country of Spain,[61] and the self-managed enterprises that became the backbone of the Yugoslav economy after 1950.[62] The former grew from a single workshop employing 5 people in 1956 to a federation of well over 100 primary producer cooperatives by the 1980s employing more than 20,000 people. The primary cooperatives were supported by secondary cooperatives, including an investment bank, educational cooperatives and a research and development unit. As a whole they were far more productive than conventional businesses in Spain and were quite successful in the international market. Yugoslavia, using self-managed enterprises which were essentially cooperatives operating on the basis of one employee one vote, enjoyed the second highest rate of growth of GNP per capita in the world from 1954 to almost 1970.[63] When in the early 1970s some problems were perceived with the structure of self-managed firms, they were decentralized so that in effect each firm became a federation of semi-autonomous work units.[64]

By the late 1980s it began to be seen in the mainstream that participation made for greater effectiveness in virtually every aspect of an organization's behavior, precisely because it was a more human basis for an organization.[65] Leading thinkers of the time concluded that if participation was the proper basis for running an organization, then it should no longer be grafted on to the old model. Rather, a new organization model centered on participation needed to be utilized.

The emerging participatory organizational model is very flat, with either few layers, or in its more developed form, no hierarchy at all.[66] It is the team organization composed of a collaborative circle of teams all on the same level. It is based upon commitment, equality of status and reward, joint decision making (with delegation to whomever is directly affected by a decision) and democratic communication directly among all with a need to communicate. It is a decentralized, networking organization that is really a federation, rather than a monolithic structure.[67] In order to support participation, the system of reward is changed so that it connects the employee directly to the market and the performance of the firm. This is being done for both the short and long term, with such gainsharing devices as group productivity bonuses, profit sharing and worker ownership or its equivalent (in the US often through Employee Stock Ownership Plans, or ESOPS).[68]

Perhaps the best known example of a firm that embodies most of the new model is W. L. Gore, an almost totally employee-owned high tech fiber company. In a few years Gore expanded from start up to a Fortune 500 multinational corporation employing over 5,000 employees worldwide.[69] Everyone at Gore has the same status. All are called associates. Gore is an organization composed of autonomous, interrelated teams. To work at Gore one negotiates a job with a team. Each team makes its decisions by consensus. Whenever an issue involves more than the members of a team, whoever is concerned participates in the decision. As team organizations develop, they tend to lose their organizational egos, making decisions on their merits and not just because one of the parties is a member of the larger organization.

For example, a team at the Indianapolis Ford plant concerned with obtaining high quality steel was told by the Ford foundry that they could not supply steel to the specifications required until expensive improvements could be made at the foundry. Hearing this, the team at the Indianapolis Ford plant fired the Ford foundry as a supplier.[70]

Indeed, there are now numerous examples of firms that have sufficiently devolved into federations, whose units act very autonomously, almost as separate enterprises, that are semi-independent profit centers, buying and selling where they choose either/or both inside and outside the organization.[71] Similarly, in Japan, in the 1980s and 1990s, independent enterprises have come together as federations (*Kaizens*, which at this stage operated with a combination of top down direction and collaborative participation, while externally acting as aggressive competitors),[72] while collaborative joint ventures among firms worldwide are becoming increasingly more common.

The Spread of Democratization to All Kinds of Organizations in All Sectors

This transformation has emerged in organizations of all kinds, including nonprofit enterprises and governments. For example, as early as 1981, Wake County, North Carolina ran a pilot program of thirty-nine quality circles in its agencies. After fifteen months, employee morale was up, services to the public had improved with management accepting most suggestions from employee circles, and the county had saved $151,000 in the first year in improved efficiency.[73] Osborne and Gaebler in *Reinventing Government* provide numerous examples of the full range of employee participation processes from quality circles to team process in government agencies at every level across the United States. This includes examples of services becoming more responsive to the people they serve by treating them as customers and communicating with them about their needs and how, and how well, they are served.

In an age of large nations, providing a variety of services to many people, while regulating many areas of life, making the bureaucracy participatory and representative for the people it serves and regulates is a critical matter. This is especially the case as those who make and apply policy may be geographically and socially distant from those they serve and regulate. One field in which much has been accomplished to bridge the distance between government and people, after many years is in Indian affairs.[74]

People Input into Government: The American Indian Affairs Example

Relations between American Indians in tribes recognized by the US federal government are a special case that has general relevance for the relations of all people to government. Some of the aspects of US-Indian relations are particular to the special status of Indian tribes and their members. This makes them not just another interest group. Indian nations are domestic sovereigns, within the United States, whose sovereignty the US government has always recognized in theory, but often only to a limited degree in practice. In the current "self-determination" era of federal Indian policy, begun in the 1970s, there have been ongoing efforts to improve government-to-government relations between Indian tribes and the federal government. What is relevant to all citizens is the communications model that has been put into place in an attempt to ensure that US government Indian policy, and its implementation in practice, are appropriate, and consistent with the needs and wishes of the recipients, within the limits of that policy. This requires that Indian tribes and people have a proper voice in the making and adjusting of that policy. The communications channels that have been established function no better than the people involved work with them, and are only effective to the extent external politics allows. But they often are effective, and are suggestive of what might be undertaken in other contexts.

Beginning at the tribal level, there has been effort to decentralize programs downwards, so that tribal governments who are able and willing can either run their own federal programs according to the relevant guidelines, or contract out the running of the programs. Decentralization is an important general principle. While in the post industrial age, many basic policies need to be set at national, regional, or state levels, consistent with the Indigenous principle of place, each location is different, and local people often know the particulars of their circumstances better than anyone from outside.

Moreover, the greatest opportunities for participation are at the local level, where people are in community together. When community relations are fractured, or less than optimal, increasing opportunities for people to participate inclusively locally is a strong measure for building community. It helps community members feel better about themselves in the course of increasing the quality of relations among neighbors, and improving the quality of life. At the same time, it is essential that there be clear guidelines, sufficient review from higher levels, and channels for local people to complain if they are not being properly served, or their rights are being violated. This is sometimes a problem amid the vagaries of local politics, which may involve prejudicial relationships.

Assisting decentralization of federal programs to tribal, state, and local governments in the United States, has been a change in perception beginning in the 1960s of how federalism is viewed. There has been a shift from seeing federalism as a competitive, legal structure of separation of authority, to its being conceived as a cooperative system (with competitive elements). In the newer approach, the federal government more often carries out policy by empowering the states and localities through grants in aid, with varying degrees of discretion by the recipients, than by exercising control.[75]

A relevant precedent for participation in running federal programs at the local level is that at the beginning of the "war on poverty," the local communities who received a community action program under the Equal Opportunity Act were empowered to elect their local program's governing board.[76] After numerous mayors complained, perceiving that the practice was undermining some of their power base, community action board membership was changed so that the target community, the mayor, and involved nonprofit organizations each selected one third of the board. Electing boards of directors in local programs is an excellent vehicle for participation. When that is not appropriate, advisory committees can be elected. While this provides an important voice, it is no more effective than the willingness of officials to listen to it. However, when an advisory committee is not heeded, it may be in a position to raise the community and its friends and allies in protest, which may bring about change.

Also, where an agency functions locally in a sizable jurisdiction, it is beneficial to decentralize to the various areas of the jurisdiction, and to establish interactive relations within the community, or various communities. This will promote dialogue among normally separated groups of people. Done properly, this will improve community relations and the effectiveness of operations, as well as provide valuable opportunities for participation and empowerment of community members. A good example, is community policing.[77]

The Example of Community Policing

In medium and large urban and suburban areas, standard policing is usually centralized in a hierarchical system. The main decision makers at the center are distant from, and not personally knowledgeable about, most of the areas, and the day to day police activities in those areas, they are responsible for. Police officers usually live outside the precincts in which they are stationed and patrol, and precinct stations are usually centralized in the precinct. This alone, usually means that most of the officers do not know the neighborhood, its people, and circumstances very well, nor do the people living and working in the precinct know, and have much of a relationship with, the officers who serve them. This becomes a serious problem in high crime, minority neighborhoods, with few, if any, of the officers members of the minority in question, much less residents of the neighborhood. Often this leads the citizens of the area and the police to be alienated from one another. Relations are often marked by mistrust, and sometimes fear on both sides. This situation is worsened when police incentives are to respond as quickly to calls as possible, and spend as little time as possible on each call, in order to be available for future calls. This means that police often know little of a situation they are called to, or happen to arrive at. Often they suspect, hassle, and arrest the wrong people, increasing the alienation and further lowering the quality of police service, while doing little to reduce crime or ameliorate the problems that cause it.

Outside forces can have some advantages if properly applied in certain situations. As outsiders, they are not involved in the interplay of interests in the community, and if properly directed can act impartially, with relatively little fear of personal reprisals from those against whom they act or whose interests they may threaten. There are cases early in the twentieth century in American cities (when police patrolled neighborhoods on foot, and knew their beats fairly well) where local police have been ineffective in quelling riots, because of their relationship with the rioters, where a not much larger force of national guardsmen from outside the city were able to swiftly restore order. But the very distance that members of an outside force have from the community undermines their effectiveness in the long run, and in worst cases can make the police more of a problem than an aid to a community. Those in the community (e.g. gangs and war lords) who benefit from weakening the policing force can easily exploit the situation to turn people in the community actively against the police. The harder the police try to act proactively through massive raids and hit and run operations, the more they are likely to turn the community against them as innocent community members are likely to be insulted, hassled, injured, and even killed with little real effect in reducing crime or maintaining order.

Evidence of the loss of trust that can occur in the community from overly aggressive policing can be seen in the 2004 experience of Milwaukee, Wisconsin.[78] There, black residents became outraged at hearing that a biracial man at a party had been severely beaten by several white off-duty police officers. The incidents sparked protests and a seventeen percent reduction in 911 calls to police. The effect lasted over a year and resulted in an approximate net loss of 22,200 calls for police service in impacted black neighborhoods.

A particularly bad example of overly aggressive policing by officers alienated from the community occurred in Detroit, in the 1960s, when a special force of officers was put together to try to act proactively against crime in the inner city. At first the new strike force ("STRESS") was welcomed by the people in the neighborhoods, as they suffered from a great deal of crime.[79] Very quickly, however, the citizenry began to fear the STRESS officers more than the criminals. The officers, almost all white from outside the mostly African American neighborhoods they patrolled—apparently were caught up in racial profiling and stereotyping. They continually over reacted to calls, hassling people, who had nothing to do with the complaint, and collectively shooting more people than the rest of the Detroit police force combined. Eventually, the unit was disbanded after it mistakenly got into a shootout with fellow officers who were on a stake out.

By contrast, officers who are integrated into the community and work with it, with many of them stationed around the community (and have both sufficient professional training and independent oversight of their actions to keep them honest and impartial) are likely to be knowledgeable of the community and its people. They are likely to be well informed of community developments and concerns and supported by the community. This type of "community service" or "neighborhood patrol" policing tends to be effective both proactively, in ameliorating situations that tend to cause or promote crime, and after the fact in catching perpetrators and retrieving stolen property. The key is that the patrolling officers meet and collaborate with concerned community groups, leaders, and people in developing plans and taking action.

A good example is the experience of turning a low income housing project plagued by crime in Indianapolis, Indiana into a relatively secure area.[80] The transformation was accomplished by having the police meet with housing project management (which agreed to initiate and work with a tenants association, run by the tenants), the tenants' association, and neighborhood organizations in the surrounding area. In addition, the mostly white police officers teamed up with local black ministers to go door to door to survey the largely black tenants on their concerns.

Plans were mutually developed with the participants agreeing to take responsibility for various actions. Management hired a new security service and agreed to evict tenants quickly who were arrested for selling drugs, which was a major part of the crime problem. With the approval of the tenants, the police blocked off some vehicle accesses to the project to make it easier to monitor activity. This was important because much of the crime was caused by outside drug sellers and buyers coming into the project which had been a convenient place to do business.

The police also obtained agreement of the prosecutor's office to take swift action against those charged, and from federal authorities to act quickly against those arrested for gun possession. Tenants took responsibility for informing the authorities of criminal activity and situations which might lead to crime. Within a few months, the housing project had become so crime free that the major concern of the tenants was that the police would consider the area so secure they would stop working with the tenants and crime would return to the project.

At its best, community policing becomes a team effort among police or peacekeeping forces, local citizen groups, social institutions and services, and individual citizens.[81] For example, if there is a drug problem around a school, it may be advantageous to take a team problem solving approach by bringing together representatives of, and having ongoing meetings and other communication among, school personnel, parents, students, police, relevant public and private social services, and neighborhood residents and organizations. Where violence and/or crime in an area are found to be caused by intergroup hostility or conflict (which is a problem in both domestic and international peacekeeping situations) a variety of conflict resolution and peace building techniques can be employed.[82] These can be carried out either by the police or peacekeepers in collaboration with others or by special facilitators or service organizations. To make this approach effective, the policing force needs to be well trained in conflict resolution and peace building techniques, and how to apply them in culturally appropriate ways for the people involved. Thus peace building may be carried out effectively by having peacekeepers collaborate directly with facilitating and peace building groups and the community involved.

Policing is most successful when it functions not as a totally independent force, seeing its role in isolation from other community functions, but as an integrated participant in community team work that empowers community people in all of their peaceful purposes. Police operating in this manner not only help keep the peace, but also play an important role in helping people take charge of their lives and develop their communities humanely, while encouraging further participation by the citizens involved. Furthermore, the problem solving-oriented interagency collaboration with community member involvement in these cases is a good general model for overcoming the overly narrow foci that agencies tend to have when operating isolated from each other in hierarchical systems. This causes conflicting policies, duplication of effort, unmet needs, and often inadequate and inappropriate service. Moreover, attempts to set up interdepartmental coordinating committees in hierarchically structured and functioning organizations often suffer from organization ego-generated turf struggles, and turf-protecting influenced compromises that are not the best solutions to problems.

When problem solving-focused consensus building team process is employed, the results are usually much better holistic courses of action. This is even more the case when each of the participating groups or organizations functions on an inclusive participatory basis so that the coordinating teams develop synergy from bringing their diverse perspectives, approaches, experiences, and talents to bear to create a well working unified solution to problems.[83]

Communication between the People and the Agency: American Indian and Related Experience

To ensure appropriate and effective services and/or regulation, community dialogue with administrators is also needed beyond the local level. American Indians, beginning with the Nixon administration, gained a communications channel within each of the federal agencies that dealt with them in a major way. An Indian Desk was established to act as a liaison with Native nations and organizations in all the federal agencies that dealt significantly with Indians.[84] At first, many of those who held the position had significant other duties in the agency, which in some cases prevented them from doing much as a contact person. Even when these people were quite active, the position often was assigned only to the person, so when they left, no one replaced them. Only when the position was institutionalized, given enough time and resources, did it become continually effective. Moreover, just having a liaison is insufficient. Especially where there are cultural differences between the community members and the bureaucrats, and there are unique circumstances in the concerned community, the liaisons need to know enough about the people they are a contact point for to be effective, as do others in the agency who deal with the population in question. Consequently, some agencies, such as some parts of the Environmental Protection Agency (EPA), have trained their relevant personnel in "Indian 101", and hired qualified Indians to work in the agency.

Coordination of operations among a number of programs working with the same population or geographical area is important, in order to avoid contradictions, duplications, and other problems. In the spring of 1975, for example, the extremely complex Department of Health, Education, and Welfare established the HEW (later HHS) Intra-Departmental Council on Indian Affairs, supplementing it in 1979 with the American Indian Advisory Group, chartered to function for two years. In January 1979, the Department of Agriculture established an agency wide Native American task force. The purpose was to improve the effectiveness of the department's programs as they apply to Indians. The task force was chaired by the Assistant Secretary for Rural Development, and included the assistant secretaries for Conservation, Research and Education, Food and Consumer Services, and International Affairs and Commodity

Programs. The task force reported to the secretary quarterly, beginning in March 1979. Policy Issues that the chairman believed to be beyond the role of the task force were referred to the secretary for consideration by the Program and Budget Review Board. All agencies of the department were authorized and directed to cooperate with the task force and to supply personnel for it on a temporary basis, as might be requested by the chairman.

Coordinating bodies of this kind can be extremely helpful if they are permanently institutionalized. However, for them to be effective, the leading members (or a sufficient number of the members) of the coordinating body must have an understanding of the concerns and cultures of the people in question, their current situations, and the relation of the relevant programs to the developing situations of the concerned communities.

In the case of the Department of Agriculture task force, the high position of the members provided them with appropriate organizational authority to be effective, but since each of the members had a number of concerns, of which Native American affairs were but a small part, there was no assurance that the understanding and orientation of the task force members would be appropriate and would not merely strengthen the perpetuation of misguided paternalistic policy and implementation. While this might have been corrected by appropriate staffing, the possibility of that occurring, and continuing, depended upon who the secretary, chair, or other key members happened to be. Experience with Indian Desks shows that this crucial matter needed to be institutionalized in the official make up and formal charge to the coordinating body. While such formal arrangements do not assure the appropriate operation of any entity, they can greatly increase the likeliness that it will operate as intended, and provide a touchstone for review and correction of its functioning.

Since Indian affairs were the purview of numerous federal department and agencies, it was appropriate to establish coordination at the top of the executive branch, in order to ensure consistent policy without contradictions or duplications across federal programs, and to provide Indigenous Americans with input and dialogue at the center of executive policy. After an appropriate, but short-lived start with the National Council on Indian Opportunity under the Johnson administration, this was first institutionalized during the Clinton administration, in two vehicles.[85]

First, an annual meeting was launched in which all federally recognized tribes were invited to the White House for discussion of Indian affairs. Key people from the departments regularly involved in Indian affairs participated. It has proved to be a useful vehicle for enhancing government-to-government relations, and for enhancing holistic consideration of Indian affairs, as well as for discussing specific major problems.

To make this discussion truly inclusive, it would be useful to include representatives of "urban Indians," since more than 60 percent of Native Americans now live off reservation, mostly in cities (while most federal agencies and programs are primarily focused upon reservations). It should be noted that the first of these annual meetings, followed by the National Indian Listening Conference, jointly sponsored by the Departments of Interior and Justice with participation from Housing and Urban Development, with the heads of all three departments in attendance, led directly to a series of reforms both within departments (e.g. the creation of the Office of Tribal Justice in the Justice Department) and at the top of the administration that have institutionalized Indian relations.

The most important of these initiatives was the establishment of the second national coordinating vehicle, The Working Group on American Indian and Alaska Natives as part of the Domestic Policy Council. The Council (as of January 1997) was composed of twenty high ranking members of executive departments (such as the Under Secretary of Agriculture for Rural Development, the Chief of Staff of the Department of Commerce, and the Principal Deputy Assistant Secretary for Congressional and Intergovernmental Affairs of the Department of Energy) and other agencies (such as the Office of Management and Budget), plus designated staff in each agency, and was chaired by the Secretary of the Interior.

There was, however, one major problem with the organization of the Working Group as it was constituted at the end of the Clinton administration. The Secretary of the Interior, as chair, was presented with a conflict of interest between his responsibilities to his department and the requirements for coordinating Indian policy as a whole. He had pressures from a number of constituencies in his department, along with concerns for maintaining his power and authority to function effectively as department head. Moreover, the Secretary of the Interior as an equal with other department heads, had to work cautiously and diplomatically with other departments. As a result of this dual difficulty, energy was drawn away from the Secretary's ensuring that the BIA and other Interior agencies dealt adequately with current major issues, while communicating well with the tribes. This meant that the Working Group was unable to move swiftly or effectively to solve major problems that crossed departmental and agency jurisdictional boundaries in such crucial fields as gaming and the handling of toxic wastes.

Additionally, little was done to improve the extremely varied quality of tribal communications infrastructure, so that all tribal governments and their members could receive up to date information from, and provide timely input to, all federal agencies. What needed to be done was to move the coordination (and chairing) of the Indian Working Group entirely into the White House as part of the Intergovernmental Working Group with equal status for tribal governments with state and other governmental entities. There it would be able to operate from above the level of the departments with a clear institutional interest in, and the full authority to, effectively coordinate Indian policy and its implementation in dialogue with the tribes. The council was moved to the Domestic Council of the White House during the Obama administration, but the Secretary of the Interior continued to be its chair.[86]

Despite its limitations under the Clinton administration, the Working Group was the initiator, after appropriate consultation, of a number of reforms and took enumerable steps to see that government-to-government relations were operating on a regular and proper basis throughout the executive branch. These steps included the establishment of permanent Indian Desks or offices in all agencies that regularly dealt with, or had an impact upon, Native Americans. Several presidential memoranda were drafted for the heads of agencies and departments, first, "directing them to engage in continuing government-to-government relations with federally recognized tribal governments," and then requesting the departments and agencies to report what government-to-government procedures they had instituted, as a step in "ensuring that the President's directive is properly implemented."[87]

There are some Indian examples at the state level of policy voice into government, and coordination of policy, that may have a general application to major interests of groups, such as consumers of public health services, farmers, and small businesses.[88] In the state of Washington, for instance, the concerned tribes formed the American Indian Health Commission for Washington State to provide policy advice and collective communication with the state on health matters. The Commission communicates regularly with a variety of state and local health agencies, while each Washington tribe appoints its own representative to the Indian Policy Advisory Committee in the Washington Department of Social and Health Services. The department also has appointed a liaison person for Native American/Alaska Native issues who is actively involved with the Commission, playing an instrumental role in avoiding and solving problems.

In Washington, Indian policy as a whole is coordinated from the top of the executive branch, by the Governor's Office of Indian Affairs (GOIA). The Office recognizes that tribes have different needs, priorities, and objectives that are broader than economic development. It acknowledges that two-way communication and training are essential to its many efforts. GOIA has enhanced government-to-government relation between state agencies and tribes through promoting dialogue, increasing the number of qualified Native Americans employed in state government, and providing education to agency staff on Indian issues and communication.

The resulting collaboration has brought about advances in policy in economic development, natural resources management, and social and cultural issues. Those concerned about policy for the population in general, or for specific groups, such as low income people, could organize, and the state, or a set of its agencies could organize similar channels of communication.

Other Special Cases and the Need for Affirmative Action

While some aspects of the American Indian input into government are a special case, it should be noted that there are other situations that may need vehicles that normally are not open to all in the same way. In many countries, for example, there are Indigenous nations which have experienced, and still are, undergoing depredations from, or with the acquiescence of, government that need to be brought to an equal position with other citizens. While the general principle needs to be to treat people on an equal basis, where people are not equal, placing the social order out of balance, some type of affirmative action may be needed as a temporary measure, until balance is restored to the social-economic-political system.

Thus, after the freeing of slaves in the United States, the federal government established the Freedmen's Bureau in order to facilitate former slaves in attaining full membership in the society and economy.[89] In an attempt to overcome the disadvantages faced by poverty, the Equal Opportunity Act was passed to undertake "a war on poverty" during the Johnson administration. Various affirmative action programs were put into place aimed at overcoming the continuing disadvantages that many people faced from past and continuing discrimination.[90] Similarly, In India, when the caste system was officially ended, but its deleterious effects for some citizens continued, a system of affirmative action was established for members of what had been the untouchable caste.[91]

Any special program to correct inequities only is legitimate so long as those inequities have not been redressed, and only to the extent that it moves to redress them. Otherwise new inequities are created, or old ones continued. The Indigenous principle is that a major social goal is to create and maintain harmony in the community, and between communities, and with the environment. And when harmony and balance, or as the Diné would say, "beauty," have been lost, efforts need to be made to restore them.[92]

The Legitimate Role and Function of Interest Groups

Normally, sufficient channels need to be created for all citizens to have input into decisions that affect them *on an equal basis.* In a mass society, it is impossible for every individual to participate directly. Thus, there is a legitimate role for interest groups in order to represent people, to aggregate separate voices so that they can be heard. However, the power of the groups must be directly proportional to the number of people they represent, times the strength of their interest. In addition, the groups themselves need to be representative of their members—ideally operating according to principles of inclusive participatory democracy. To be sure that all interests (and each person has numerous interests), and that all people and interests are fairly represented in a balanced way, it is desirable to have as many groups as possible. As Rousseau has said, the closer the number of interest groups comes to the number of people, the more perfectly representative the system is likely to be.[93] Thus, the interest group system, as well as the offices of government, needs to fit the Indigenous principle of a broad diversity of power, which needs to be as balanced as possible with the actual interests of people.

In a properly balanced system, interest groups can play an important role in transmitting the will of the people to the legislative and executive bodies. In today's complex world, the latter necessarily need to be given leeway in filling in the details of legislation. Often this is through rule making authority within broad guidelines set by the legislature. Moreover, top executives and agencies serve as major proposers of legislation on the basis of the expertise that arises from their specialization, and input from citizens. This function can be carried out through all of the usual methods of lobbying and petitioning. These can be practiced more easily, and rapidly, in the age of the internet, so long as the net and e-mail service remains neutral and equally and freely accessible.

In addition, the lobbying process needs to be kept completely transparent, and guided by an enforceable set of ethics to prevent, so far as possible, any sort of bribery. Bribery can be any kind of favor, not only monetary payment, or the giving of gifts. To help prevent this, there need to be regulations requiring a sufficient time to pass after a person in legislative or executive decision making position leaves office, before s/he can work as a lobbyist, or be employed by an organization, a legislator, or official who directly makes decisions concerning them, such as deciding to whom a government contract should be awarded. However, it is also advisable to establish additional arrangements for all the significantly concerned groups to take part in consensus decision making processes to develop proposals for a decision by government bodies.

The EPA in the late 1980s, for example, initiated a process for developing regulation by bringing all the interested parties (primarily representatives of environmental groups, business and the agency) together to participate in consensus decision making. Any of the parties could withdraw from the process at any time. But, if they accepted the final agreement, they could not challenge it in court. As in traditional tribal governance, the process of dialogue takes time, but usually results in better decisions than competitive processes because of the attempt to accommodate all of the concerns and interests of those affected in order to create a viable policy. By contrast, decisions in competitive processes tend to be the result of the ability of the individual contenders to force the inclusion of as much of their position as possible in the final outcome. Compromises tend to be determined more in terms of including the diverse agendas of strong pressure groups than in achieving a well working policy as a whole.

The setting of new standards for the contents of gasoline in 1991 used the inclusive process initiated by EPA.[94] Often, when the process fails to produce a consensus it is still useful. Agreement is invariably reached on many of the issues, leaving only a narrow range of questions, which have already been well framed by the discussion of the concerned parties, for decision by the agency. Several states, including Indiana, California, and Florida have taken such an inclusive approach to promoting energy conservation and pollution reduction in the generation of electric power.[95]

In the past, there had been no incentives for power companies to operate efficiently or to encourage customers to conserve energy. Using an inclusive process, power companies, environmental groups and consumer group representatives have sat down together along with state officials to develop regulations that meet the primary concerns of all the parties.[96] This has resulted in measures which saved consumers money, reduced energy use, and pollution through allowing power producers to benefit financially from encouraging consumers to be energy efficient.

This involves recreating one of the strengths of traditional Indigenous societies, finding means or incentives to encourage people to act in the general interest, by making it in their personal interest to do so. Such incentives can be moral, political, and social as well as economic. But, they can only be effective to the extent that the structure and functioning of the incentives in practice actually encourages the socially or organizationally desirable behavior. Sometimes, common apprehension of not finding a solution to a major problem can be an effective inducement to take part in a consensus building process, if all the concerned parties understand that their views and interests will be respected and included in the outcome. For example, Search for Common Ground assisted some communities in the United States in defusing the very divisive issue of abortion, by bringing together the full range of concerned people in each community in problem solving dialogues.[97]

For such inclusive processes to function properly, particularly in government, there are a number of requirements. First, the process must be truly inclusive, involving all the interested parties on an equal basis. Otherwise, it is only a vehicle of hierarchical, special interest driven, competitive government. For example, during the presidency of the first George Bush, Vice President Dan Quayle's Competitiveness Council involved only big business leaders and government personnel in blocking new federal regulation that business did not want, regardless of its impact on the rest of the country.[98] Indeed, the George W. Bush administration was widely known for including only a narrow range of interests and actors—including oil companies—in its decisions, and of exacerbating divisiveness in US politics. Equally bad was the older practice of having only the Business Advisory Council, composed of the leadership of big business, meet regularly with the top officials in the Department of Commerce and various cabinet members in exclusive sessions, paid for by the Department, at the Homestead in Hot Springs, Virginia, and other expensive resorts.[99]

Second, the power of the parties in the process needs to be reasonably equal, to the extent of their interest, in order for the outcome to be equitable. If, for example, in the early 1990s EPA gasoline content decision making process, the oil industry could have gotten most of what it wanted by going directly to Congress, that could have perverted the consensus process in its favor by threatening to pull out of the discussions if it did not receive most of what it wanted at the expense of everyone else.

Third, there need to be reasons, or incentives, for those interested to participate and the consciousness of the parties must be such that they are open to participating. For example, if the petroleum companies had had sufficient power to get the regulations they wanted in a satisfactory time through EPA, and didn't care about the wellbeing of the other parties, the companies would not have bothered to join in the consensus process. However, even if they were generally significantly more powerful politically than the other parties, the oil companies would have joined in the consensus decision process, with only a small advantage, if the delay and/or uncertainty of not participating had been sufficient.

Where parties are in an ongoing relationship, as were members of traditional Indian communities, they may well find it in their long-term advantage to join in a collaborative problem solving process by consensus, rather than bargaining competitively. This has been the case where employers and labor unions, from experience, have gained sufficient trust in jointly managing team process for mutual benefit. For example, where labor-management collaboration has resulted in greater productivity, leading to increased profits and wages, the two parties may find it advantageous to work out labor contracts by mutual problem solving. This may be useful, not only for obtaining a better deal for both parties, but for maintaining the trust necessary to continue to carry out effective team process in the workplace.[100]

The point is, that well working consensus decision making involves the creation of a close relationship with the other parties in which each party gains its own ends by helping the other parties attain their goals. It also involves people really listening to each other, and dialoguing with each other to produce a flow of meaning. Too much of contemporary discourse over issues consists of deafly shouting at each other. This solves nothing, but has a tendency to escalate the shouting, even to breaking into violence.

Experience taught Native peoples the value of inclusive decision making and reharmonizing processes to keep the peace. Nonviolent conflict resolution and training has been successfully applied in the United States, particularly with young people, to reduce violence.[101] Experience with nonviolent conflict resolution, and with instituting team process in workplaces, demonstrates that what is necessary to get people to appreciate and use mutually respectful means of communication and decision in contemporary society is developing a participatory culture through appropriate participatory education (discussed below and in chapter 8). Most people prefer such modes of interrelating once they come to understand them and learn the skills involved in using them.

Currently, government in the United States and much of the world faces a series of related crises both in internal operations and external relations. Some of these difficulties relate to the way in which we conceptualize and operate governmental processes. By failing to recognize the extent to which governance is, in principle, a collaborative and empowering enterprise, we have greatly increased the costs of its operation, limited its effectiveness, and distanced it from the people.

Thus, reforms that equitably increase citizen and employee participation in the operation of governmental bodies, build team work among governmental agencies and in other ways debureaucratize government operations are useful developments, consistent with traditional principles of band and tribal governance.[102] To accomplish this it is necessary to develop a collaborative culture, even as American Indians, and Indigenous people around the world, did millennia ago. An important aspect of this is making all organizations participatory, especially workplaces, for several reasons, including that a major element in learning to be participatory is to participate in consensus decision making.

Developing a Collaborative Culture

What is important for the general development of more collaborative culture is that the emergent participatory organization is based on the idea of joint decision making on the basis of mutual respect: of group problem solving in order to meet everyone's needs. In a complex age, teams need to be composed of different people with different ways of perceiving and thinking and different talents, and often different expertise. Thus, team members quickly learn to listen to each other and support one another.

Diversity is a virtue. The strength of the team is the uniqueness of the individuals that compose it, and the team can only succeed through inclusiveness: through taking everyone's concerns into account. Conflict becomes an opportunity for mutual advancement. Moreover, in the current age of increasingly rapid change, to be an effective team member, one needs to be continually open to new ideas and insights. Work, and indeed life, become a process of continuing education.

Furthermore, the complexities of decision making in the workplace increasingly mirror the complexities of decision making in the world in general, including in major areas of public policy such as balancing the requirements of the environment, the economy, etc. Therefore, team process in the workplace encourages holistic thinking, considering all aspects of a problem or situation in making the best practicable balanced decision which is increasingly the approach necessary in making good public policy decisions.

It is obvious, and confirmed by research, that if a person is immersed every day at work in such a culture, that this will tend to make them more thoughtful, concerned collaborative neighbors and citizens at every level from the neighborhood to the planet.[103] Studies show that people who are more involved in decision making at work tend to be more involved in the community. Moreover, people whose work requires them to carefully study issues and to approach difficulties through problem solving after listening to all points of view and considering all sides of the problem will approach public problems in a more knowledgeable and intelligent manner. They will tend to elect people who will proceed in the same way in government (and in political campaigns), and will encourage the media to speak to them on a higher level.

In addition, if workplaces require people who are group problem solvers, then there will be pressure on education to provide just such employees. Indeed, there have been a number of pressures on education to move in that direction for some years, and that is precisely the thrust of the current "child needs centered" educational reform movement. The principle of mutual respect of team process for treating intrinsically equal people individually according to their uniqueness, works to focus education on meeting the learning and related support needs of each student in order that they can attain the collective goal of receiving appropriate education.[104]

At least in Europe, the organizational revolution is bringing with it the rise of collaboration between the public and private sectors in education. This is increasingly part of the new educational reform movement in the US, though it is not well developed.[105] In Germany for example, the large number of young people who do not go on to college are engaged in vocational education programs in collaboration with businesses, ensuring that school education provides the relevant skills for participation in work and the job market.

Apprenticeships with businesses also provide opportunities for students to explore possible future carriers, while giving the participants concrete practical experience that is helpful in giving citizens an understanding of practical public policy problems. To the extent that the businesses involved have become participatory, student involvement in them will tend to increase the student's participatory education.

Furthermore, to the extent, and *only to the extent,* that such education is sufficiently, and sufficiently equally provided for all young people and is paired with appropriate public policy to create and maintain adequate job opportunities for everyone, the relevance and meaningfulness of the participatory education experience can be a significant force for overcoming youth alienation at school and in general.[106] For a long time, lack of sufficient and equal education has been a major failing in the United States with its "savage inequalities" of educational opportunities.[107] In recent years the situation has only gotten worse.

Changes in education and workplace social process and culture can create a new consciousness. If these were adequately developed, they would tend to have a significant impact on moving the balance of opposed forces favoring and opposing positive socio-economic-political transformation that the United States has been experiencing for some time in a positive direction in almost all areas. Positive movement in one area will generally tend to increase the likelihood of positive movement in the others. However, the correlations are complex, and not totally or equally reciprocal.

For example, the kind of mutual respect, in team process and related education, for each person (organization, group, culture, etc.) and approaching problems holistically with concern for mutual gain in the process, can set an appropriate basis for dealing positively and effectively with the problems of diversity that are extremely divisive in contemporary America and internationally. This should tend to be the case because the consciousness involved focuses attention on long run self-interest, which must include the needs of others. It would also likely occur because the new workplace system tends to move toward more equal compensation at work, while encouraging an outlook that favors public policies that move toward moderation of extreme differences of income. This would be best if it included raising the situation of those with lower incomes through providing opportunities for becoming more equal rather than through direct transfers.[108]

The holistic thinking of the new workplace and related education tends to move people toward finding ways to use technology that are helpful, or neutral toward human beings and the environment. This is true precisely because such thinking orients one toward considering the full range of factors and long term consequences of actions, which is increasingly essential given the short run thinking that continues to create vast environmental problems.[109]

This kind of thinking, which also includes considering problems from the points of view of everyone involved, requires seeking out the full range of views and relevant information. This is made easier by the new information technology if it remains open and neutral, which in turn has a democratizing tendency when used in this way. Conversely, while the gestalt of the new culture approves of *appropriate* monitoring of human activities in order to gain useful and *empowering* information for making mutually respectful decisions, the entire approach mediates against using the technology (or older means) for increasing hierarchical control. The exception is in specific cases when doing so is appropriate, and perhaps empowering. For example, using monitoring technology to allow persons with destructive tendencies to work or go to school rather than to be confined in jail or mental institutions.

Section 3: Moving to Reinvent Government

Stephen M. Sachs

The rise of the participatory workplace has begun to produce a new approach to government and public policy making and administration that goes beyond traditional left-right, conservative-liberal, and other, dichotomies. This approach moves toward producing more dialectical, innovative problem solving and harmonious approaches to the whole field of governance. It does so because it is inclusive, and pragmatic rather than dogmatic. There are currently many versions and expressions of this rising approach (or set of approaches). One of the best known is set out by David Osborne and Ted Gaebler in *Reinventing Government*.[110] It is a very significant work because it documents the rise of a new approach on the American political scene. Where traditional American conservatives (i.e. traditional conservatives such as Milton Friedman and Ronald Reagan) and New Deal Liberals (e.g. Hubert Humphrey and Lyndon Johnson) were caught in an either/or argument on many issues, the "new politics" attempts to integrate the concerns of both positions. However, with the limited extent to which workplace participation had developed in fall 2019, the United States was still in the midst of a strong counter trend of polarized, often more ideological, politics stemming from growing income inequality.

For example, conservatives argue that government needs to be small, doing little regulation and providing few services, because doing more involves government becoming bogged down in an undemocratically unresponsive, inefficient, costly bureaucracy. Conversely, liberals argue that government must provide many services and engage in considerable regulation because there is a public need that can only be met by government.

New politics would agree with both, saying that there are many public needs that government is required to make representative decisions about, but the conservatives are right about the ills of bureaucracy. Government needs to act to debureaucratize, while maintaining representative ways to guide public policy. But government does not necessarily need to carry out all policies itself. Under this approach, government would have a responsibility to make policy about the matters in question, but decide case by case whether to carry it out itself.

To have the time and energy to make and change such policy efficiently, at low cost, responsively, and appropriately, government often would engage in "steering rather than rowing"[111]: setting the policy and reviewing its being carried out, but selectively deciding where it was better to carry out the policy directly, contract out administration, and/or create mechanisms and incentives to achieve the policy goals. They would have minimal need for direct administration. For example, rather than provide job training directly or by contract, government would provide vouchers to eligible people usable at accredited training programs. This would reduce bureaucracy, increase individual choice, and keep training relevant and efficient through choice driven competition, which could involve either or both private and public providers.

The most interesting aspect of *Reinventing Government* is that the work is not just a theoretical tract, but a first attempt at mapping new approaches and methods which in the 1990s were actually being applied in the US. Thus it presents a partial documentation of the consciousness related with team process beginning to appear significantly in public affairs.[112] Although a more inclusive and holistic consciousness has only beginning to emerge, there are numerous signs that its emergence may be a growing trend.

It appears that this has been in progress beneath the surface of the extreme political struggles of the Obama administration years. For example, a 1996 survey research showed the emergence of "transformational values" in 25 percent of the US adult population: a new subculture, who wished to rebuild neighborhoods and reduce family and street violence. They would usually do so by prevention rather than by getting tough. The new subculture would clean up and protect the environment, accepting the costs of doing so. Many of them feel that nature is sacred, and favor a decentralization of power based, generally, with more participatory decision making. In addition, surveys of people extensively engaged in computer networking tend to show the rise of participatory and empowerment oriented attitudes.[113]

A similar trend was noted in the rise of "the new historicism" school of literary criticism among scholars of literature, which H. Aram Veeser, describes:

> As the first successful counterattack in decades against this profoundly anti-intellectual ethos, New Historicism has given scholars new opportunities to cross the boundaries separating history, anthropology, art, politics, literature, and economics. It has struck down the doctrine of noninterference that forbade humanists to intrude on questions of politics, power, indeed on all matters that deeply affect people's practical lives—matters best left, prevailing wisdom went, to experts who could be trusted to preserve order and stability in "our" global and intellectual domains.[114]

It remains to be seen whether, in the current world and national political struggles, these developments, and other cultural changes mentioned in the introduction to part II of this book, will manifest in a more inclusive participatory society, essentially applying Indigenous governance principles appropriately for the current period, with an eye to future developments. But there is no question that these developments are examples of what is needed to move significantly in that direction.

It should be noted that the development of the new consciousness has been, and almost certainly will continue to be, a dialectical rather than a linear and/or zero sum process. Many forces are involved coming from different directions. The organizational revolution, supported by the information revolution, has been the most important of the positive forces for larger change. Similar thinking and processes have also been developing essentially independently, that have been interacting synergistically with the organizational and informational revolutions to enhance participatory culture.

Two examples of the many parallel developments are a growing use of collaborative decision making in professional organizations, which began before the coining of the term "team process," and the increasing use of conflict transforming or similar participatory dispute resolution processes in many settings, that have a variety of roots spanning the peace movement, traditional and new age spiritual paths, and professional mediation and arbitration.[115]

The Positive in the Negative

It is important to note that the so-called "negative" forces and developments have also been playing a role in the development of the new consciousness and related processes. For example, the rise of increasingly serious and widespread environmental problems has spurred environmental consciousness. Increasing polarization in communities has fostered the broader application of inclusive, participatory dispute resolution processes. And worsening crime rates and violence in the 1980s encouraged the application of community policing. Indeed, the driving force behind the organizational revolution, which author Stephen Sachs's analysis indicates as the most important single development and force for positive transformation, is itself largely the product of increasingly prevalent dysfunction with the traditional organization paradigm combined with the pressure of increased worldwide competition in the market, and pressure to conserve limited resources in the public and nonprofit sectors.

The question, then, is, is this new form of organization really emerging, or is it just a current trend? After all, if we are in the midst of an organizational revolution, we aren't very far along as yet, and in any case revolutions often do not end up where one would think they are going. Moreover, there are counter trends in contemporary organizations, such as downsizing, use of new information technology to increase top down control, and growing differences in income between top executives and beginning employees in large American firms, as well as increasing concentration of wealth in a few hands.

There are a number of reasons to think that the general model is in fact emerging, even though some of the details may not end up as we would now perceive them, and doubtlessly there will be new developments. First, participatory organizations generally are far more effective than hierarchical organizations. Indeed, the tightness of the world economy in the 1980s and 1990s was driving the revolution, worldwide.

However, the trend toward the internationalization of business (including the increasing portability of capital), and further concentration of capital in fewer hands,[116] has been a counter trend, first lessening the pressure of competition, therefore lessening the pressure to make organizations more effective by increasing their democratization. Secondly, democratization in all sectors, is viewed by many in top hierarchical positions as a limitation upon, if not a threat to, their power and position. This can be seen, for example, in the attempts by a number of billionaires to repress voting, greatly weaken unions, and, buy key media. The last of these has been intended in order to influence public opinion by spreading propaganda, and limiting the availability of information and views that run counter to their perceived interest.[117] Should these forces succeed, the result could be a world dominated by hierarchically managed international cartels. Fortunately, this trend is also feeding a counter movement, that includes the rise of movements and groups such as Occupy and Moveon.Org, in the United States, and broad protest movements around the world.

The change in reward systems, including the spreading of ownership of capital, as well as the decentralizing of decision making and hence power in the organization, *if fully enough developed* would mitigate much of that danger. To prevent undo monopolization, and to allow the development of diversity of ownership of capital and power, will require enlightened public policy. The increasing growth of multinationals now makes that impossible to be achieved by single nations. Thus it is imperative that appropriate transnational methods for doing this be developed. However, the spreading of "free trade" agreements such as NAFTA, has primarily benefited multinational cartels, and has yet to get many people to move from senses of national interest, to join in a new sense of global interest.[118]

But what of the counter trend to the rise of real participation in the workplace through downsizing, increased scrutiny and control of employees, etc. to deal with inefficiency in hierarchical organizations in the face of tight market competition? The answer seems to be fairly clear from both theoretical analysis and practical experience that such tactics may be beneficial in short run situations. However, they are counterproductive in the long run. There are two problems with downsizing. The first is that downsizing is usually not just a method for making firms more efficient by trimming labor. It is usually taken to reduce costs, which it does, but generally involves reducing output. Thereby, it reduces both income and market share.[119] A company in financial difficulty from failing to make timely progress in solving operational problems may have no choice except to cut back on its operations. But, if it does nothing more, it only makes a momentary gain while reducing its competitive position and market power which weakens the firm's ability to do well in the market in the future.

Moreover, large scale reduction of the workforce almost always leaves remaining employees feeling expendable and wondering if they are soon to be fired. Hence employee morale and commitment go down, lowering productivity and quality of effort, which is a direct disadvantage for any organization. Moreover, in an age where quality of product and employee attentiveness to operations increasingly are critical factors, the negative effect of lowered morale and commitment become increasingly damaging over time.

The same is true of increasing the use of top down control techniques, that also have the disadvantage that someone has to be paid to do the monitoring. One of the advantages of switching to team process, where employees have a real stake in the outcome of their work, is that supervising costs can be reduced very substantially as teams move to self-monitoring out of commitment, using all the information that they can obtain to find ways to improve their performance. In the team process organization the increased information about performance becomes a vehicle for empowerment and new energy. In a hierarchical control setting, the gains that can be made from using the increased information are limited by the direct financial and indirect human costs of obtaining and applying that information. Moreover, experience shows that committed people with sufficient education regularly make better decisions about how to use that information to improve their own work than outside managers or experts who are not directly involved in the work process. This is precisely because those involved in a process are in a position to know it better than anyone else. Further, those who participate in controlling their work tend to take ownership in it, usually becoming more concerned about doing the job well then those who are merely paid to undertake it.[120]

The coming into being of the information age is clearly an important factor in favor of an organizational form that is based upon problem solving and networking.[121] The industrial age made it possible to make huge numbers of the same thing, though not with the quality of individual craft work. The computer now makes it possible to mass produce different things, with the variation programmed into production, with the programming instantly adjustable. Many of the products can be made more finely with computer assisted production than was traditionally possible with individual craft work. This means that we are entering an age where all business, including manufacturing, is service oriented. This is the reason for the rise of the customer orientation, first in business, and increasingly in government and nonprofit organizations. An example of this is the broad popularity of TQM: total quality management. The required customer orientation fits perfectly with the outlook of participatory organizations. The customization to each particular need requires the decentralization and possibility of direct customer contacts of a participatory networking organization.

But there is one potential complex of problems to be overcome. First, the high tech, problem solving, participatory organization requires highly educated employees. Second, it is becoming possible to undertake increasing volumes of all kinds of work with less and less labor input. In this situation, it is possible that there will be a growing divide between a smaller number of people with high paying jobs, and a larger number of people unemployed or underemployed in low-paying jobs, often struggling with multiple employments to try to get by. To avoid this outcome, two current situations need to be changed.

First, the current uneven quality of schools in the United States continues to produce only a limited number of qualified potential information workers. This situation needs to be transformed so that schools are generally of high quality providing most everyone with education necessary to obtain good jobs.

Second, public policy continues to encourage firms to hire fewer employees working many hours, rather than many employees working fewer hours. One example of a policy that discourages employing more people working less hours is having firms, rather than the general public or individuals, pay for health care and other benefits per individual, and not per work period or per dollar in direct compensation. This encourages paying overtime rather than hiring new employees. Thus, public policy needs to be changed to encourage hiring more workers, working less hours. This could eventually lead to full employment with a shorter work week.

It appears, therefore, that because of its high performance, the participatory organization is likely to emerge in some form that is beneficial to its members. But the extent to which the new developments will be beneficial to national societies and to the planet depends upon foresight and sensitivity in public policy from the neighborhood to the world.

It is now clear that as the world moves into the information age, it is experiencing the rise of a participatory form of organization. This rise has taken place over several stages for a considerable time. The final result is not yet certain. But there is a clear trend which, if it continues in its current direction, may not only make organizations more efficient and working life more humane, but has the potential to contribute significantly to the creation of a more peaceable culture, and hence to a more peaceable world, founded upon a participatory society and culture.

Building the Foundation: Participatory Culture

Ultimately, ownership-control arrangements and regulations, and organizational structures are not enough to ensure participatory organizations or fully representative and open public discussion in the wider society. A culture of respect for all people and the positive value of all participating, hearing all views, and appreciation of the synergy that arises from inclusive dialogue, are a critical foundation for a participatory community or society.

There is also an educational aspect of inclusive participation.[122] This involves first, learning the value of diversity, combined with a focus on solving problems, based on fact finding and analysis, rather than ideology. This requires taking part in a common process to find the best policies or actions, and avoiding blaming people, which is divisive, in the course of choosing courses of action.

Second is developing a set of skills. This begins by developing the ability to problem solve analytically, rather than jumping directly from a problem to a solution. This means learning to effectively illuminate problems, identify and understand options, and make or create the best choices among the alternatives, or by combining elements of them.

Since this is a collective process, next comes a set of communicating and interacting skills. The first of these is learning to listen empathetically, so as to appreciate and honor each person's perspective (regardless of whether one agrees with their views), and listening clearly, in order to hear accurately what they are really saying. Too often people hear what they assume others are going to say. This often happens when people debate. The aim is to dialogue and not to debate: to share concerns, not to argue for positions.

Next, is speaking supportively, always honoring the other persons, acknowledging their concerns (whether or not one agrees with their opinions). If someone's behavior or performance is a problem, one needs to speak to suggest improvement. It is usually best to praising the person's [group's] positive behavior, before suggesting where and how improvement can be made. The idea is to focus on the positive to the extent possible, so that the feeling of mutuality of the group or community is maintained and strengthened, in the common effort of creating the best practicable decisions and actions.

To promote and maintain the quality of the process, it is important to enhance the participants' ability to act, and to speak to encourage everyone to participate and to support the process of participation. It is usually best, especially for leaders, to begin by presenting problems, and to ask everyone how they see them, rather than presenting solutions. That way, everyone is included in deciding. Everyone can help facilitate the process by drawing others into it, especially those who have said little or nothing. Any participant can help find other ways to see the question at hand when the discussion gets bogged down, or participants fall into arguing instead of dialoguing. The idea is to come together to identify and solve problems or develop a plan toward some goal. By collectively defining it, there is a proper basis for proceeding to consider alternative ways for finding (or creating) solutions or plans. Having heard everyone's thoughts on what to do, everyone can be and feel collectively involved in choosing or creating the best way to proceed. The main job of group leaders is to act as facilitators, to help the process move ahead in a good and inclusive way (as traditional tribal leaders usually did), rather than attempting to move the group toward specific decisions. Some of these skills are more essential in small group decision making, than in mass processes, but all of them are important in every arena of public discussion.

In the information age, education for participatory democracy also needs to include learning how to find information, particularly on the internet. There, it is especially important to know how to evaluate what are and are not good and accurate sources of information, ideas, and approaches to issues and problems. The most important learnings are how to learn; how to perceive, think analytically— understanding the need to see issues and problems from the full range of relevant perspectives; and how to find the information that one needs. It is also necessary to learn at least basic civics: how political, economic, and social systems function; have some knowledge of geography: human, political, economic, environmental, etc. Also. one needs to attain the skills and information needed for everyday living and working. For a participatory society, it also helps to learn that life is a never ending process of education.

Ensuring the Dispersion of Power

A crucial aspect of traditional Indigenous societies, and a necessity for any well working democracy is the wide dispersion of power, in all its forms. In practice people need to have an approximately equal voice and influence, with essentially equal access to sources of information, and whatever services, including education, are necessary to provide for basically equal participation. All also need to have an equal opportunity in life, including in developing carriers, in the economy, etc. On the political side, in the postmodern, age this requires not only political, but ultimately virtually all institutions, to operate on the basis of inclusive participatory democracy, with political authority widely dispersed. This includes having no undue power or concentration of power in any office or agency—and with all political and governmental functions carried out with transparency (except in limited cases where secrecy or protection of privacy is legitimate). All governmental bodies and actions must be subject to review and appropriate corrective action for any improprieties that may occur.

As to the structure of government, there are a variety of forms that meet the basic American Indian principles of participatory democracy and practical effectiveness in the current era. The need for dispersion of political power in a nation of any size needs to involve a federalism in which the central government sets the basic guidelines of policy in order to ensure coordination of policy and protection of basic rights. Within those guidelines the states or provinces need to do the same within their jurisdiction. So far as is practicable, policy ought to be carried out at the local level to meet local conditions. This is potentially more democratic because the geographical distance between the people and the government is closest, with the voting power of people the greatest as there are fewer of them in local jurisdictions, and the ratio of people to their elected officials is the smallest.

There are some caveats to this. Today, the most important decisions need to be made at the national and international level, because local and regional economies and environments are more closely interlinked than ever before, really constituting national and international economies and environments. With the development of electronic communications, citizens may know more about what is happening, and what their representatives and administrative officials at the higher levels are doing, particularly at the national level, than at the lower, and especially the local level.

Also, in the smaller arenas of the states and localities, there are often a smaller number of interests and points of view, that at times can lead to more skewed policies, and a higher likelihood of people being discriminated against and having their rights violated than is likely to occur with higher level decision making. Thus, in the current era, decentralization needs to be balanced with sufficient higher level decision making and vehicles for review of the lower levels, compared with a century ago, and even more so since the time of contact. Indeed, one of the reasons for writing the US Constitution and abandoning the Articles of Confederation, which closely followed the examples of the Haudenosaunee, Wendot, and Muskogee federations, was even then the need to have national decision making power in many fields, including commerce.[123] The practice learned from Indian nations no longer sufficed for the early United States, in having strong legislatures, requiring a consensus agreement to make decisions, a weak executive, and almost all domestic authority in the states.

Concerning the structure of government, some argue that a parliamentary form of government is more democratic than a presidential model with a separation of powers and checks and balances. The parliamentary form usually encourages multiple parties, and, hence more views in the legislature that need to be taken into account to develop decisions. In a parliamentary system, governments can be changed more quickly at need, or change in public view. However, either type system can work quite democratically and effectively if elections are frequent and fair enough, the system of communication among the people and between the people and the government are open and equally available, and if power in all forms is sufficiently equal and balanced.

Moreover, in a two-party system that is not overly polarized, the aggregating of the variety of citizens' views can take place in the public discussion and election process, with candidates attempting to encompass the views of sufficient people to win the election. As in a participatory society the political parties need to function quite democratically, the same would tend to be the case in primary elections, providing a large number of people to vote. This is likely the case in highly participatory societies, but often a problem in less participatory "democracies", such as the United States. There, voter turnout is usually low in primaries, and non-presidential elections—and indeed not very high even in Presidential elections.

There are also other considerations, depending upon the circumstances. For example, France moved from a standard parliamentary system to a strong presidential system in the 1950s, because of widely fractured public opinion represented by numerous parties which had difficulty agreeing on policy decisions. The parties were able only to form fragile governments that fell frequently, unable to keep governing coalitions together.[124]

The Articles of Confederation, in addition to the above reason, were replaced by the Constitution because of the need for a stronger executive and a need to have a legislature that did not require unanimous approval of all bills, as it was too difficult to build a complete consensus (as well as the need to have the national government be able to finance itself by raising its own taxes).[125] But a presidential system can also have an overly strong president, or executive agencies may have too much power. There are critics of the US government in the period of the war on terror who charge that too much power has accrued to the President. There is also considerable concern that the National Security Agency (NSA) and other security services have undue surveillance power that seriously undermines democracy.[126]

Whatever the form of government, it needs to operate in a balanced way to reflect democracy. Leaders in traditional Indigenous societies are facilitators, who, because they have been selected for their virtues, including wisdom, may be influential in guiding discussion. They are not themselves the decision makers in what should be a collective process. The same ought to be the case in contemporary government. The United States Congress, for example, would need reforms to meet these principles.[127] As of the end of 2016, the leadership has too much power to control the legislative process. For example, in the House of Representatives, the speaker and the rules committee can control what comes to the floor for a discussion and vote, indicating what parts of a bill can and cannot be amended, and how long discussion can take place.

While efficiency is necessary to realize democracy, and it may be appropriate for an elected small body or single person to initially set the agenda, their decisions ought to be overruleable by simple majority vote. Among other issues in the Senate, the ability of any senator to put a hold on a bill or a presidential nomination, preventing the measure from coming to the floor, is most undemocratic. The filibuster—though reduced in its application in 2013—which requires a 60 percent majority of the entire Senate to stop discussion and allow a vote, is too extreme. It is wise to have devices to protect minorities, and to briefly slow discussion so that measures are not rushed through without sufficient consideration. However, a majority of the entire body, not just of those who are present and voting, ought to be sufficient to overcome any blocking or delaying procedure.

For a government to be democratic, terms of office need to be appropriately short, but need to be long enough, and perhaps staggered, to provide sufficient continuity. Also, the Indian origin practice of recall elections, along with legislature and citizen initiated ballot measures (as exemplified by California's propositions), are good practices for well-balanced participatory political systems. These usually function very well in truly democratic regimes. However, these, and other "democratic" practices often do not work well where there is an imbalance of power, especially concerning money.

Ensuring a Dispersion of Economic Power

Extremely important to the proper functioning of a participatory (or any) society is a dispersion, and approximate equality, of economic power. Philosophers as diverse as Aristotle and Marx have pointed this out. Aristotle set forth in *The Politics*, Book IX, Ch. 2, one needs to emphasize the middle. A stable and well working society, in the best case would have a middle class with more members than the poor, and more wealth than the rich. Liberal democratic theorists have usually indicated the importance of a sizable and strong middle class for a well working democracy. Karl Marx and Friedrich Engels went one step further saying that the ultimate society needed to become a classless society.[128]

A well working participatory society needs to have a balanced economy, without any person, group or class of people having so much more wealth than others, or so much control of economic institutions, that they would have more say than everyone else. Undo concentration of economic power can lead to unfair lobbying, un equal political advertising, control of or advantage in the media, and other undo economic leverage. Similarly, it is important that there not be a large group, or class, of people who are so much poorer than everyone else, that they cannot participate on an essentially equal basis. Moreover, it is important that there not be such great differences in wealth, essentially in class, that it causes such a wide difference in interest and outlook that if creates distinct and largely incompatible factions within society. This makes it difficult or impossible to find the common interest.[129]

Maintaining a balanced, egalitarian economy is the American Indian tradition. All citizens were considered family, who needed to be included in the reciprocity of tribal relations, as is shown in chapter 1. Even the somewhat more hierarchical, but still quite participatory, Northwest Coast tribes largely used their excess wealth for potlatches, huge giveaways that redistributed much of the excess (and destroyed some of it).[130] Thus even they were consistent with the usual Indian nation practice of harmonizing community economy. As the Comanche state it, the principle was to remember our relationships, which involves responsibility, bringing about reciprocity, which results in redistributive justice.

Approaches to Maintaining a Balanced Economy

The best way to achieve and maintain a balanced equalitarian economy varies with the circumstances and conditions of society. In the post-industrial age we need to use different means than those which were effective in smaller, traditional Indigenous societies. A number of approaches have been proposed. Some favor centralized planning based on need, to take money and greed out of the distribution process. To date, however, centralized planning, as used by the Soviet Union, much of Eastern Europe, and North Korea, has proven to be very inefficient. It also broke down into an oligarchic form of state capitalism, with monopolistic state owned companies attempting to manipulate and lobby the system for their own benefit.[131] Communist China has modified central planning, including employing a considerable amount of private enterprise operating under a somewhat regulated market. While this arrangement has led to considerable economic development, the Chinese government itself is concerned that this has been accompanied by great inequalities in wealth and living standards.[132] Further, huge development projects have caused direct harm to large numbers of people and the environment in the short run, with further human harm in the longer term.[133]

One might speculate that perhaps with improved computing, and significant feedback, centralized economic planning might become feasible. However, this would be a modification of a top down hierarchical approach, and like the implementation of the cybernetics approach to organization in the 1940s, discussed above, would likely only somewhat improve a defective hierarchical approach. What would be needed would be a switch to inclusive participatory decision making. In the case of planning, what would be needed would be a switch to decentralized planning, with the role of the center as facilitator and coordinator.

The opposite approach to attempting to achieve a balanced economy has been that of capitalist libertarians. They seek to remove the political advantage of wealth from the economy, by minimizing government regulation and provision of services. They would "leave everything to the market," which is seen as producing and maintaining an equilibrium when not interfered with. This seems appealing, especially if one begins with strong antitrust legislation to initially limit participation in the economy to small businesses. But there are several fundamental problems with this approach that make it unworkable, at least in industrial and post-industrial society.[134] First is the fact that markets are created by governments, and operate according to the rules and procedures that governments do (or do not) establish. The economic outcome, including which firms succeed and fail is greatly influenced by what the rules are.

Second, while smaller firms may tend to be more efficient than larger ones, planned and serendipitous events continually occur which increase the market power of some firms, and reduce that of others. This gives firms with more market power more advantage over others than the natural advantage of being below a certain optimal size provides. A firm with more capital can advertise more to sell more than poorer competitors, or can keep prices lower, longer, in order to win a price war, driving competitors out of business.

They also can buy in larger volume, attaining lower prices, etc. Thus in a minimally regulated market, there is a natural tendency for some firms to gain market power, leading to their gaining additional market power, leading to a concentration of capital, unbalancing the market, and ultimately moving it towards monopoly and oligopoly. This creates major differences in wealth and power, undermining democracy.

Additionally, the capitalist libertarian approach, by emphasizing the profits and loses of individual firms, fails to take into account the very important areas of externalities. Externalities are the costs and benefits to society and people that do not show up on a firm's balance sheet. An example of an externalized cost is harmful pollution that injures people and the community, without payment by the polluter, Contrary to the libertarian approach, the pollution needs to be taxed or regulated. Similarly, public goods, such as education and other services, are not adequately provided for in the Libertarian approach. Private firms and charitable acts will not supply them sufficiently, and on an equitable basis. Equitable access to services is often necessary to provide the equal opportunity necessary for people to participate in the economy on an equal basis: a requirement to keep the economy in balance and to maintain equal inclusive political participation.

In the twenty-first century, a market of relatively small businesses is usually necessary for a participatory economy, but government action of various kinds is necessary to keep the market in balance—preventing oligopoly and monopoly from arising—while providing necessary public goods and regulating to minimize the costs of externalities.[135] A market of relatively small businesses can achieve the economies of scale of large enterprises, by forming networks or cooperatives to purchase in bulk, as IGA (Independent Grocers Association) supermarkets do. The stores are individually owned, but agree to buy certain products from the association, while stores in the same marketing area coordinate sales and advertising.[136] Similarly, small firms can band together to provide research, as the Mondragon Cooperatives, discussed above, do through the federation's research division. Alternatively, firms could subscribe to research organizations for the right to use their products or patents, and/or research could be undertaken or funded by public organizations (government or nonprofit), as the US government has long done in the United States[137] For example, a great deal of medical research in the US is funded by government grants, and a fair amount by charitable organizations, such as the American Cancer Society.

The Role of Taxes in Balancing the Economy

An important instrument for maintaining a balance of relations in contemporary society in terms of keeping wealth relatively equal is the taxing system. The main two vehicles that are usually appropriate for doing that are a sufficiently graduated income tax and an inheritance tax. The graduation needs to be steep enough to prevent fortunes to grow large enough to begin to significantly unequalize wealth at any time, and especially, across generations. Normally, to raise revenue, it is preferable to use graduated taxes, based on people's ability to pay, rather than to use regressive sales and excise taxes. Sales and excise taxes can be used, however, as incentives against socially undesirable behavior—such as high sales taxes on tobacco to discourage its use, and taxes on carbon dioxide emissions to encourage more efficient use of fossil fuels, and switching to renewable energy, to counter global warming. Also, reasonable sales and excise taxes, often as user fees, can be used to have people pay their share of public goods they use, such as fees for playing on a public golf course. However, such taxes or fees ought not to be so high that they tend to discriminate economically against lower income people.

Income taxes can be used for regulatory purposes, particularly in granting deductions or tax credits for certain desirable purposes. An example is a tax credit for installing solar electricity on a building, to counter global warming, or to assist people in isolated areas, away from power lines, to have electricity. However, the use of income taxes for regulatory purposes ought not to go so far as to make the tax code overly complex, nor should it be allowed to provide unwarranted advantages to particular interests. The granting of tax exemptions and credits certainly ought not to extend to the point of creating large differences in wealth, or otherwise unbalancing the economy. If in a particular case the tax code cannot be used for regulatory purposes without creating significant injustices or imbalances, then it should not be used for regulatory purposes.

Appropriate Regulation and Services

Just what regulations and public goods are needed or desirable depends on the particular circumstances, but there are a few general guidelines. To the extent that it is practical, it is advisable to regulate via incentives, rather than by commands.[138] Public goods include investments in human capital, community infrastructure, and institutions, as well as services. So far as practical, the emphasis on services and human capital investments ought to be empowering people, and only providing income—or its equivalent, such as food, or food vouchers, as a temporary supportive part of empowerment. For example, people might receive grants while they are undertaking education or skill training. In addition, public support can quite properly be provided where empowering people to earn income is not feasible or appropriate, as with people who are sufficiently disabled or ill, or have earned their pensions.[139] To provide equal opportunity with empowerment, and to keep the economy and human relations in balance, education and health care need to be easily accessible and inexpensive, of sufficient and essentially equal quality for all. Similarly, there needs to be sufficient social insurance equally available in ways that are empowering and do not create dependence, to support people hit by the accidents of life, such as illness, injury, loss of employment from a change in technology, shift in the market, etc.

In this technologically advancing age, automation is reducing the amount of labor required to operate the economy. As this occurs, the number of hours of work each week need to be reduced to maintain full employment. This requires making available adequate and readily accessible education and job related training, along with incentives for businesses to hire more employees rather than to require overtime. For people who are partially disabled, are older, or need a shorter or less strenuous work week, appropriate part-time work could be made available. This can allow them to continue to be and feel they are contributors to society. As the regular workweek becomes shorter, that would create opportunities for additional public or private enterprises and increased employment in education and recreation which would enhance the quality of life.

In a participatory society people tend to feel a part of society by supporting each other, on an individual and institutional basis. They can feel that they are contributors to it, both through contributing their voice to decision making, and through taking actions with a social benefit. Therefore, it would often be beneficial to have all citizens take part in a period or periods of public service, which could include military service, to the extent that was necessary. Public service could include involvement in all kinds of projects, as was done in the US New Deal with agencies such as the Civilian Conservation Corps, or currently with AmeriCorps and the Peace Corps.[140] Adjustments could be made so that many citizens with disabilities would be able to serve.

For a twenty-first century economy to function well, there is a legitimate need to raise capital for business and government. For businesses, selling stock and issuing bonds are often legitimate ways to do that. Governments may tax and borrow money, usually through bonds. Similarly, charging reasonable interest rates related to the cost of money and level of risk is normally proper, except where higher or lower rates would be more appropriate public policy. An example is providing low interest loans for investment in designated low income areas.[141]

However one problem that is widespread in contemporary economies that needs to be prevented by regulation is avoiding parasitic speculation that very often skews markets, artificially impacting prices. This sometimes causes considerable wealth disparities. It has also been involved in huge and very expensive scandals. Examples of this are the mortgage crisis that set off the 2007 Great Recession, and skewed pricing and supply problems in the years since 2007 because of speculation on commodity prices, including oil, aluminum, and food.[142] A graduated income tax that is quite high at the top may dampen speculation. It may also help keep executive salaries relatively low, by making it more advantageous to leave money in a business, and having less money available to speculate with. Another proposal is to have a small tax on every stock, security, or commodity trade to discourage pure speculation.[143]

Section 4: Returning to Harmony

Stephen M. Sachs

Dealing with Torts and Crimes with Restorative Justice

Native societies worked strongly to create and maintain harmony and balance, and used a variety of means to return to harmony when relations within a person or between people or groups were out of balance.[144] When dealing with acts that Western society today considers crimes and torts (civil injuries), the emphasis was on restoring harmony between the parties. This might involve punishment or compensation for harm as part of the harmonizing process. So far as possible, when someone had committed an offense, the emphasis was upon reintegrating the wrongdoer back into society as a good citizen. Only in extreme cases, where reintegration seemed unattainable and the offender was considered sufficiently dangerous, was a perpetrator exiled or killed.

By contrast, in the United States and other Western societies the emphasis in crimes long has been first in retribution, and most often only secondarily, if at all, providing restitution to victims, and rehabilitation for offenders. This has usually left victims of crimes, and sometimes their communities, unrestored from the harms of crimes. There often have been high recidivism rates among those convicted of crimes. One aspect of this is that in many instances those who have been convicted, on completing their sentences have been greatly limited in their ability to obtain desirable employment.

As with the history of organizations in the West, discussed above, there have long been some modifications occasionally introduced into the corrections model in North America to deal with its short-comings. An example of this has been providing psychological services to convicts, and halfway houses to provide employment and ease convicts' reintegration to society. More recently, an alternative approach, restorative justice, has been applied in the United States, beginning in the 1970s, in different forms and to different extents, that derives directly from American Indian experience.[145]

Empowering and Healing

Restorative justice, when fully applied, is an attempt to restore solid relationships among all those who have suffered loss from a criminal act: the victim, other members of the community—individually and/or collectively—and, if possible, the offender.[146] For the victim, involvement in the process is very often quite empowering and healing. The victims have the opportunity to know what is being done about the harm done to them, and perhaps be able to discover why the harmful act was committed, while being heard through telling their stories. As with participatory decision making, simply having a voice in many instances is extremely important to the speaker. Often the victim is able to receive restitution from the perpetrator, either concretely, or symbolically. Where concrete restitution is not possible, the restorative justice process can be augmented by victims' compensation from the government or community. An example is the California Victim Compensation Program,[147] that helps pay bills and expenses resulting from certain violent crimes. Victims of crime who have been injured or have been threatened with injury, in many instances, are eligible for assistance. It may also be possible for the victim to receive an apology from the perpetrator.

For communities, restorative justice provides an opportunity to be involved in matters of concern to them. This is not possible in standard Western judicial proceedings, where the full responsibility is with the appropriate level of state government.[148] Crime affects communities, making them stakeholders, as secondary victims, when it occurs in their midst. Having a role in a criminal proceeding allows the community and its members to establish forums to address issues of crime, support victims in their midst, while building a sense of mutual accountability and strengthening the bonds of community. It encourages community members to take on their obligations for the welfare of their members, encompassing victims and offenders. This action fosters conditions that promote healthy communities, much the way citizen participation in community policing, discussed above, can be empowering in building healthy communities and reducing crime.

For a high proportion of offenders, restorative justice has been found to be extremely important, in several dimensions.[149] While it is not always proper for offenders to be directly involved with victims in a restorative justice process, they can still be involved indirectly. The participation of offenders, in whatever form, is important as it pressures those who admit their guilt to face up to what they have done, and to see the impact of their behavior. Depending upon the circumstances, this also often provides an opportunity for offenders to move toward making things right, at least with an apology. This usually is not accepted unless it appears genuine, with understanding of the harm inflicted, which offender' participation confronts them with. Further, in many instances the offender can provide restitution. In cases of minor offenses involving property damage, or minor injuries, this may involve the perpetrator repairing the damage, or earning the money to pay for the repair or compensation. All of these aspects of offender participation tend to enhance rehabilitation. Recidivism rates are generally lower for offenders who have gone through a restorative justice process than an adversarial criminal justice process.[150] This is partly the case because one aspect of restorative justice is to consider and take steps to assist the offender in attaining rehabilitation, and where appropriate, reintegration with the community. This may involve such actions as the offender participating in substance abuse programs, undertaking counseling or psychological treatment, undertaking anger management, nonviolence training, or other appropriate education, and supervised probation or halfway house living. Probation and halfway house living can be used instead of, or following incarceration, as is appropriate.

Principles of Restorative Justice

In situations where the offender is also a victim, though their offense is not an appropriate response to their victimhood, the restorative process needs to lead s/he to understand the inappropriateness of the offender's action. Steps also need to be taken to correct that injustice, as the ultimate aim of restorative justice is to return all the parties, and at times the community, to balanced, harmonious relations. To do this requires examining each case holistically, to understand the full set of relations involved, and to work to bring them into harmony. This is more complex than the normal workings of Western criminal justice systems that focus narrowly on the offender's act in isolation, though mitigating (or aggravating) circumstances may be taken into account in sentencing. A key to working well with offenders—as with everyone else—is to speak and act with respect: to support, not criticize people, but to criticize inappropriate and harmful behavior and work to correct wrong thinking. This includes honoring a person's views and experience in a mutually respectful dialog, to try to assist people in moving to be more fully who they really are.

Thus, the underlying principles of restorative justice flow as follows.[151] Crimes and equivalent harms are a violation of people and of interpersonal relationships. Since we are all related, interconnected, the violation creates an obligation on all parties, including the offender, to restore proper relationships, so far as possible. Where relationships were previously imperfect, the aim is to improve them, the need for which may be illuminated by a harm.

Restorative justice processes may take any number of a wide variety of forms and be applied for different purposes.[152] In twentieth-century North America, much of their use has been as alternative sentencing programs, following a standard judicial process to determine guilt.[153] This has had some special applications in the development of drug courts, that can focus on rehabilitation,[154] in family courts, in dealing with domestic sex crimes[155] and in juvenile courts and restorative programs, where young people are widely considered generally more open to social and psychological reeducation.[156] Restorative justice is sometimes also used more broadly as the process for handling crimes, as remains the case in some Indigenous nations, as exemplified by Navajo peacemaking courts.[157]

Section 5: Inner Harmony and Outer Harmony

Phyllis M. Gagnier and Stephen M. Sachs

Ho'oponopono, a Form of Restorative Justice

Following the Indigenous model, restorative justice can be utilized in civil law in dealing with all harms and injuries. It is so used outside the legal system in some institutions, including workplaces and schools.[158] One example is the application of the Native Hawaiian problem solving process, *ho'oponopono*, a form of restorative justice, applied by a variety of social services, beginning in Hawaii in the 1970s.[159] Although varying slightly in form, *ho'oponopono* follows the same basic principles of the Indigenous and restorative processes previously discussed. It is:

> A method for restoring harmony that was traditionally used within the extended family. According to Pukui, it literally

means "setting to right… to restore and maintain good relationships among family, and family and the super natural powers."[160]

While first used in mainstream application to solve a case involving traditional Hawaiians, the practice quickly spread in Hawaii to include non-Hawaiian clients and practitioners in a variety of social service activities involving the resolution of conflicts and the restoration of relationships. *Ho'oponopono* was applied, for example, to resolve family and business disputes. It also was applied as an alternative mental health strategy to solve clients' psychological and psychiatric problems.[161] Since the 1980's, *ho'oponopono* has been applied internationally, with many variations, as a method of conflict resolution in many settings.[162] In addition, a version of *ho'oponopono* has become internationally popular as a meditation method for individuals to attain inner harmony.[163]

The Need for Good Inner Dialogue for Good Citizenship and Well Working Democracy

Ultimately, to have good relations with others, requires harmony within oneself. A major factor in making inclusiveness successful in traditional Indigenous societies has been their emphasis on continual work at healing and returning to harmony, both within each person and among people and groups. One of the difficulties today in restoring harmony in many North American Native communities, and also in obtaining peace in much of the Middle East, is that not enough has been achieved in overcoming the trauma suffered by a great many individuals from past conflict and repression[164] In agreement with Native traditions, John Dewey linked good psychological health, and continual reflection and reevaluation of one's assumptions, conclusions, and habits of thought and action, in order to have a citizenry able to carry out effective democracy, as is discussed in the development of the American philosophy of pragmatism section of chapter 4. One cannot be truly open to others unless one continually undertakes the work of being open within oneself.

There are many methods for effectively undertaking this inner work. Some of these are offered by various schools of psychology. Others are found in the Eastern and other spiritual traditions that have become widely popular in the West since World War II, discussed in the introduction to part II. Many are to be found in the traditional ways of Indigenous societies and in their adaptations to contemporary circumstances. One of these is *ho'oponopono*.

Author Phyllis M. Gagnier, a longtime conflict resolution facilitator, has found *ho'oponopono* extremely helpful in restoring and sustaining her own inner balance, that is essential to good physical, mental and spiritual health, and relating well with others:

> Somewhere in the process between diagnosis, treatment, and recovery from cancer, I learned of the *Ho'oponopono* Practice. I was consulting with an ordained (Spirit-Directed Healer, Oneness Blessing Facilitator) Spiritual Counselor, who is now a friend. During a process, he introduced me to *Ho'oponopono*. Upon hearing the words of the mantra on his CD, I immediately felt my body relax, My body's response was so obvious that we both perceived it as intuitive. Prior to leaving his home, he created a CD with downloaded *Ho'oponopono* music and chants for me. This was 2012, the year of my breast cancer diagnosis, treatment, and journey into the world of responsible healing. Today, in 2019, I have experienced and continue to experience the relevance and impact of the *Ho'oponopono* Practice in my healing and recovery process. I remain committed to restoring and preserving my health. Consistently, *Ho'oponopono* Practice has been and is one of my choices of healing modalities.
>
> Over these 7 years, my experience with the *Ho'oponopono* Practice includes actively engaging in practicing, researching, reading, and, registering for the *Ho'oponopono* Practitioner Certification Program in October 2016,

and the Advanced *Ho'oponopono* Certification Program in September 2017, by Dr. Joe Vitale, Dr. Ihaleakala Hew Len, and Mathew Dixon. Through this self-created learning process, I discovered in the *Ho'oponopono* Practitioner Certification Program the evolution and origin of the modern Self I-Dentity *Ho'oponopono* Practice I am engaging in.

The Traditional *Ho'oponopono* Practice originated in Hawaii. Vitale, Len, and Dixon state that the Hawaiian dictionary defines *Ho'oponopono* as a "mental cleansing: family conferences in which relationships were set right through prayer, discussion, confession, repentance, and mutual restitution and forgiveness." They explain that in the word *Ho'oponopono*, the "*ho'o* is a particle used to make an actualizing verb from the following noun. In English we would use 'to' before a noun. In *Ho'oponopono*, ho'o creates a verb from the noun pono."[165]

They further explain that pono is defined as:

goodness, uprightness, morality, moral qualities, correct or proper procedure, excellence, well-being, prosperity, welfare, benefit, true condition or nature, duty; moral, fitting, proper, righteous, right, upright, just, virtuous, fair, beneficial, successful, in perfect order, accurate, correct, eased, relieved; should, ought, must, necessary... [and as] to put to rights; to put in order or shape, correct, revise, adjust, amend, regulate, arrange, rectify, tidy up, make orderly or neat.[166]

According to Vitale, Len, and Dixon, Mary Kawena Pukui, a preeminent Hawaiian scholar, wrote that *Ho'oponopono* was a practice in Ancient Hawaii. This is supported by oral histories from contemporary Hawaiian elders. She described *Ho'oponopono* as a practice of extended family members meeting to "make right" broken family relations. Some families met daily or weekly to prevent problems from erupting. Other families met when a member became ill, feeling and believing that illness was caused by the stress of anger, guilt, recriminations, and lack of forgiveness.[167]

Information shared by Vitale, Len, and Dixon states that usually the most senior member of the family conducted the process and gathered the family together. If for any reason the family was unable to work through a problem, they turned to a respected outsider. The process began with a prayer. A statement of the problem was made, and the transgression discussed. Family members were expected to work problems through and cooperate, and not "hold fast to the fault."

Periods of silence were taken to reflect on the entanglement of emotions and injuries. Everyone's feelings were acknowledged. Confession, repentance, and forgiveness took place. Everyone released (kaka) each other, letting go. They cut off the past ('koi) and together they closed the event with a ceremonial feast, called pani, which could include eating lime kala or kala seaweed which symbolizes the release. The belief was that Ho'oponopono corrects, restores, and maintains good relationships among family members and with their gods or God by getting to the source of trouble.[168]

Gagnier is of Algonquin heritage and has facilitated considerable conflict resolution, education, and other consulting services with Indian tribes and organizations. She was invigorated by her research, as she worked with *Ho'oponopono* for personal peace and healing:

I inhaled this, previously unknown to me, history with mixed emotions. Memories of my studies, professional services, and experiences in the Field of Conflict Resolution flooded my mind. I felt validated for the many years of openly advocating for our Indigenous Communities to be respected for their Cultural Traditional processes in solving problems; to be encouraged to study their Traditions; to be supported to return, where relevant, to their Traditions; to be acknowledged for continuing to follow their Cultural Traditions. While searching for a PhD Program in Conflict

Analysis-Problem Solving, I repeatedly considered the University of Hawaii. I recalled disclosing to a friend that "there's something in Hawaii." When I learned of *Ho'oponopono*, I experienced moments of regret that I hadn't pursued my inclination. These feelings were followed by appreciation that Hawaii came to me.

The process of *Ho'oponopono* learned by Gagnier seems to be a contemporary adaptation two steps removed from the Traditional *Ho'oponopono* Practice. Again, according to Vitale, Len, and Dixon in the Ho'oponopono Practitioner Certification booklet, Kahuna Lapa'au Morrnah Nalamaku Simeona is responsible for the modern version of *Ho'oponopono*, which she shared throughout the United States, Asia, and Europe. Born May 19, 1913, and died February 11, 1992, she is recognized as the first kahuna lapa'au (healer) to create an updated modern version of the ancient *Ho'oponopono* Practice, which she called Self I-Dentity through *Ho'oponopono* (SITH). Morrnah used the Traditional *Ho'oponopono* Practice since she was age two, later revamping the process yet retaining the 'essence' of the 'ancient wisdom.' For 10 years, she owned and operated health spas at the Kahala Hilton and Royal Hawaiian Hotels. She was a practitioner of the lomilomi massage. She combined her healing form of *Ho'oponopono* and massage which she offered to many clients including celebrities, i.e., President Lyndon B. Johnson, former first lady Jackie Kennedy, and golf pro Arnold Palmer.[169]

Her modification of the Traditional *Ho'oponopono* practice, of forgiveness, repentance, and reconciliation, to the realities of modern day begin through Divine Inspiration in the mid-1970s. Her new system, Self I-Dentity *Ho'oponopono*, uses Traditional techniques to create a working partnership among the three parts of the mind (self) which she calls by Hawaiian names, Unihipili (child/subconscious), Uhane (mother/conscious), and Aumakua (father/superconscious). The concept is that when this 'inner family' is in alignment a person is in rhythm with their Divinity. When this balance occurs life begins to flow. Thus, *Ho'oponopono* helps restore balance in the individual. Praying to the Divine Creator and connecting problems with Reincarnation and Karma resulted in this unique new problem-solving process that became self-help for the individual rather than the Traditional *Ho'oponopono* Practice of group process. The basic principles, however, remain the basis of the application of *Ho'oponopono* in contemporary interpersonal and inter-group conflict resolution.[170]

Morrnah's legacy involves presenting her new modern form of Self I-Dentity *Ho'oponopono* in trainings and lectures which include a presentation to the United Nations; presentations to nearly a dozen states in the US; presentations in more than 14 countries including Germany, the Netherlands, Switzerland, France, Russia, and Japan. Other presentations were made to medical, religious, business, and educational institutions including the University of Hawaii and Johns Hopkins University. She founded Pacifica Seminars and the Foundation of "I" Inc., which helped to spread her *Ho'oponopono* process. She was named a Living Treasure of the State of Hawaii in 1983 by the Hongwanji Mission of Honolulu and the Hawaii State Legislature.[171]

She summarized:

> *Ho'oponopono* is a profound gift that allows one to develop a working relationship with the Divinity within and learn to ask that in each moment, our errors in thought, word, deed, or action be cleansed. The process is essentially about freedom, complete freedom from the past.[172]
>
> We can appeal to Divinity who knows our personal blueprint, for healing of all thoughts and memories that are holding us back at this time....[173]
>
> Peace begins with me.[174]

According to Dr. Joe Vitale, the credit for expanding Morrnah's new modern version of Self I-Dentity *Ho'oponopono* goes to Dr. Ihaleakala Hew Len, a psychologist who worked and traveled with Morrnah for more than nine years. Using Self I-Dentity

Ho'oponopono, Dr. Hew is known for healing a ward of diagnosed criminally insane patients, without ever seeing them, at the Hawaii State Hospital. His process represents an advanced new perception of total responsibility.[175]

Gagnier found this to be an essential component in her healing process:

> It is this core of "total responsibility" that I connect with. In the 1960s, Summerhill was quoted as saying, "Total freedom is total responsibility." At the time, I was impacted by this view. I perceived it as exemplifying personal integrity. With a diagnosis of cancer for the second time, I am committed to dig deep to learn what role I have and I am playing in my body's deterioration rather than settle for "my body has betrayed me." At the time I learned of the *Ho'oponopono* Practice, I experienced an innate sense my healing is an "inside job."
>
> I actually find comfort in the "total responsibility" concept. I feel myself shifting from self-blame to self-empowerment, thus experiencing a shift in my perceptions and emotional states, a process I am familiar with, since it is the basis of the professional training services I offer in Brain-Based Emotional Intelligence.
>
> I am intent on healing myself. I became clear that in *Ho'oponopono* Practice healing means "Loving Myself."[176] With this clarity, I received the insight of my need to include Self Compassion, in my healing practices, as an antidote for the shame that accompanied my experiences with cancer.
>
> Wow! I continue to wonder about the impact on children, today, if their families were practicing either Traditional *Ho'oponopono* Practice or Self I-Dentity *Ho'oponopono?* What clarity would they experience? What insights would they receive?
>
> Through the many months of recovery, I have integrated my *Ho'oponopono* Practice with other healing modalities, particularly Appreciation and Self

Compassion processes. To date, my *Ho'oponopono* Practice remains front and center, my "foundation," whether I am reframing a belief, shifting negative self-talk, releasing a memory, neutralizing a self-imposed meaning, feeling shame, terror, unsafe, safe, courage, motivated, lifting a moment of suffering, appreciating a blessing, or listening for inspiration.[177] [Details on Gagnier's experience with her practice are in this endnote.]

However one undertakes it that fits one's background and evolving circumstances, as John Dewey emphasized, it is important both for our personal health and development, and for our being able to participate as good citizens in a healthy democracy, that we continually reexamine our attitudes, habits, thinking, and experience for our personal and our communities' growth. A good inner restorative justice practice is a prerequisite for a well-functioning interpersonal and inter-group restorative justice process.

Restorative Justice and Conflict Resolution

Stephen M. Sachs

Restorative justice practices are related to the whole expanding field of conflict resolution and transformation. This encompasses a large number of participatory processes for solving interpersonal and inter group (or institution) problems, as well as a number of inclusive participatory strategic planning methods. Good examples of large and small scale participatory processes for transforming conflict into collaboration, and to prevent open conflict through inclusive dialogue are the work of the National Coalition for Dialogue and Deliberation, the Network for Peace Through Dialogue, and Search for Common Ground. An excellent example of a participatory strategic planning process employed to restore community harmony and empower effective community actions is the Indigenous Leadership Interactive System (ILIS), discussed above.[178] The rise and expansion of these participatory processes, particularly since World War II, is an indication of the increasing relevance of traditional Indigenous principles, values, and ways of being for the wider world of the twenty-first century.

In the fully participatory society, applying Indigenous values, restorative justice would be the general approach used to find justice in both the criminal and civil law. It would be used informally, in various forms, as appropriate, in many institutions and organizations for dealing with inappropriate behavior. It is important to note that restorative justice uses punishment and compensation, when and as appropriate, as criminal and civil courts in the West have been doing for centuries. The difference is that restorative justice is broader, focusing on people and the full set of relations involved in each case or situation.

The Principle of Place: Applying Principles and Programs Appropriately for Each Situation

It is important to be aware that, like any social institution or device, restorative justice has to be instituted according to the culture and needs of the specific situation to which it is being applied, and adjusted appropriately as the circumstances change. Bruce Miller for example, reports that the attempt to apply the Maori family group counseling model, favored by the Canadian government for sentencing diversion programs for First Nations, to the Sto:lo Nation in British Columbia, functioned rather poorly, with much community resistance, because it did not fit the traditions and situation of the community. This led to developing a revised approach, beginning with discussions with people in the Sto:lo community.[179] Indeed, participation by the people involved is usually critical to developing a well working program. Miller reported that one of the major reasons for the failure of the South Island Justice Project, a diversionary project among Salish communities in British Columbia, was failure to consult with the people of the communities. They agreed with the principles of the project, but found the top down approach of developing and implementing it caused it not to meet the needs of the community.[180]

The importance of involving everyone involved in applying a principle, process, or program extends across the full range of human activity. Among the fields discussed in this chapter, for instance, organizational democracy demonstrates this again and again.

Lesieur, for example, describes the change that occurred in a book manufacturing plant when the Scanlan Plan was instituted.[181] This is a team participation process on the shop floor, offering teams that saved the firm money a share of the savings. Just prior to its initiation, the plant engineers had come down to the book binding department and made a study, on the basis of which they designed and installed, over a long holiday weekend, an assembly line to replace the tables on wheels that workers rolled from station, moving books through the various stages of the binding process.

On their return, the book binding employees were angry at the change, for two reasons. First they knew from experience that it would not work well (which it did not), and second, they were annoyed at it being imposed on them. With the initiation of the Scanlan Plan at that time, one of the engineers came down to discuss the problem of improving the production process with the book binders. He first had to gain sufficient trust among the binders for them to be willing to engage in a meaningful discussion. He achieved this by pointing out some problems in what the engineers had designed, and admitting that the engineering study on which the assembly line was based was undertaken at an unrepresentative time. He then had to find appropriate communication methods. On finding that the binders could not readily work with blueprints, the engineer brought the binders an adjustable model of the assembly line. Then the book binders dialogued with the engineer to resolve the conflict and develop a flexible production system to fit changing conditions in the shop, which fit the employees' work needs, and that was up to the technical standards of engineering.

Consequently, production efficiency and employee morale and commitment increased.

Similarly, author Stephen Sachs found in interviewing Indianapolis police officers about the initial launching of the community policing process, discussed above, that the officers were unhappy with its being forced on them from headquarters. Again, the complaint was twofold. The officers did not appreciate a major change in their work being forced on them. But they also quickly observed that there were problems in the implementation that were immediately obvious to them, but not to the top brass who did not work the streets. Among the problems was that the incentives for police officers were not changed with the shift from a rapid response patrol model to a community relations approach. Officers were now ordered to spend time observing the neighborhoods in which they worked, and talking to residents about crime and safety related issues. But they were still being evaluated on the basis of how little time they spent on any task, and how quickly they moved on to the next call. It was only when the top officers in charge of the program talked with those carrying it out that the contradictions were removed. The new program, then, began to function well with a corresponding rise in how the police people involved felt about it.

This brings us back to the two-part principle of place, which is fundamental to everything discussed in this chapter. First, each location in place and time is different, so that appropriate general principles have to be applied in accordance with the specific needs of each situation. Second, each person needs to be respected and has a different way of seeing, or perspective, that needs to be included to make good decisions: decisions that people will own and support. By doing this the community will include everyone, and all will feel included. This leads in turn to all citizens supporting, and being concerned about the community as a whole, and each other. This is essential for the harmony and wellbeing of one and all.

Notes to Chapter 5

1. Stephen M. Sachs, "Remembering the Traditional Meaning and Role of Kinship in American Indian Societies, to Overcome Problems of Favoritism in Contemporary Tribal Government," *Indigenous Policy* 22, no. 2 (2011).

2. Larry L. Naylor, *Cultural Diversity in the United States* (Indianapolis, IN: Greenwood, 1997).

3. Natalia Simanovsky, "Multiculturism in Canada: A Model for Other Countries," *Nonviolent Change* 26, no. 3 (2012). This article was written for the Common Ground News Service (CGNews), March 12, 2012, www.commongroundnews.org, who distributed it with copyright permission granted for publication. While this is the direction in which multiculturalism has been moving in Canada, it is important to note that its attainment is not complete, as exemplified by the continuing struggles of First Nation people in Canada with the Canadian government over a wide variety of issues. See "International Developments," *Indigenous Policy* 23, no. 3 (2012).

4. Lewis Fischer, *American Constitutional Law*, 3rd ed. (Durham: Carolina Academic Press, 1990), 550.

5. Ibid., 573.

6. Ingrid van Biezen, *Financing Political Parties and Election Campaigns: Guidelines* (Strasbourg, France: Council of Europe Publishing, 2003), http://www.coe.int/t/dghl/monitoring/greco/evaluations/round3/Financing_Political_Parties_en.pdf; "Campaign Finance: Comparative Summary," Library of Congress, http://www.loc.gov/law/help/campaign-finance/comparative-summary.php.

7. Dianne Russell, http://dianerussell.nationbuilder.com/fair_elections_act (unfortunately this webpage no longer works); "Senator Bernie Sanders: We Need Public Funding of Elections," FedUpUSA, September 14, 2012, http://www.fedupusa.org/2012/09/senator-bernie-sanders-we-need-public-funding-of-elections/; "Campaign Finance," Bernie Sanders: US Senator for Vermont, http://www.sanders.senate.gov/legislation/issue/campaign-finance.

8. "1992 Presidential Debate with George HW Bush, Bill Clinton & Ross Perot," YouTube, December 22, 2010 [televised October 6, 2008], http://www.youtube.com/watch?v=Jg9qB_BIjWY.

9. A summary of early, absentee, and mail voting in the United States: "Absentee and Early Voting," National Council of State Legislatures,

October 29, 2018, http://www.ncsl.org/legislatures-elections/elections/absentee-and-early-voting.aspx.

There is also the question of the voting system. The United States, with a few local exceptions, and a partial exception with the Electoral College in selecting the president, has always used a system of voting for individual candidates. The candidate with the most votes wins the election (and in some state and local elections, there is a runoff between the top two candidates, if there are more than two, and no one achieves a majority in the initial election). The system tends to support having only two parties. While it promotes stability, it does not necessarily lead to representative outcomes. Where there are more than two candidates, having the person with the most votes win may not bring about a representative result, even with a runoff between the top two candidates. What may be more representative—though it takes some education to get people to understand it—is a preferential ballot, also known as ranked-choice voting or instant runoff, in which each voter may vote for all the candidates in order of preference. This, in effect, asks the voter that, if your first choice is eliminated for too few votes, what is your second, third, fourth, etc., choice. If someone gains a majority on the first round, they win. But if not, the candidate with the lowest votes is eliminated, and those who voted for that person as first choice have their second preference vote used. If a candidate now has a majority, then s/he is the winner. If not, the candidate with the lowest votes (among those still in the race) is eliminated, and their next choice not already eliminated is counted, and so on for as many rounds as it takes until someone achieves a majority.

For example, there are four candidates who on the first round win the following percentage of the vote: A (a conservative), 29 percent; B (a liberal), 27 percent; C (a liberal), 25 percent; D (a socialist), 19 percent. D is eliminated, and her second-round votes are counted with the following result: A, 31 percent; B, 33 percent; C, 36 percent. No majority yet, so A is eliminated, and the next still in the race votes for A are counted resulting in B, 55 percent, and C, 45 percent, so B is elected, and overall is probably the most representative candidate.

Ranked-choice voting was being used in local voting in eleven US cities in 2016. These included Cambridge, Massachusetts; Minneapolis, Minnesota; Portland, Maine; and San Francisco, California. Maine instituted statewide rank choice voting in 2016, first going into effect in primary elections in 2018. The state did so after a number of three-candidate races for governor in which the winner attained a plurality, but not a majority of the vote. Preferential balloting is also used in Irish and Australian national elections. Analysts have pointed out that if this system had been used in the US presidential election in 2000, Al Gore would have won Florida and the national election, rather than G. W. Bush. In 2016, Donald J. Trump would not have won the Republican nomination for president if this system had been used. See Katherine Q. Seely, "Maine Adopts Ranked-Choice Voting; What Is It, and How Will It Work?," *New York Times*, December 3, 2016, http://www.nytimes.com/2016/12/03/us/maine-ranked-choice-voting.html?ref=todayspaper&_r=0, reported.

10. Benjamin R. Barber, *Strong Democracy: Participatory Politics for a New Age* (Berkeley: University of California Press 1984), 273–81, 307; Theodore Lewis Becker and Christa Daryl Slaton, *Future of Teledemocracy* (Westport, CT: Praeger, 2000). On electronic journalism, see Lewis A. Friedland, "Electronic Democracy and the New Citizenship," *Media, Culture, and Society* 18 (1996): 185–212.

11. "Channel 97," City of Stockton, California, http://www.stocktongov.com/government/departments/manager/pub97.html.

12. Becker and Slaton, Future of Teledemocracy.

13. James S. Fishkin's 1991 proposal is reported, along with other discussion of electronic citizen deliberation in Friedland, "Electronic Democracy and the New Citizenship." The September 2019 dialogues among 526 representative Americans is reported in Emily Badger and Kevin Quealy, Photographs by Chad Batka and Celeste Sloman, "These 526 Voters Represent All of America. And They Spent a Weekend Together," *New York Times*, Oct. 2, 2019, https://www.nytimes.com/interactive/2019/10/02/upshot/these-526-voters-represent-america.html.

14. Ibid.

15. P. Bourdieu and L. J. D. Wacquant, *An Invitation to Reflexive Sociology* (Chicago: University of Chicago Press, 1992).

16. R. D. Putnam, "Bowling Alone: America's Declining Social Capital," *Journal of Democracy* 6, no. 1 (1994): 6–78.

17. J. P. Kretzmann and J. L. McKnight, *Building Communities from the Inside Out: A Path toward Finding and Mobilizing a Community's Assets* (Chicago: Center for Urban Affairs and Policy Research/Acta, 1993).

18. Friedland, "Electronic Democracy and the New Citizenship."

19. Raymond Schillinger, "Social Media and the Arab Spring: What Have We Learned," *Huffington Post*, September 20, 2011, http://

www.huffingtonpost.com/raymond-schillinger/arab-spring-social-media_b_970165.html; Caitlin Dewey, "How the Middle East Uses Social Media, in Four Charts," *Washington Post*, December 19, 2012, http://www.washingtonpost.com/blogs/worldviews/wp/2012/12/19/how-the-middle-east-uses-social-media-in-four-charts/.

20. Friedland, "Electronic Democracy and the New Citizenship."
21. Jane Mansbridge, *Beyond Adversary Democracy* (New York: Basic, 1980).
22. Friedland, "Electronic Democracy and the New Citizenship."
23. Ibid.
24. The issue of at what point it is necessary and proper to regulate expression while maintaining openness and equal access is a complex one. The proper answer depends open the circumstances. There are numerous court cases on this issue in American legal history. Among the many works discussing them is: Gregory Maggs and Peter Smith, *Constitutional Law: A Contemporary Approach* (Interactive Casebook Series), 4th ed. (St. Paul, MN: West Academic Publishing, 2019), part IX. A comparative summary of the approaches of thirteen nations to this set of issues is. "Limits on Freedom of Expression," Library of Congress, June 2019, https://www.loc.gov/law/help/freedom-expression/index.php.

On appropriate limits on young persons' time before computer and T.V. screens, see "How Media Use Affects Your Child," KidsHealth from Nemours, reviewed by Elana Pearl Ben-Joseph, December 2016, http://kidshealth.org/parent/positive/family/tv_affects_child.html; Padma Ravichandran and Brandel France de Bravo, "Young Children and Screen Time (Television, DVDs, Computer)," National Research Center for Women and Families, 2012; and Neza Stiglic and Russell M. Viner, Effects of screen time on the health and well-being of children and adolescents: a systematic review of reviews, BMJ Open, January 3, 2019, https://www.ncbi.nlm.nih.gov/pmc/articles/PMC6326346/.

25. Edgar Cahn, *No More Throw-Away People: The Co-Production Imperative* (Washington, DC: Essential, 2000); Time Dollar Institute, 2012 (unfortunately this webpage no longer works).
26. TimeBanks, http://timebanks.org/.
27. Ibid.
28. As author Stephen Sachs observed in a year of fieldwork in 1973–74, the Yugoslav system of social and workers' self-management operated moderately democratically in practice at the local level, but the political system became increasingly less democratic as one

moved upward from the local to the national level, because as one moved further and further beyond the local level the leadership of the oligarchic (but not totalitarian) League of Communists increasingly was also the leadership of other major organizations. The main problem at the local and enterprise level, which also frustrated democracy at higher levels, was cultural, as most of the cultures of Yugoslavia did not have democratic traditions, and general education taught participatory democracy only in theory, with no opportunity to experience it in school, while managers, technical experts, and those with higher education were taught to make decisions, rather than act as facilitators. The Yugoslav experience demonstrates the requirement of participatory democratic structures to develop and function on the basis of participatory culture and education, if they are in fact to function participatively, as is discussed below. Rousseau, who learned much from American Indians, makes this point in *The Social Contract*, including in chapter XII.

29. Stephen M. Sachs, "Some Reflections Upon Workers' Self-Management in Yugoslavia," *Journal of the Hellenic Diaspora: Critical Thought on Greek and World Issues* 4, no. 1 (1977), reprinted as *Workplace Democracy Paper #4* (Washington, DC: Association for Workplace Democracy, 1981); David Riddell, "Social Self-Government in Yugoslav Socialism," in *Where It's At: Radical Perspectives on Sociology*, eds. John Howard and Stephen Deutsch (New York: Harper and Row, 1970); Stephen M. Sachs and Nahoma Sachs, "Political Participation in a Macedonian Village," paper presented at Midwest Political Science Association Meeting, Chicago, 1974.

30. LaShonda M. Stewart, Steven A. Miller, and R. W. Hildreth, "Participatory Budgeting in the United States: A Preliminary Analysis of Chicago's 49th Ward Experiment," *New Political Science* 36, no. 2 (2014): 193–218.

31. Christopher Holman, "Reconsidering the Citizens Assemblies on Electoral Reform Phenomena: Castoriadas and Radical Citizen Democracy," *New Political Science* 35, no. 2 (2013). In the case of Jackson, Mississippi, at the instigation of the mayor, the city organized community meetings to get public input on issues and to develop innovative approaches to problems. As of April 2017, Jackson had for some time been employing "people's assemblies" in neighborhoods throughout the city to empower and involve people in giving input on issues that affected them, and to put pressure on city government

to act according to popular will (Kate Arnoff, "From Movement to Mayor," *In These Times*, June 2017).

32. Holman, "Reconsidering the Citizens Assemblies on Electoral Reform Phenomena," 205.

33. Holman, "Reconsidering the Citizens Assemblies"; "Improving Democracy in B.C.," Citizens' Assembly on Electoral Reform, http://citizensassembly.arts.ubc.ca; "Making Every Vote Count: The Case for Electoral Reform in British Columbia," Citizens' Assembly on Electoral Reform, 2004, http://citizensassembly.arts.ubc.ca/resources/TechReport(full).pdf; "British Columbia Citizens Assembly on Electoral Reform," Citizens Assembly on Electoral Reform, http://www.citizensassembly.gov.on.ca/en-CA/docs/Weekend%20Five/The%20Cases%20of%20B.C.%20and%20The%20Netherlands.pdf. The 260-page "Technical Report" contains detailed descriptions and evaluations of every stage of the citizen assembly process in British Columbia.

34. "Technical Report," 66–67.

35. Ibid., 72–73.

36. Information about the Dutch government constituting a Citizens' Assembly on Electoral Reform is at "Ministerie van Binnenlandse Zaken en Konindrijksrelaties," Rijksoverheld, www.burgerforumkiesstelsel.nl; "Improving Democracy in B.C.," http://citizensassembly.arts.ubc.ca; "Citizens' Assembly," Wikipedia, https://en.wikipedia.org/wiki/Citizens%27_assembly.

37. On the Irish citizens' assemblies see ibid.; "Citizens' Assembly (Ireland)," Wikipedia, https://en.wikipedia.org/wiki/Citizens%27_Assembly_(Ireland); "Citizens' Assembly Set to Be Up and Running By October," RTÉ, July 13, 2016, http://www.rte.ie/news/2016/0713/802272-citizens-assembly/; Elaine Loughlin, "Judge Mary Laffoy to Chair Citizens' Assembly," *Irish Examiner*, July 28, 2016, http://www.irishexaminer.com/ireland/judge-mary-laffoy-to-chair-citizens-assembly-412775.html; Ronan McGreevy, "Citizens' Assembly on Eighth Amendment to Meet Next Month: The Constitutional Ban On Abortion Will Be First Item On the Agenda For New Grouping," *Irish Times*, September 10, 2016, http://www.irishtimes.com/news/ireland/irish-news/citizens-assembly-on-eighth-amendment-to-meet-next-month-1.2787112.

38. LaDonna Harris, Stephen M. Sachs, and Barbara Morris, *Re-Creating the Circle: The Renewal of American Indian Self-Determination* (Albuquerque: University of New Mexico Press, 2011), chap. 4, sec. 1.

39. Ibid., chap. 1, sec. 2.
40. MoveOn.Org.
41. Ivan Boothe, "The Occupy Movement: What Democracy Looks Like," *Nonviolent Change* 26, no. 2 (2012).
42. "Welcome to NCDD," National Coalition for Dialogue and Deliberation, http://ncdd.org/.
43. Network for Peace through Dialogue, http://networkforpeace.com.
44. Search for Common Ground, www.sfcg.org.
45. Mass movements, such as the Arab Spring, in both the short and long run, may or may not be effective in bringing democratizing equalitarian change. The issue here is not what makes for a successful movement, or whether a particular movement is successful, but whether such movements have a democratizing tendency, which the Arab Spring movements have had. The tendency is there, regardless of whether the democratic movements, for example, in Syria, have been lost in the collapse of the country into a terrible civil war, or have become greatly reduced in Egypt, amid political developments including the army reasserting power. Moreover, while such movements have their ebbs and flows, from a long-term perspective, the beginning score of years of the twenty-first century appears to be a period of increase in such movements.
46. Stephen M. Sachs, "We Face a Critical Moment as the World Moves into a New Period," *Nonviolent Change* 27, no. 1 (2013).
47. Harris, Sachs, and Morris, *Re-Creating the Circle*, chap. 4, sec. 1.
48. Ibid., chap. 1.
49. University of Foreign Military And Cultural Studies, *Red Team Handbook* (Fort Leavenworth, KS: Author April 2012), https://www.act.nato.int/images/stories/events/2011/cde/rr_ufmcs.pdf; Caroline E. Zsambok, *Advanced Team Decision Making: A Model and Training Implications*, ARI Research Note 95-02 (Fairborn, OH: Klein, 1994) [for the US Army Research Institute for the Behavioral and Social Sciences].
50. Peter Kropotkin, *Mutual Aid: A Factor in Evolution* (Lawrence, KS: Digireads, 2010); John Simmons and William Mares, *Working Together* (New York: Knopf, 1983); Paul Bernstein, *Workplace Democratization: Its Internal Dynamics* (New Brunswick, NJ: Transaction, 1980); Stephen M. Sachs, "The Interaction of Forces for and Against Political and Social Transformation," *Proceedings of the 1997 American Political Science Association Meeting* (Washington, DC: American Political Science Association, 1997).

51. The dysfunctional aspects of hierarchy in organizations are discussed in Chris Argyris, "The Individual and the Organization, A Problem of Mutual Adjustment," *Administrative Science Quarterly* 2 (1957). For more detailed analysis of some of the aspects of the psychological and other problems encouraged by hierarchy see L. Coch and J. R. P. French, "Overcoming Resistance to Change," *Group Dynamics*, ed. by D. Cartwright and Z. Zander (Evanston, IL: Row, Peterson, 1953); Robert Blauner, *Alienation and Freedom* (Chicago: University of Chicago Press, 1964); Charles Walker, "The Problem with the Repetitive Job," *Harvard Business Review* 28 (May 1950); Nancy Morse, *Satisfaction in the White Collar Job* (Ann Arbor: University of Michigan Press, 1953); Seymour Melman, *Decision-Making and Productivity* (Oxford, UK: Basil Blackwell, 1958).

52. Paul Bernstein, *Workplace Democratization: Its Internal Dynamics* (New Brunswick, NJ: Transaction, 1980); Alan S. Blinder, ed., *Paying for Productivity: A Look at the Evidence* (Washington, DC: Brookings Institution, 1990); Edward E. Lawler III, Susan Albers Mohrman, and Gerald E. Ledford Jr., *Employee Involvement and Total Quality Management: Practices and Results in Fortune 1000 Companies* (San Francisco: Jossey-Bass, 1992); Haig R. Nalbantian, ed., *Incentives, Cooperation, and Risk Sharing: Economic and Psychological Perspectives on Employment Contracts* (Totowa, NJ: Rowman & Littlefield, 1987).

53. Frederick Taylor, "The Principles of Scientific Management," [1916] in *Classics of Organization Theory*, 3rd ed., ed. J. Stephen Ott (Pacific Grove, CA: Brooks/Cole, 1992); Frederick Taylor, *Scientific Management* (New York: Harper and Row, 1947).

54. Stephen M. Sachs, "Workplace Revolution, Education, and Political Transformation," *Proceedings of the 1991 American Political Science Association Meeting* (Washington, DC: American Political Science Association, 1991).

55. Ibid.

56. For example, see Frederick J. Roethisberger, "The Hawthorne Experiments," in *Management and Morale* (Cambridge, MA: Harvard University Press, 1941).

57. For an example of the cybernetics or communication approach to organizations see Jay Galbraith, "Information Processing Model," in *Designing Complex Organizations* (Reading, MA: Addison Wesley, 1973), chap. 2, and reprinted in Jay M. Shafritz and J. Stephen, *Classics of Organization Theory*, 3rd ed. (Pacific Grove, CA: Brooks/Cole, 1992). 308–15.

58. Curt Tausky, *Work Organizations: Major Theoretical Perspectives*, 2nd ed. (Ithaca, IL: F. E. Peacock, 1978); William Ouchi, *Theory Z: How American Business Can Meet the Japanese Challenge* (Reading, MA: Addison-Wesley, 1981); Simmons and Mares, *Working Together*; Stephen M. Sachs, "Uncertain Verdict: In the Auto Industry the Participation and Quality of Worklife Programs Have Mixed Results," *Workplace Democracy* 11, no. 2 (1984).

59. F. E. Emery and Einar Torsrud, *Form and Content in Industrial Democracy* (London: Tavistock Institute, 1969), 51–67.

60. Executive Board of the West German Trade Union Federation (DGB), "Co-Determination in the Federal Republic of Germany" and Helmut Schaur, "Critique of Co-Determination," in *Workers' Control: A Reader on Labor and Social Change*, ed. by Gerry Hunius, G. David Garson, and John Case (New York: Random House, 1973).

61. Discussed in Henk Thomas and Chris Logan, *Mondragon: An Economic Analysis* (London: George Allen and Unwin, 1982); Alastair Campbell, et al., *Worker Ownership: The Mondragon Achievement* (London: Anglo-German Foundation for the Study of Society, 1977); Terry Mollner, *Mondragon: A Third Way* (Shutesbury, MA: Trustee Institute, 1984); A. Gutierrez-Johnson and William Foote Whyte, "The Mondragon System of Worker Production Cooperatives," *Industrial and Labor Relations Review* 31, no. 1 (1977), 18–30; A. Gutierrez-Johnson, "Compensation, Equity, and Industrial Democracy in the Mondragon Cooperatives," *Economic Analysis and Workers' Self-Management* 12 (1977), 267–89; Robert Oakeshott, "Mondragon: Spain's Oasis of Democracy," in *Self-Management: The Economic Liberation of Man*, ed. Jaroslav Vanek (Baltimore, MD: Penguin, 1975), 290–96; Germal Medanie, "Mondragon: Your Add Is About to Run Out," *Grassroots Economic Organizing Newsletter* 10 (September/October 1983).

62. Josip Obradovic and William Dunn, *Workers' Self-Management and Organizational Power in Yugoslavia* (Pittsburgh, PA: University Center for International Studies, University of Pittsburgh, 1978); Ichak Adizes, *Industrial Democracy: Yugoslav Style; The Effect of Decentralization on Organizational Behavior* (New York: Free Press, 1971).

63. Jaroslav Vanek, *The Participatory Economy: An Evolutionary Hypothesis and a Strategy for Development* (Ithaca, NY: Cornell University Press, 1971), chap. 4. Additional information is available in Martin Schrenk, Cyrus Ardakan, and Nawal A. El Tatawy, *Yugoslavia: Self-Management Socialism and the Challenges of Development; Report of a Mission Sent to*

Yugoslavia, World Bank Country Economic Report (Baltimore, MD: Johns Hopkins University, 1978).

64. Sachs, "Some Reflections upon Workers' Self-Management in Yugoslavia."

65. Simmons and Mares, *Working Together*; Douglas McGregor, "The Human Side of Management," *Management Review* (1967), reprinted in *Classic Readings in Organizational Behavior*, ed. J. Steven Ott (Pacific Grove, CA: Brooks/Cole, 1989): 66–73.

66. Sachs, "Workplace Revolution, Education, and Political Transformation."

67. Ibid.; Gifford Pinchot and Elizabeth Pinchot, *The End of Bureaucracy and the Rise of the Intelligent Organization* (San Francisco: Berrett-Koehler, 1993), particularly pt. 1–2, chap. 11, 13, 16.

68. Bernstein, *Workplace Democratization*, especially chap. 5; Blinder, *Paying for Productivity*; Lawler III, Mohrman, and Ledford Jr., *Employee Involvement and Total Quality Management*.

69. Doug Raynor, "W. L. Gore: Creating a Business Without Bosses," *Workplace Democracy* 12, no. 2 (1985).

70. Unpublished research in the 1980s by Stephen Sachs.

71. Pinchot and Pinchot, *The End of Bureaucracy and the Rise of the Intelligent Organization*, chap. 4, pt. 2.

72. Hedrick Smith, *Rethinking America* (New York: Random House, 1995).

73. "Pilot Program Saves County $151,000," *Workplace Democracy* 9, no. 3 (1982).

74. Harris, Sachs, and Morris, *Re-Creating the Circle*, chap. 3.

75. Morton Grodzins, *The American System: A New View of the Government of the United States* (New York: Rand McNally, 1966); Daniel Elizar, *American Federalism* (New York: Thomas Crowell, 1973).

76. David Greenstone and Paul E. Peterson, *Race and Authority in Urban Politics: Community Relations and the War on Poverty* (Chicago: University of Chicago Press, 1973); Glenn A. Bowen, "An Analysis of Citizen Participation in Anti-Poverty Programmes," *Community Development Journal* 43, no. 1 (2008): 65–78.

77. James Q. Wilson and George L. Kelling, "Making Neighborhoods Safe," *Atlantic Monthly* 263, no. 2 (1989); Jack R. Greene and Stephen D. Mastrofski, eds., *Crime and Delinquency* (New York: Praeger, 1988); Lee P. Brown, *Community Policing: A Practical Guide for Police Officials* (Washington, DC: National Institute of Justice, 1989); Herman Goldstein, "Toward Community Oriented Policing: Potential, Basic Requirements and Threshold Questions," *Crime and Delinquency* 33

(1988): 6–30; Robert Trojanowicz and Bonnie Bucqueroux, *Community Policing: A Contemporary Perspective* (Cincinnati, OH: Anderson, 1990); Mark Harrison Moore, "Problem-Solving and Community Policing," in *Modern Policing*, eds. M. Tonry and N. Morris (Chicago: University of Chicago Press, 1992); Ralph A. Weisheit, L. Edward Wells, and David N. Falcone, "Community Policing in Small Towns and Rural America," *Crime and Delinquency* 40, no. 4 (1994): 549–67.

78. Quoctrung Bui, "Calls to 911 From Black Neighborhoods Fell After a Case of Police Violence," *New York Times*, September 29, 2016, http://www.nytimes.com/2016/09/29/upshot/calls-to-911-from-black-neighborhoods-fell-after-a-case-of-police-violence.html?ref=todayspaper; Matthew Desmond, Andrew V. Papachristos, and David S. Kirk, "Police Violence and Citizen Crime Reporting in the Black Community," *American Sociological Review* 81, no. 5, (2016): 857–76, http://asr.sagepub.com/content/81/5/857.full.pdf?ijkey=fkZ2Xv6YvBo6uv4&keytype=finite.

79. Dan Georgakas and Marvin Surkin, *Detroit I Do Mind Dying: A Study in Urban Revolution* (New York: St. Martin's, 1975), chap. 8.

80. Stephen M. Sachs, "Los Angeles and Somalia: Community Service Policing and Community Empowerment," *Nonviolent Change* 8, no. 2–3 (1994), reprinted in *COPRED Peace Chronicle* 19, no. 2 (1994).

81. Veronica Coleman, Walter C. Holton Jr., Kristine Olson, Stephen C. Robinson, and Judith Stewart, "Using Knowledge and Teamwork to Reduce Crime," *National Institute of Justice Journal* 88 (October 1999).

82. Gary Shapiro, "The Neighborhood Facilitators Project in Bosnia Post-War Community Peacebuilding, from the Bottom Up, Excerpts from the Executive Summary," pt. 1, *Nonviolent Change* 13, no. 3 (1999): 17–20; pt. 2, *Nonviolent Change* 14, no. 1 (1999): 17.

83. David Osborne and Ted Gaebler, *Reinventing Government: How the Entrepreneurial Spirit Is Transforming the Public Sector, from Schoolhouse to Statehouse, City Hall to the Pentagon* (Reading, MA: Addison-Wesley, 1992), chap. 9.

84. Harris, Sachs, and Morris, *Re-Creating the Circle*, chap. 3, sec. 1.

85. Such coordination was first attempted very late in Lyndon Johnson's administration with the launching of the National Council on Indian Opportunity (NCIO). The model used had several advantages. NCIO consisted of the secretaries of the seven US government departments that dealt significantly with Indians (Interior, Agriculture, Commerce, Health Education and Welfare, Housing and Urban Development, and the Office of Economic Opportunity),

six presidentially appointed Indian leaders, and was headed by the vice president of the United States, who stood above the cabinet members. This avoided the problem in the later Clinton administration model of having the secretary of interior as chair, who had conflicts of interest on Indian issues in his own department. As an equal with the other department heads with whom he had to deal diplomatically, he was limited in his effectiveness. The problem with designating the vice president as chair is that it would depend who the vice president would happen to be, so that it would be better to have the president appoint a chair, who might be the vice president or a top White House staff member, as appropriate in the particular case. NCIO achieved some important accomplishments. However, it was short-lived (1968–1974), underfunded, and understaffed and, because of the politics of the time, the council rarely met (though its staff was quite active). Thomas A. Britten, *The National Council on Indian Opportunity: Quiet Champion of Self-Determination* (Albuquerque: University of New Mexico Press, 2014). After, and to a considerable extent from the Nixon administration to the Clinton administration, federal Indian policy was coordinated on an ad hoc basis (Harris, Sachs, and Morris, *Re-Creating the Circle*, chap. 3, sec. 1).

86. "Executive Order: Establishing the White House Council on Native American Affairs," Executive Order 13647 of June 26, 2013, Office of the Press Secretary, Press Release, June 26, 2013, https://obamawhitehouse.archives.gov/the-press-office/2013/06/26/executive-order-establishing-white-house-council-native-american-affairs.

87. White House Memorandum for Heads of Departments and Agencies from Erskine Bowles, Chief of Staff to the President, and Bruce Reed, Assistant to the President for Domestic Policy, concerning Executive Memorandum on Government-to-Government Relations. Document given to the author by Special Assistant to the Assistant Secretary of the Interior for Indian Affairs Michael Chapman.

88. Harris, Sachs, and Morris, *Re-Creating the Circle*, chap. 3, sec. 2.

89. "African American Records: The Freedmen's Bureau," US National Archives, African American Heritage, http://www.archives.gov/research/african-americans/freedmens-bureau/.

90. G. Calvin MacKenzie and Robert Weisbrot, *Washington and the Politics of Change in the 1960s* (New York: Penguin, 2008); Gareth Davies, *From Opportunity to Entitlement: The Transformation and Decline of Great Society Liberalism* (Lawrence: University of Kansas Press, 1996); Richard A. Cloward and Francis Fox Piven, "The Weight of the Poor: A Strategy

to End Poverty," *Nation*, May 2, 1966; M. Varn Chandola, "Affirmative Action in India and the United States: The Untouchable and Black Experience." *Indiana International and Comparative Law Review* 3 (1992–1993): 101, http://heinonline.org/HOL/LandingPage?collec tion=journals&handle=hein.journals/iicl3&div=7&id=&page=.

91. Chandola, "Affirmative Action in India and the United States."
92. Clyde Kluckhohn and Dorothy Leighton, *The Navaho* (Cambridge, MA: Harvard University Press, 1974); James F. Downes, *The Navajo* (New York: Holt, Reinhart, and Winston, 1972), particularly chap. 2, 3, 8.
93. *The Social Contract*, bk. II, chap. 3.
94. Jeff Smith, "Traditional Foes Agree on Gasoline Formula," *Indianapolis Star* 89, no. 73 (1991): 1, 7.
95. *Citizens Power* 18, no. 2 (1992), published by Citizens Action Coalition; Osborne and Gaebler, *Reinventing Government*, 299–395.
96. Wilson Clark, *Energy for Survival* (Garden City, NY: Anchor, 1975), chap. 3; Osborne and Gaebler, *Reinventing Government*, chap. 10.
97. Search for Common Ground, www.sfcg.org. See Susan Koscis, "Peaceful Abortion Dialogue Is Shaky But Real." *Christian Science Monitor*, June 8, 2009, http://www.sfcg.org/articles/abortion_koscis. pdf.
98. "EPA, Quale, Committee Head for Showdown," *Indianapolis News*, November 21, 1991, Al.
99. A. Lee Fritschler, *Smoking and Politics: Policy Making and the Federal Bureaucracy* (New York: Appleton Century Crofts, 1969), 46.
100. There are numerous examples of effective employee-involvement programs collapsing because of bad feelings arising over collective bargaining. A classic example is that of ARMCO steel plant in Ashland, KY. The collaborative effort of the plant's team process was a major factor in its achieving the lowest cost in the world for steel production. But because management failed to appreciate, and take into account, labor's concern on a major issue, the team process arrangement fell apart, reducing the plant's ability to keep production costs low and product quality high. See, US Department of Labor, Bureau of Labor Management Relations and Cooperative Programs, *ARMCO Steel's Quality Plus Program at Ashland Kentucky* (Washington, DC: Author, 1990). On parallel development of respectful interpersonal relations and decision making in participatory workplaces, see Bernstein, *Workplace Democratization*; Sachs, "Building Trust in Democratic Organizations."

101. Center for Nonviolent Communications, http://www.cnvc.org/.

102. See the discussion of reforming government in Osborne and Gaebler, *Reinventing Government*, which grows out of the movement for workplace democratization, involving institutions in a modern context of the traditional tribal and band principles of inclusive consensus decision making.

103. Carole Pateman, in her classic work, *Participation and Democratic Theory* (Cambridge: Cambridge University Press, 1970) first shows that theorists such as John Stuart Mill have long considered everyday participation in workplaces an excellent education for citizenship in a democratic polity (chap. 2, particularly, 28–35). She supports these theoretical predictions with pragmatic evidence, concluding (105):

> Yet we have seen that the evidence supports the arguments of Rousseau, Mill and Cole that we do learn to participate by participating and that feelings of political efficacy [necessary to make people believe that participating is worthwhile, and thus essential to motivating them to participate] are more likely to be developed in a participatory environment. Furthermore, the evidence indicates that the experience of a participatory authority might also be effective in diminishing tendencies toward nondemocratic attitudes in the individual.

Pateman's findings continue to be supported and reinforced by recent research. For example, Richard S. Beth, "How Transformationalists Think About Transformation: Themes and Implications," *Proceedings of the 1995 American Political Science Association Meeting* (Washington, DC: American Political Science Association, 1995), 63, having indicated that active participation (such as occurs on teams in participatory workplaces) tends to develop "a mindful engagement with experience in the participants that tends to make them reflective upon their relations with others, and self-reflective about their own development and action." Beth goes on to report:

> Fourth, mindful engagement with experience in the context of political practice would also foster transformation into less authoritarian or dominative forms of people's sense of, and relation to, leadership. As respondent (el) pointed out, the process of

transformation is inherently political in that it involves the transformation of power relations. When leaders proceed in mindful engagement with other participants, it will tend to transform their awareness of, and relation to, those participants toward more facilitative and collaborative styles of leadership...

Nor is it only leadership that would be transformed by the practice of responsive engagement with members. The development of group members' own sense of empowerment, or understanding of themselves as capable of participation, would also tend to transform their responses to all these kinds of leaders toward more participatory and less authoritarian forms, which in turn would require leaders to engage in less dominative styles of action.

Further empirical support is given by Jane Junn, "Participation in Liberal Democracy: What Citizens Learn from Political Activity," *Proceedings of the 1995 American Political Science Association Meeting* (Washington, DC: American Political Science Association, 1995), 28–29:

The objective of this analysis was to demonstrate empirically a particularly important hypothesis of democratic theory, that citizen participation has an educative or transformative effect on individual citizens. The results from the estimation of simultaneous equation models hypothesizing reciprocal causality reveal that citizens who are active in politics and social life are in fact more knowledgeable about politics as a result of their participation.... The findings provide support for the hypothesis that taking part in political and social life makes a difference; citizens learn about politics by being part of it. In this sense, political knowledge is not only important for democracy in its *role for* making good decisions, but instead, knowledge is also the *result of* democracy.

104. Stephen M. Sachs, "Educating for Workplace and Economic Democracy," paper presented at International Conference on

the Politics of Economic Democracy, International Sociology Association, Research Committee 10, 1987; Sachs, "Workplace Revolution, Education, and Political Transformation."

105. Smith, *Rethinking America*, chap. 5, 7.

106. Stephen M. Sachs, "The Putney School: John Dewey Is Alive and Well in Southern Vermont," *Democracy and Education* 6, no. 3 (1992): 35–41.

107. Jonathan Kozol, *Savage Inequalities: Children in America's Schools* (New York: Crown, 1991).

108. The reason for this tendency toward overcoming undesirable inequalities, when it is possible and appropriate to do so, through increasing the means for achieving reduction in difference, rather than by legislating its reduction directly, follows from the empowering action and achievement oriented gestalt of workplace team process, and the similar empowerment oriented approach of the related child needs oriented educational reforms. That is, the cultural orientation in both cases is towards empowerment for achieving ends, to the extent that that is appropriate, rather than providing the desired benefit to passive recipients. This can be seen in slightly different form in the principle of "regulating with, rather than against, the market," when possible, discussed in Osborne and Gaebler, *Reinventing Government*, chap. 10, favoring approaches that use incentives rather than commands, to the extent practicable, as this tends to move away from a control, toward an empowerment oriented, approach.

109. Stephen M. Sachs, "Climate Change, Environmental Decay, and Indigenous People: Indigenizing the Greening of the World," *Indigenous Policy* 19, no. 2 (2008).

110. An examination of the text of Osborne and Gaebler, *Reinventing Government*, will show that it stems directly from the kind of thinking engendered by the rise of team process in the workplace, though from that beginning it necessarily (to be consistent with such thinking) extends beyond it in considering matters of public policy, as is seen in comparing the author's ten principles of governance with the new workplace principles. In Osborne and Gaebler's version of the new politics, government needs to proceed, so far as is practicable, as: 1) catalytic government: steering rather than rowing; 2) community-owned government: empowering rather than serving; 3) competitive government: injecting competition into service delivery; 4) mission-driven government: transforming rule-driven organizations into purpose-oriented units; 5) results-oriented government:

funding outcomes, not inputs; 6) customer-driven government: meeting the needs of the customer, not the bureaucracy; 7) enterprising government: earning rather than spending; 8) anticipatory government: preventing rather than curing; 9) decentralized government: moving from hierarchy to participation; 10) market-oriented government: leveraging change through the market.

111. Ibid., chap. 1.

112. This is well spelled out in Will Marshall and Martin Schram, *Mandate for Change* (New York: Berkeley, 1993), and exemplified by the designation of Vice President Gore to head a "Reinventing Government" commission to lead reform the federal bureaucracy. See Al Gore, *Creating A Government That Works Better and Costs Less: The Gore Report on Reinventing Government* (New York: Random House, 1993). Since the 1990s, a strong "conservative" reaction has become a strong force in American politics, running completely counter to this line of thinking, and these types of policies. But this emergent thinking remains in the population, and may well be a harbinger of change in the longer run.

113. Paul H. Ray, *The Integral Culture Survey* (Sausalito, CA: Institute for Noetic Sciences, 1996).

114. See H. Aram Veeser, *The New Historicism* (New York: Routledge, Chapman, and Hall, 1989). The relation of this approach to the emerging consciousness is evident in some of the editor's comments:

Conventional scholars—entrenched, self-absorbed, protective of guild loyalties and turf, specialized in the worst senses—have repaired to their disciplinary enclaves and committed a classic *trahison des clercs*. As the first successful counterattack in decades against this profoundly anti-intellectual ethos, New Historicism has given scholars new opportunities to cross the boundaries separating history, anthropology, art, politics, literature, and economics. It has struck down the doctrine of noninterference that forbade humanists to intrude on questions of politics, power, indeed on all matters that deeply affect people's practical lives—matters best left, prevailing wisdom went, to experts who could be trusted to preserve order and stability in "our" global and intellectual domains. (ix)

A newcomer to New Historicism might feel reassured that, for all its heterogeneity, key assumptions continually reappear and bind together the avowed practitioners and even some of their critics: these assumptions are as follows:

1. That every expressive act is embedded in a network of material practices;
2. That every act of unmasking, critique, and opposition uses the tools it condemns and risks falling prey to the practice it opposes;
3. That literary and non-literary "texts" circulate inseparably;
4. That no discourse, imaginative or archival, gives access to unchanging truths nor expresses inalterable human nature;
5. Finally...that a critical method and a language adequate to describe culture under capitalism participate in the economy they describe.

The New Historicists combat empty formalism by pulling historical considerations to the center stage of literary analysis...New Historicists have evolved a method of describing culture in action. (xii)

The motives are clear. By forsaking what it sees as an outmoded vocabulary of allusion, symbolization, allegory, and mimesis, New Historicism seeks less limiting means to expose the manifold ways culture and society affect each other...New Historicism renegotiates these relationships between texts and other signifying practices, going so far (as Terence Hawkes has observed) as to dissolve "literature" back into the historical complex that academic criticism has traditionally held at arm's length. It retains at the same time, those methods and materials that gave old fashioned literary study its immense interpretive authority...By discarding what they view as monologic and myopic historiography, by demonstrating that social and cultural events commingle messily, by rigorously exposing the innumerable tradeoffs, the competing bids and exchanges of culture, New Historicists can make a valid claim to have established new ways of studying history and a new awareness of how history and culture define each other. (xii–xiii)

The emergence of indicators of consciousness change that are appearing across a wide spectrum of fields and activities fits Jean Gebser's finding that the world is moving from "three dimensional" to "four dimensional" consciousness, *The Ever-Present Origin* (Athens: Ohio University Press, 1953). Interestingly, it also fits the pattern of more positive outcomes in moving from the "fourth world" to the "fifth world" of the Hopi prophecies as described in Thomas Mails, *The Hopi Survival Kit* (New York: Stewart, Tabori, and Chang, 1997).

115. John Paul Lederach, *The Little Book of Conflict Transformation* (New York: Good Books, 2003); John Paul Lederach, "Conflict Transformation," Beyond Intractability, 2003 (updated April 2017), http://www.beyondintractability.org/essay/transformation/.

116. David Korten, *When Corporations Rule the World* (San Francisco, CA: Berrett-Koehler, 1995); Robert McChesney and John Nichols, "Dollarocracy: How Big Money Undermines Our Democracy and How We Can Take It Back," *The Nation*, September 16, 2013.

117. Jane Mayer, "Covert Operations: The Billionaire Brothers Who Are Waging a War against Obama," *New Yorker*, August 30, 2010, http://www.newyorker.com/reporting/2010/08/30/100830fa_fact_maye; Rory Carroll, "Activists Protest Koch Brothers' Links to Purchase of *Los Angeles Times*," *Guardian*, May 14, 2013, http://www.theguardian.com/media/2013/may/14/los-angeles-times-los-angeles.

118. Korten, *When Corporations Rule the World*.

119. Smith, *Rethinking America*, chap. 2, 9.

120. Frederick Lesieur, *The Scanlan Plan: A Frontier in Labor Management Cooperation* (Cambridge, MA: MIT Press, 1958).

121. Peter F. Drucker, *The New Realities* (New York: Harper and Row, 1989); Peter F. Drucker, *Post-Capitalist Society* (New York: Harper and Row, 1993).

122. Harris, Sachs, and Morris, *Re-Creating the Circle*, chap. 4, sec. 1.

123. Andrew C. Mclaughlin, *A Constitutional History of the United States* (New York: D. Appleton-Century, 1936); Merrill Jensen, *The New Nation: A History of the United States during the Confederation, 1781–1789*

(New York: Vintage, 1950); Max Farrand, *The Records of the Federal Convention of 1787*, 3 vols. (New Haven, CT: Yale University Press, 1911).

124. Nicholas Atkin, *The Fifth French Republic* (Basingstoke, UK: Palgrave Macmillan, 2004).

125. McLaughlin, *A Constitutional History of the United States*; Jensen, *The New Nation*; Farrand, *Records of the Federal Convention*.

126. David E. Sanger and Charlie Savage, "Obama Is Urged to Sharply Curb N.S.A. Data Mining," *New York Times*, December 18, 2013, https://www.nytimes.com/2013/12/19/us/politics/report-on-nsa-surveillance-tactics.html; Brad Bannon, "The Epitome of Executive Overreach: The Bush Administration's Abuse of Power Has Sadly Continued Under Obama," *U.S. News and World Report*, June 6, 2013, http://www.usnews.com/opinion/blogs/brad-bannon/2013/06/06/government-overreaches-with-verizon-phone-record-collecting; "Glenn Greenwald: NSA Analysts Have Access To 'Powerful and Invasive' Search Tools," *Huffington Post*, July 28, 2013, http://www.huffingtonpost.com/2013/07/28/glenn-greenwald-nsa_n_3667083.html?ncid=edlinkusaolp00000009.

127. The rules by which Congress functions can be found at "Resources A to Z: Rules, Precedents, and Procedures," Congress.gov Resources, https://www.congress.gov/resources/display/content/Resources+A+to+Z#ResourcesAtoZ-R. A shorter comparative description of the House and Senate procedures is Paul Rundquist, Judy Schneider, and Lorraine H. Tong, "House and Senate Rules of Procedure: A Comparison," CRS Report for Congress, updated April 7, 1999, https://digital.library.unt.edu/ark:/67531/metadc824716/m2/1/high_res_d/97-270_1999Apr07.pdf. A quick reading of the latter will show that power is highly centralized in the leadership, especially in the House, while in the Senate any member can delay (put a hold) on many measures. Also, on many matters it takes sixty of one hundred votes to end debate if one or more senators wish to filibuster and block a measure from coming to a vote. The concentration of leadership has become even more narrowed since the study was made.

128. Robert C. Tucker, *The Marx-Engels Reader*, 2nd ed. (New York: W. W. Norton, 1972), 133–35, 505, 535, 593, 665.

129. Rousseau, *The Social Contract*, bk. II, chap. 11.

130. Irving Goldman, "The Kwakiutl of Vancouver Island," in *Cooperation and Competition among Primitive Peoples*, ed. Margaret Mead (New York: McGraw-Hill, 1937), 180–209.

131. Ladislav Rusmich and Stephen M. Sachs, *Lessons from the Failure of the Communist Economic System* (Lanham, MD: Lexington, 2003), pt. 1.

132. Bingqin Li and David Piachaud, *Poverty and Inequality and Social Policy in China* (London: Centre for Analysis of Social Exclusion, London School of Economics, 2004).

133. Andrew Jacobs, "Plans to Harness Chinese River's Power Threaten a Region," *New York Times*, May 4, 2013, http://www.nytimes.com/2013/05/05/world/asia/plans-to-harness-chinas-nu-river-threaten-a-region.html?ref=todayspaper; Ian Johnson, "China's Great Uprooting: Moving 250 Million Into Cities," *New York Times*, June 15, 2013, http://www.nytimes.com/2013/06/16/world/asia/chinas-great-uprooting-moving-250-million-into-cities.html?ref=todayspaper; Edward Wong, "Central China Hit by Drought, as Reservoirs Become 'Dead Water,'" *New York Times*, May 16, 2011, http://www.nytimes.com/2011/05/17/world/asia/17drought.html?ref=world; Edward Wong, "Three Gorges Dam Is Said to Hurt Areas Downstream," *New York Times*, June 2, 2011, http://www.nytimes.com/2011/06/03/world/asia/03china.html?ref=todayspaper.

134. Rusmich and Sachs, *Lessons from the Failure of the Communist Economic System*, pt. 2.

135. Ibid.

136. Independent Grocers Alliance, https://www.iga.com/about/about-iga.

137. "Where Discoveries Begin," National Science Foundation, www.nsf.gov; "Online Grants Management for the NSF Community," National Science Foundation, www.research.gov; "Siemens: Ingenuity for Life," Siemens, http://www.usa.siemens.com/ [keyword search for "US Government Sponsored Collaborations"]. An example of a private nonprofit organization funding research is the American Cancer Society, http://www.cancer.org/.

138. Osborne and Gaebler, *Reinventing Government*, chap. 10.

139. Ibid., chap. 2.

140. "Civilian Conservation Corps," Civilian Conservation Corps Legacy, http://www.ccclegacy.org; "Records of the Civilian Conservation Corps [CCC]," National Archives, https://www.archives.gov/research/guide-fed-records/groups/035.html; "Civilian Conservation Corps," History.com, https://www.history.com/topics/great-depression/civilian-conservation-corps; "Make the Most of Your World," Peace Corps, www.peacecorps.gov; AmeriCorps: Corporation for National Community Service, http://www.nationalservice.gov/programs/americorps.

141. See "California Enterprise Zones," California Department of Housing and Community Development, 2013, http://www.hcd. ca.gov/fa/ez/.

142. Richard S. Grossman, *Wrong: Nine Economic Policy Disasters and What We Can Learn from Them* (New York: Oxford University Press, 2013); David Kocieniewski, "A Shuffle of Aluminum, but to Banks, Pure Gold," *New York Times*, July 20, 2013, http://www.nytimes.com/2013/07/21/ business/a-shuffle-of-aluminum-but-to-banks-pure-gold.html?_r=0; Bernie Sanders, "Wall Street Greed Fueling High Gas Prices," CNN, February 28, 2012, http://www.cnn.com/2012/02/28/opinion/ sanders-gas-speculation/index.html; "Is Speculation the Reason for High Oil and Gasoline Prices," Econ Matters, May 6, 2011, http:// www.econmatters.com/2011/05/speculation-does-not-explain-high-oil.html; Nicholas Maystre, Econ Matters, May 6, 2011, http://www. econmatters.com/2011/05/speculation-does-not-explain-high-oil. html (unfortunately this webpage no longer works); "UNCTAD: High Frequency Trading and Speculation Leads to Higher Prices," Real News.com, November 1, 2012, http://www.therealnews.com/t2/ index.php?option=com_content&task=view&id=31&Itemid=74&jum ival=8894.

143. Jim Zarroli, "How Bernie Sanders' Wall Street Tax Would Work," NPR, February 12, 2016, https://www.npr.org/2016/02/12/466465333/ sanders-favors-a-speculation-tax-on-big-wall-street-firms-what-is-that; "Financial Transaction Tax," Wikipedia, https:// en.wikipedia.org/wiki/Financial_transaction_tax. On the problems with speculation also see "The Problem with Commodity Speculation," Stop Gambling on Hunger, http://stopgamblingon-hunger.com/the-problem/; "Did Speculation Fuel Oil Price Swings?: Speculation Affected Oil Price Swings More Than Supply And Demand," *60 Minutes*, CBS News, http://www.cbsnews.com/news/ did-speculation-fuel-oil-price-swings-08-01-2009/.

144. Harris, Sachs, and Morris, *Re-Creating the Circle*, chap. 1, sec. 2; chap. 4, sec. 2.

145. On Indigenous origins, see Howard Zehr, *The Little Book of Restorative Justice* (Intercourse, PA: Good Books, 2002), 4, 11–12, 43; Rupert Ross, *Returning to the Teachings: Exploring Aboriginal Justice* (Toronto: Penguin, 1996).

146. Zehr, *Little Book of Restorative Justice*.

147. "California Victim Compensation Program (CalVCP)," State of California, http://www.vcgcb.ca.gov/victims/.

148. Zehr, *Little Book of Restorative Justice*, 17–18.

149. Ibid., 16–17, 47–57.

150. Ada Pecos Melton, "Indigenous Justice Systems and Tribal Society," in *Justice as Healing: Indigenous Ways, Writings on Community Peacemaking, and Restorative Justice from the Native Law Centre*, ed. Wanda D. McCaslin (St. Paul, MN: Living Justice, 2005), 119, 165 n. 8.

151. Zehr, *Little Book of Restorative Justice*, chap. 2; Kay Pranis, Barry Stuart, and Mark Wedge, *Peace Making Circles: From Crime to Community* (St. Paul, MN: Living Justice, 2003), chap. 1–2.

152. Zehr, *Little Book of Restorative Justice*, chap. 3.

153. Ibid.

154. Pranis, Stuart, and Wedge, *Peace Making Circles*.

155. Kristy Johnston, "Alternative Road for Victims of Sex Crime," *Fairfax New Zealand News*, December 22, 2013, http://www.stuff.co.nz/national/9544771/Alternative-road-for-victims-of-sex-crime.

156. Maria Hantzopoulos, "The Fairness Committee: Restorative Justice in a Small Urban Public High School," *Prevention Researcher* 20, no. 1 (2013): 7–10; Susan Duncan Hanley and Ida Dickie, "Family Group Conferencing: A Pilot Project within the Juvenile Court System in Louisville, Kentucky," *Prevention Researcher* 20, no. 1 (2013): 11–14.

157. Philmer Bluehouse and James Zion, "*Hozhooji Naat'aanii*: The Navajo Nation Justice and Harmony Ceremony," in *Native Americans, Crime, and Justice*, eds. Marianne O. Nielsen and Robert A. Silverman (Boulder, CO: Westview, 1996), 181–82; James Zion and Elsie B. Zion, "*Hazho's Sokee'*—Stay Together Nicely: Domestic Violence under Navajo Common Law," *Native Americans, Crime, and Justice*, 96–102, 170–78.

158. "Uses Outside of Criminal Justice," Centre for Justice and Reconciliation, http://www.restorativejustice.org/press-room/06outside?searchterm=restorative+justice+in+workpl; "Restorative Justice in the Workplace," Mediation Services, April 27, 2011, http://mediation-serviceswpg.wordpress.com/2011/04/27/restorative-justice-in-the-workplace/.

159. Victoris Shook, *Ho'oponopono: Contemporary Uses of a Hawaiian Problem Solving Process* (Honolulu: University of Hawaii Press, 2002).

160. Ibid., 10.

161. Ibid., 96–97.

162. Shannon Sumrall, "*Ho'oponopono*," Advanced Behavioral Consultants, http://www.healthsurvey.com/hoopono.htm; J. Brinson and T. A. Fisher, "The *Ho'oponopono* Group: A Conflict Resolution Model for

School Counselors," *Journal for Specialists in Group Work* 24, no. 4 (1999): 369–82.

163. "What Is Huna?," Ancient Huna, http://www.ancienthuna.com/ho-oponopono.htm. Also keyword search for "*ho'oponopono*" on bing.com. Some information on the discussion below comes from a booklet on *Ho'oponopono* by Joe Vitale and Mathew Dixon. Also from the experience of Phyllis M. Gagnier, who in October 2016 registered for the *Ho'oponopono* Practitioner Certification Program, and in September 2017 registered for the Advanced *Ho'oponopono* Certification Program by Joe Vitale, Ihaleakala Hew Len, and Mathew Dixon; from Joe Vitale, Ihaleakala Hew Len, and Mathew Dixon, "*Ho'oponopono* Practitioner Course Certification," a forty-two-page eBook with eight videos over six hours and Zero Limits Music by Mathew Dixon, available at "*Ho'oponopono* Practitioner Course Certification," 2017, http://www.hooponoponocertification.com; and the "Advanced *Ho'oponopono* Course Certification," a twenty-six-video seminar style instruction class totaling eight hours (with nine featured speakers) and nine audio files totaling four hours.

164. Unresolved historical trauma and work to overcome it are discussed in Harris, Sachs, and Morris, *Re-Creating the Circle*, chap. 2, 4, 5 (to which Phyllis M. Gagnier is a contributing author).

165. Vitale, Len, and Dixon, "*Ho'oponopono* Practitioner Course Certification," 5.

166. Ibid., 5–6.

167. Ibid., 6.

168. Ibid., 6–7.

169. Ibid., 9; Joe Vitale and Ihaleakala Hew Len, *Zero Limits* (New York: John Wiley, 2007), ix.

170. Vitale, Len, and Dixon, "*Ho'oponopono* Practitioner Course Certification," 9; Vitale and Len, *Zero Limits*, 44.

171. Vitale, Len, and Dixon, "*Ho'oponopono* Practitioner Course Certification," 10–11; Vitale and Len, *Zero Limits*, [unnumbered page opposite dedication page].

172. Vitale and Len, *Zero Limits*, [unnumbered page opposite dedication page].

173. Ibid., 147.

174. Ibid., ix.

175. Vitale, Len, and Dixon, "*Ho'oponopono* Practitioner Course Certification," 12, 14; Vitale and Len, *Zero Limits*, ix.

176. Vitale and Len, *Zero Limits*, features *Ho'oponopono*, including a comparison between Self I-Dentity *Ho'oponopono* and traditional *Ho'oponopono* practice. Gagnier particularly benefited from Ihaleakala Hew Len, "Who's in Charge?," [Appendix C], 209–23.

177. Developing one's own inner practice, appropriately for one's nature, background, culture, and ongoing circumstance is extremely useful for personal and social development. Author Stephen Sachs has been engaged in doing this through a combination of psychological, philosophical, and eclectic spiritual work based in a universalist (or ecumenical) Sufism, including learning from many traditions and experiences. Phyllis M. Gagnier has developed an evolving personal inner methodology out of a variety of experiences, in which her work with *Ho'oponopono* has been vital to her processes of healing and has been a stabilizer in the steady and turbulent times of her healing processes. She notes:

My years of experience, teaching and practicing mindful awareness, understanding, acceptance, commitment, action as a viable learning process, are serving me well. This sequence was Divinely Inspired after I read Victor Frankl's "Man's Search for Meaning." In my *Ho'oponopono* Practice I am learning ACCEPTANCE.

- Accepting I am unconditionally totally 100% responsible for my healing ("taking ownership"). My practice is to accept the problem and own it. In so doing, I've reached the emotional state of embracing the problem with Love and perceiving the problem as a Gift.
- "It's not your fault but it is your responsibility," Joe Vitale. (Vitale and Len, *Zero Limits*, 177)
- Accepting I am healing myself from the inside out ("inside job"). In my practice, I focus within me rather than look for answers outside of me.
- "Who looks outside, dreams; who looks inside, awakes," Carl Jung (Vitale and Len, *Zero Limits*, 11). Accepting I am embracing the ancient Traditional *Ho'oponopono* Practice and the Self I-Dentity *Ho'oponopono*. In my practice, this means "to make right," "to rectify an error." I accept my errors arise

from thoughts tainted by painful memories, traumas, from the past which can cause imbalance and disease.

- "Allowing your toxic thoughts to be first, you automatically experience imperfection in the way of disease, confusion, resentment, depression, judgment, and poverty."
- Dr. Ihaleakala Hew Len. (Vitale and Len, *Zero Limits*, 51)
- Accepting I am knowing my *Ho'oponopono* Practice offers me a choice to neutralize and release toxic energy while engaging in problem-solving processes done entirely within me.
- "You cannot be denied anything that is perfect, whole, complete, and right for you when you are your Self first. Being your Self first you automatically experience perfection in the way of Divine Thoughts, Words, Deeds, and Actions," Dr. Ihaleakala Hew Len. (Vitale and Len, *Zero Limits*, 51)

With my *Ho'oponopono* Practice I am LEARNING:
- To take mindful awareness of my thoughts seriously.
- To understand my thinking by asking myself questions.
- To clarify by differentiating my fear based thoughts, my trauma memories, my fixed mindsets, my unreleased beliefs, my attachment to nonfactual meanings, my memories replaying, my inspiration.
- To face shame.
- "Every man takes the limits of his own field of vision for the limits of the world," Arthur Schopenhauer. (Vitale and Len, *Zero Limits*, 19)

COMMITTED ACTION: In ancient Hawaiian Traditional *Ho'oponopono* Practice, the individual petitions Love (Divinity) to rectify his/her errors within, acknowledges being Sorry, asks for Forgiveness for whatever is inside that manifested the problem, expresses Gratitude that Love transmutes the errors.

I am deeply committed to engage in problem solving my evolving health issues utilizing noninvasive methods. For me,

Traditional *Ho'oponopono* Practice and Self I-Dentity *Ho'oponopono* is noninvasively "SAFE."

Thanks to my experiences with my *Ho'oponopono* Practice I mindfully chose COMMITMENTS:

- To perceive cancer, manifested in me, as an opportunity rather than view myself as a victim.
- To reframe my "fear of cancer" rather than act from memory and societal mindsets.
- To see through my "eyes of Love" rather than the lens of limitation with attached meanings.
- To take action from inspiration (Divine Love) rather than controlled beliefs.
- To know the more I heal what comes up, the more I get in tuned alignment with my Divinity.
- To transmute shame by feeling a balance of Compassion for myself and for others.

In my *Ho'oponopono* Practice I use the following Self I-Dentity *Ho'oponopono* problem solving processes:

- I acknowledge my Divinity (God, Life, Universe, Higher Power, Divine Guidance, Divine Presence) by saying, "I Love You." For me, I am connecting to the Divine within me. I am speaking my Truth to my Divine Presence. I am evoking my Spirit of Love. I am in an authentic relationship with myself. Experiencing this state frees me to listen to Divine Inspiration and act on its message to me. I am now able to say this mantra of "I Love You" naturally and easily as I go about my daily living. "I Love You" has become a song I hear in my head.
- I express my Repentance (Contrition) by saying, "I'm Sorry." For me, this represents I am taking ownership of the fact my thinking is a false belief or a memory or a mindset or is misaligned with my Heart Intelligence and my Divine Guidance. When I say the "I'm Sorry" mantra, I experience humility.

I have programmed my brain to the extent I now can say "I'm Sorry" and feel it while in the midst of present time experiences.

- I ask for my Forgiveness by saying, "Please Forgive Me." I am asking forgiveness for myself for my erroneous thinking, for being unconscious, for being asleep. No self-blame, no guilt, just a sincere honest request for forgiveness said to me, for me, by me.

- Dr. Ihaleakala Hew Len says, "You don't say 'Please forgive me' to the Divine because the Divine needs to hear it, you say it because you need to hear it" (Vitale and Len, *Zero Limits*, 113).

- I focus on my Appreciation by saying, "Thank You." I am Trusting the power of the Divine to transform and transmute my errors in thinking and behaving.

- "Appreciation is the Heart of Healing," Phyllis M. Gagnier.

- I perceive these Self I-Dentity *Ho'oponopono* problem-solving processes as integral components in my responsible healing choices. I know I have choices, not control. I've learned the delicate fine line between giving up, letting go, and "unconditional surrender." I utilize the problem solving processes as tools to "clear-cleanse" the stuck negativity blocking the flow of my Divine Guidance to me.

- "Cleansing helps reduce the mortgage on your soul," Dr. Ihaleakala Hew Len. (Vitale and Len, *Zero Limits*, 163)

- "The Updated *Ho'oponopono*, a process of repentance, forgiveness, and transmutations, is a petition to Love to void and replace toxic energies with its self. Love accomplishes this by flowing through the mind, beginning with the spiritual mind, the superconscious. It then continues its flow through the intellectual mind, the conscious mind, freeing it of thinking energies. Finally, it moves into the emotional mind, the subconscious, voiding thoughts of toxic emotions and filling them with its self," Dr. Ihaleakala Hew Len. (Vitale and Len, *Zero Limits*, 67)

I am the Beneficiary of the Wisdom Inherent in the Hawaiian Traditional *Ho'oponopono* Practice and the Self I-Dentity *Ho'oponopono.*

When I entered my present journey into the world of responsible healing, I was already apologizing to my body, talking to my cells, thanking my Body Wisdom, visualizing Light Energy, asking for forgiveness, collecting my observations, looking for patterns, and journaling

Overwhelmed, my mind was looking for "a way out." My emotions-feelings felt "raw" to my bones. The memory of, at age twelve, witnessing a priest, who proclaimed he was the direct descendent of Jesus, unable to heal my paraplegic father kept surfacing and resurfacing. Since that traumatic moment of the priest administering the "last-rites" in my Presence, I've looked through a lens filled with questions about healing.

"My Deepest Secret is that I Know Healing is Possible."

Experiencing the state of "healing is possible" became my quest. The more I researched, read, experienced the practice of using the Self I-Dentity *Ho'oponopono* mantras, I perceived the "essence" of Traditional *Ho'oponopono* Practice was inclusive of "healing is possible." I dedicated my energy to mindfully clearing the "old tapes, programs, attachment to memories, judgements," that replayed in my mind. I faced the fact that every time I perceived a problem, I was present. I viewed myself as pulling the weeds in my mind, one by one. Yes, it was and is slow, tedious, and sometimes deeply difficult work. "What is my alternative?" I ask myself. I feel it is my Divine Guidance that inspired me to shift my perception from "difficult" to "gift."

I'll admit it took some courage to finally see and feel "cancer as a gift." I know the Self I-Dentity *Ho'oponopono* mantras helped me get through, what seemed to be endless layers, of what I call "cancer fear based perceptual society mindsets." The depth of the language of violence within the "cancer culture" distressed me. I realized I needed to override the hard wired concepts and emotions that I encountered within the medical system, the family-friends system, and the community. With *Ho'oponopono* mantras, I found a comforting way to approach accepting my responsibility for the life I created for myself. I observed that the more I practiced the mantras, trickles of Hope grew into the possibility of restoring my life to Divine Inspirational Guidance.

In the depth of excruciating pain, I clarified the fine line between giving up, letting go, and surrender. I "got" I have choice, not control. Sincere unconditional surrender is the key, for me, to empower my choice to enter "the zero limits" zone and feel the reality that "healing is possible." I understand Buddhists call this space "the void." With these insights as my compass, I set about clearing my thoughts, listening for Divine Inspirational Guidance, allowing new energy to flow, and taking action.

I discovered the mantra "I Love You" gets me to zero limits. The Love energy seems to transmute my "stuckness." I, on occasion, have experienced while sincerely repeating the "I Love You" mantra the Peace that passes all understanding. For a brief fleeting moment, I have said out loud, "I Love You Cancer." Tapes and self-judgments come up like lightning flashes in the Arizona desert, although, when I just wrote this, I immediately visualized the ocean and the sky and mentally tossed the toxicity into those spaces.

As I continue my journey in responsible healing, I am transitioning into restoration and preservation. I am bringing with me direct experience with the Hawaiian Traditional *Ho'oponopono* Practice and Self I-Dentity *Ho'oponopono* as powerful transformational healing choices. I can unequivocally attest to the impact the processes have in broadening my world of possibility and in creating a pathway that connects me to the Love inside of me, resulting in the hope of my experiencing a new life of healthy wellbeing through allowing the expression of Divine Inspirational Guidance.

I move inward knowing my core is Divinity, focused on living my life from Divine Inspirational Guidance from where and from whom all Blessings flow. The miracle of living now in the moment with clarity, receiving Light in, giving Light out, is my "NewNormal" action.

With my practice of *Ho'oponopono* I received Divine Inspiration and created four mantras.

CELL
Cruising into the Heart of my Soul
Embracing the Love of my Divine Guidance
Letting the Radiance of my Pure Energy fill me
Loving the Wisdom of my Body
—Phyllis M. Gagnier

It is my purpose, in sharing my story, to honor, express appreciation, and give credibility to the Truth that the Hawaiian Traditional *Ho'oponopono* and Self I-Dentity *Ho'oponopono* practice are powerfully relevant and powerfully impact my journey into the world of responsible healing. 9 years later, I know with certainty, that my practice of Ho'oponopono expanded my evolvement to allow, to receive and to feel Unconditional Love, which embodies Unconditional Forgiveness, for my Body, my Mind, my Spirit.

In my "Patient to Patient Conversations" writing, I have encouraged and continue to encourage everyone to develop and evolve their own inner practices as fits them and their circumstances.

Owau no ka "I"
I am the "I." (Vitale and Len, *Zero Limits*, 123)

Ka Maluhia no na wa a pau, no ke'ia wa a mau a mau loa aku.
The Peace for always, now and forever and ever-more. (Vitale and Len, *Zero Limits*, 197)

178. For more information and resources concerning conflict transformation and resolution: Peacemakers Trust, http://www.peacemakers.

ca/; "Welcome to NCDD," National Coalition for Dialogue and Deliberation, http://ncdd.org/; "Welcome to ACT," Alliance for Conflict Transformation, http://www.conflicttransformation.org/; National Conflict Resolution Center, http://ncrconline.com/.

179. Bruce G. Miller, *The Problem of Justice: Tradition and Law in the Coast Salish World* (Lincoln: University of Nebraska Press, 2001), 156–62.

180. Ibid., 194–99.

181. Lesieur, *The Scanlan Plan.*

Chapter 6: Returning to Reciprocity: Reconceptualizing Economics and Development

Stephen M. Sachs, Christina A. Clamp, and Donna K. Dial

Section 1: Reconceptualizing Economics and Development

Many of the world's current major problems are directly related to the narrow, reductionist[1] approach of much of mainstream economics (particularly neoclassical economics), whose focus is on economics as profit and loss mostly of the individual firm or economic actor, with inadequate concern for public goods or externalities (though some economists, including many macro-institutional, environmental, and certain socialist economists, do much better).[2]

This is particularly the case concerning the environmental crisis, discussed in the chapter below, "Indigenizing the Greening of the World: Applying An Indigenous Approach to Environmental Issues." But it is also the case with much of the suffering and violence troubling the world. Failure to develop and maintain adequate, balanced economies, providing high levels of employment and fulfilling human needs in a sufficient and relatively egalitarian manner (as developed in the previous chapter) has produced and worsened many damaging developments, though there are also other causes.

For example, much of the turmoil in the Middle East since 2000 has economic causes and accelerants. The Arab Spring in Tunisia, and across the region, for instance, arose in part from very high youth unemployment and other economic problems.[3] Similarly, the Syrian Civil War was triggered by the government's failure to deal with the huge number of impoverished people forced off their farm land by the agriculture destroying drought,[4] an impact of global warming induced climate change. This environmental crisis resulted largely from business and government economic values which focused primarily on profits with little concern for externalized costs and public goods, and a development model which emphasized the maximizing of unending growth, measured largely in terms of gross national product (GNP), emphasizing increasing income (especially corporate profits) and jobs, but little else. Similarly, racism has become much more serious because of economic inequities, as when jobs, and/or good jobs, are hard to get, many people feeling threatened look for someone to blame, and all the more so if they are viewed as competitors for jobs.[5] This can be seen in western Europe in 2014, suffering from a tenuous economy and high unemployment, in the rising feelings against Middle Easterners and North Africans (mostly Muslims), as well as East Europeans coming to their countries either directly or indirectly in large part for economic reasons.[6.]

From a Native viewpoint, as previously discussed, economics needs to be about relationships, and working to maintain, and recreate a balanced web of relations among people,

Thus economics is primarily a sociology[7] that includes not only relations among people, but also with the environment of which it is becoming clearer and clearer that human beings are a part, and have to take into account for their own welfare. American Indian societies, and Indigenous nations around the world, have generally done quite well in creating and maintaining such balances. Out of practicality, they have refrained from taking more from their environment than needed, and have undertaken long term, as well as short and medium term, planning in their decision making, taking into account their relations with the environment, and among the members of their band, tribe, or confederacy. Similar short, medium, and long term planning is needed in contemporary societies.

Moreover, as developed in the last chapter, decision making about economics as well as other aspects of public policy needs to be participatory. That requires an informed citizenry and transparent governmental and economic processes. Further, from the point of view of pragmatic Indigenous peoples, policy approaches, and the policies themselves, need to be based on principles and factual findings long observed as being correct and viable (today one would say based on sound science): aimed at appropriate ends and in fact designed to attain, or at least sufficiently move toward, them. As is developed here, much of mainstream economic policy meets neither standard, and an alternative approach is needed.

An important factor in the socio-economic success of most traditional tribal societies has been that assisting others, particularly those less well off, and the nation as a whole, has been highly honored. Advancing one's own interest at the expense of the community, including accumulating without sharing, has been considered dishonorable. In tribal and band societies, community pressure—positive and negative—generally has been sufficient incentive to keep almost all community members advancing community interests in the course of furthering their own interests. This was partly so because as a practical matter in labor intensive communities people needed the cooperation and support of each other, Indeed, a major aspect of being tribal is identifying with the community to the extent that one feels good about oneself largely in terms of one's ability to contribute to and assist the community and its members.

At the current stage of societal evolution, such moral and public opinion incentives are helpful, but insufficient to achieve socially beneficial behavior, particularly in what is normally considered economic activity. Today, significant economic incentives quite often are necessary as a major instrument to keep individual economic and business behavior socially beneficial, and to keep society in balance. Mainstream market economic theory, going back to Adam Smith, John Locke, David Ricardo, and their colleagues, claims to achieve this through competition in the market. But the failure of current economic incentives to adequately take into account externalities and public goods, combined with imbalances in the economy, resulting from and contributing to, great differences in market power, causes the contemporary market economy to often divisively promotes private interest over the public good. Thus, as some socialist critiques of capitalist markets assert, instead of promoting the general welfare, too often the concept of the invisible hand of the market is a cover for the dirty hand of the antisocially behaving economic actor.[8]

Creating, Maintaining, and Restoring Economic Balance

Economic systems, whether they are market based or take some other form, are human creations, put into effect by governments. These systems operate following the decisions and non-decisions made consciously or unconsciously by those who create, maintain, and modify them. The outcomes of the interactions within an economic system, as within a game, are determined by the actions (and non-actions) of the participants—including those who are supposed to carry out or enforce the "rules" of the system or game, in given circumstances. This includes how perceptive and creative participants are in understanding and acting upon their opportunities. Economic systems will function differently according to the circumstance, and may be modified or transformed either by changes in circumstance, or by conscious or unconscious actions or inactions by those who govern the system.

For example, a market system often tends to concentrate wealth over time in fewer and fewer hands, as those with some advantage or good fortune gain market power, which allows them to further increase their share of market power and wealth. Consequently, an egalitarian "free" market may be transformed into an oligopolistic or monopolistic economic system with no change in governance.

But changes in governance—in the rules that actually apply—may also change, or prevent a change, in the operation of the system.

As developed at length in the previous chapter on politics, Native societies generally functioned quite well for almost all their members because they operated in a participatory equalitarian fashion on the basis of mutual respect, dispersing and essentially equalizing power, including economic power and wealth. To obtain equivalent benefits for citizens of communities today, the same equalitarian values need to be applied to create, maintain, and renew participatory societies. In the economic sphere this requires establishing and maintaining relatively equal distribution of wealth and control of economic institutions, and, indeed, of economic, as well as all other sources of power.[9] This can only be attained and maintained in a fully participatory society, with a participatory economy, in which virtually all institutions, including economic institutions are participatory. Such an economy, except for very small enterprises, would be composed of democratically operated worker cooperatives, and supporting participatory institutions, such as the Mondragon cooperatives, briefly considered in the preceding chapter on politics, and discussed more fully below.

But, just having an economy of democratically run business and related institutions is not sufficient. For instance, in the case of Yugoslav self-management, as was shown in the preceding chapter, without adequate antitrust laws and other regulation and balancing actions, in what some called *laissez faire* socialism, the market moved rapidly toward a quite oligopolistic economy. Movement toward oligopoly and monopoly is a multifold problem. As discussed in the last chapter, concentration of power undermines political democracy.

It also is an economic aberration, first because it skews the market towards the interests of the larger firms that can use their market power for their own economic interest over others, so that market forces no longer function for economic efficiency. For example, a large firm with more resources can hold out longer in a price war than a more efficient smaller one that may be able to offer better products at lower cost. If the larger firm can drive enough of its competition out of business through temporarily sustaining losses by selling at below cost prices, then, in the absence of effective competition, it can later raise prices as high as the market will bear.

Larger firms also have advantages of economies of scale that increase their market power over smaller ones. For example, a large firm may receive discounts for purchasing in larger quantities, leading to lower costs. In addition, a large firm can attract more customers through a greater ability to advertise, than a smaller firm offering the same product with higher quality, even at a lower price. Thus, larger less efficient firms can gain monopoly positions allowing them to charge more than properly operating market forces allow, and to readily sell lower quality or less desirable products to consumers, who due to the absence of meaningful competition have little or no choice. There are also diseconomies of scale. For instance, beyond a certain point, the larger an organization becomes, which at least potentially gives it more power, the less efficient it becomes, as the Mondragon cooperatives, discussed below, discovered.[10]

A major problem for the effectiveness and economic efficiency of firms as they grow is the increase in communication and coordination costs. In hierarchical organizations this usually leads to increasing numbers of managers with a rising ratio of managers to productive workers in an increasing number of layers of organization. As discussed in the previous chapter, this increases the cost of communication and lessens the accuracy of information on which higher-level decisions are based, while lowering the accuracy of understanding of decisions as the communication distance grows.

Democratic organizations have a similar rise in communication costs with growth. Either teams become unwieldy as they grow, or as the firm enlarges the number of teams expands, requiring additional coordinating teams, and more time discussing issues. In both the case of hierarchical and democratic organizations, the larger the organization becomes, often above two hundred to three hundred members, the less people know and understand each other. Like everything else, this has some advantages, but these tend to be outweighed by the disadvantages. A partial solution to the problems of size is decentralizing the firm to become a federation. In the postmodern world of great complexity, this well may be the best practical approach to balancing the needs of organizational and economic efficiency with other aspects of effectiveness, but it is important to note that it does not fully minimize economic and organizational costs related to size.

One aspect of the problem of size was the subject of a study of the financial sector in the United States by Stephen G. Cecchetti and Enisse Kharroubi on behalf of the Bank for International Settlements. Published in February 2015 under the title "Why does financial sector growth crowd out real economic growth?,"[11] the authors found that financial sector "growth disproportionately harms financially dependent and R&D-intensive industries."

For instance, large banks, in order to protect their investments, tend to invest in firms that have sufficient collateral, often in real property. But these are often the less entrepreneurial organizations than those that are researching and making new developments that in the medium and long term contribute more to the economy. Thus large financial institutions underfund research and development, and developers of new ideas and products often need to seek funding from smaller venture capital organizations. But as money becomes more concentrated in large financial organizations, less funding becomes available for venture capital. In addition, as financial institutions grow and become a larger portion of the economy, they attract an increasing number of talented people who otherwise would apply their brainpower and productivity in organizations directly producing and developing products and services. Moreover, as the financial sector has grown in the United States, it has more and more been found to act for its own and not society's advantage. Further, the financial sector accounted for 15 percent to 25 percent of the overall increase in wage inequality from 1980 to 2006.[12]

Thus government must be vigilant in foreseeing, understanding and correcting developing imbalances in market power, and other misbalancing forces and practices, that naturally will occur quite frequently, employing whatever means are appropriate. This can include such measures as changes in: regulations, taxes, subsidies, services, government interventions in purchasing, ease of obtaining credit, and so forth. But this also requires strategic planning to harmonize public and private interest and power for the public good.[13]

The "Economic" Advantages of a Democratic Economy

An economy well balanced in terms of equality of wealth, and economic and market power tends to be more efficient, productive, and stable than one hierarchically structured in terms of wealth and power.[14] To begin with, the basis of a modern economy is "bottom up." Experience has shown that "trickle down" economic policies produce less total wealth. When money is available at the bottom and middle of the economy it is more quickly spent in the community, particularly in socially more valuable items, and recirculated with a multiplier effect, than is the case with money at the top of the economy. Thus, the same amount of wealth has a greater power when it is more evenly distributed in a society than when it is concentrated in fewer hands. Similarly, with higher employment, more people are contributing to the economy, and fewer simply taking from it.

Thus austerity policies which try to balance government budgets, by lowering spending, generally have the negative effect of lowering employment and making less money available to consumers. This reduces consumer spending and economic activity. This in turn tends to reduce sales, and may deflate prices, lowering tax revenue, and hence government income. The result tends to be a continuing downward spiral, as has occurred in the Great Recession beginning in 2008 in Spain,[15] Portugal,[16] and Greece (where the economy shrank 25 percent),[17] and in Germany in the 1930s, helping to bring Hitler to power.[18]

By contrast in the Great Depression of the 1930s in United States, the New Deal spending on programs and people stopped the collapse, and expanded the economy through investing in infrastructure of many kinds and assisting people, largely by putting them to work in rebuilding the economy. This also increased education and training, which in an expanding technological age is essential for individual and societal economic advancement. But when the government cut back on spending in 1937, the recession increased, until returning to more public spending curtailed it.[19] The economist J. M. Keynes advocated governments spending money and increasing public debt in the downturn of economic cycles, and balancing that by increasing taxes relative to spending in strong economic times to pay off public debt and build up a surplus, while curbing inflation.[20]

The approach of cutting taxes, particularly on the wealthy, rather than increasing government spending, has been a much less effective means of stimulating the economy. Government spending significantly increases the amount of money going to low and middle income people, who spend most of it, giving the economy a boost. By contrast, with tax cuts, people of low to moderate incomes receive a relatively smaller amount of money, which may increase their spending, but only to a limited extent; or may not increase spending, to the extent people use the additional money to pay bills or reduce debt.

Meanwhile, only a small portion of the larger amount of money that tax cuts give to wealthier people gets spent. While the well-to-do may be more able to make investments that would lead to more job creation, there is no incentive to do so if there is little or no demand for additional products or services.[21] Thus during the recent Great Recession of 2008–12, many large firms simply sat on large amounts of saved capital, and much unneeded money held by wealthy individuals went into speculative spending, which contributed very little to the economy. Indeed such speculation often creates bubbles, which when they break, bring economic downturns, which can become deep recessions or depressions. Bubbles form as a result of commodities being overvalued, and then break when it is widely perceived that the commodity is overpriced. This has happened repeatedly in US history,[22] including the real-estate collapse which triggered the stock market crash that began the Great Depression, and the 1980s Savings and Loan Scandal and the insecure mortgage scandal of the early 2000s that brought on the Great Recession.[23]

Consequently, there have been calls for highly graduated income taxes, which aim to promote equality of wealth and discourage speculation, as well as small transaction taxes on sales of securities that also tend to discourage speculation. Indeed, the great economic collapses in modern economies have generally taken place when income disparities and concentration of wealth have been quite great, in large part because of the factors discussed above. (It is important to note in dealing with actual situations, that many factors are always involved and one needs to look at the uniqueness of each situation in order to have a good understanding of it. This is too often missed in the reductionist oversimplification of neoclassical economic theory).

A society or an organization which supports all its members makes a financial investment that reaps considerable economic reward for the whole society, in addition to improving the overall quality of life. Social research makes this very clear. For example, on the basis of surveying the literature in the field, the 2007 GAO Report to Congressional Requesters, *Poverty in America: Economic Research Shows Adverse Impacts on Health, Status and Other Social Conditions as well as on the Economic Growth Rate*, found:

> Economic research suggests that individuals living in poverty face an increased risk of adverse outcomes, such as poor health and criminal activity, both of which may lead to reduced participation in the labor market. While the mechanisms by which poverty affects health are complex, some research suggests that adverse health outcomes are due, in part, to limited access to health care as well as exposure to environmental hazards and engaging in risky behaviors. For example, some research has shown that increased availability

of health insurance such as Medicaid for low-income mothers led to a decrease in infant mortality. Likewise, exposure to high levels of air pollution from living in urban areas close to highways can lead to acute health conditions. Data suggest that engaging in risky behaviors, such as tobacco and alcohol use, a comparatively sedentary life-style, and a low consumption of nutritional foods can account for some portion of the health disparities between lower and upper income groups. The economic research we reviewed also points to links between poverty and crime. For example, one study indicated that higher levels of unemployment are associated with higher levels of property crime. The relationship between poverty and adverse outcomes for individuals is complex, in part because most variables, like health status, can be both a cause and a result of poverty. Regardless of whether poverty is a cause or an effect, the conditions associated with poverty can limit the ability of individuals to develop the skills, abilities, knowledge, and habits necessary to fully participate in the labor force.

Research shows that poverty can negatively impact economic growth by affecting the accumulation of human capital and rates of crime and social unrest. Economic theory has long suggested that human capital—that is, the education, work experience, training, and health of the workforce—is considered one of the fundamental drivers of economic growth. The conditions associated with poverty can work against this human capital development by limiting individuals' ability to remain healthy and develop skills, in turn decreasing the potential to contribute talents, ideas, and even labor to the economy. An educated labor force, for example, is better at learning, creating, and implementing new technologies. Economic theory suggests that when poverty affects a significant portion of the population, these effects can extend to the society at large and produce slower rates of growth. Although historically research has focused mainly on the extent to which economic growth alleviates poverty, some recent empirical studies have begun to demonstrate that higher rates of poverty are associated with lower rates of growth in the economy as a whole. For example, areas with higher poverty rates experience, on average, slower per capita income growth rates than low-poverty areas.[24]

Also, people who feel supported generally feel good about themselves and the community that empowers them, and though other factors are involved, generally achieve more and contribute more to their communities. Moreover, providing quality education and training to all who have the ability to succeed in education appropriate to them is essential for the high quality workforce necessary for an economy to function well. Those who may have difficulties in achieving in educational processes, if properly supported, usually can still succeed and ultimately contribute significantly to society. Conversely, people who do not have educational opportunity or necessary support may not be employable, or may only be minimally employable. Thus, society loses their contributions to the economy and the quality of life in the community, while they become economic drags on society. If there are many such people, the failure to make the relatively small investment to support their development has a high cost to society.

In addition, social services impact productivity. For example, people who are supported by adequate health care and other services are more likely to participate in the workforce, and contribute consistently as well. Those lacking health and other services they need, usually will participate in the workforce at a lower rate, and will more often perform less well, or inconsistently. For example people who are working, but have physical or mental health problems for which they do not have adequate, or any, treatment, are more likely to miss work, work unevenly, make more mistakes, and cause more accidents than those who are healthy or have adequate treatment. This may also lead to higher turnover in organizations, bringing additional costs to employers and ultimately the economy as a whole.

The Need for Adequate Measures and Policy Driving Research

In the multifaceted world of today, maintaining a society which provides a high quality of life for all of its citizens, and is well balanced in all of its internal and external relations, as well as with the environment, not only for the moment, but into the near and more distant future, requires appropriate,[25] adequate measures and institutions to research them, with careful nonpartisan analysis to make well-crafted policy proposals. In a complex and continually changing world, in which there are always unintended consequences of actions, as well shifting conditions and needs, review of ongoing policy and its application, along with developing policy requirements, needs to be continually undertaken and reported. An instance of the kind of ongoing holistic thinking and fact finding that is required is laid out in regard to our relations with our physical environment, in the next chapter, "Indigenizing the Greening of the World: Applying an Indigenous Approach to Environmental Issues."

Examples of the kinds of research institutions which are needed include the Congressional Budget Office (CBO) which advises the US Congress on the past and likely future outcomes of existing and proposed policies, as well as on the problems and alternative means of improvement in the operation of government agencies.[26] Similarly, The Governmental Accountability Office (GAO), "the audit, evaluation, and investigative arm of the Congress, exists to support the Congress in meeting its constitutional responsibilities and to help improve the performance and ensure the accountability of the federal government for the benefit of the American people. [Staff at the GAO] examine the use of public funds; evaluate federal programs and policies; and provide analyses, recommendations, and other assistance to help the Congress make informed oversight, policy, and funding decisions."[27]

Such high-quality, nonpartisan research groups are likely needed at every level of government, and in every field of concern, to advise those public entities and the public about relevant issues and developments. In a participatory society, policy related research needs to be aimed at enhancing public discussion, through such vehicles as discussed in the preceding politics chapter, with private research organizations contributing to the discussion, while the findings of public think tanks are made readily available to the citizenry, restricted only by appropriate protections for privacy and security.

Such measures and research ought to be aimed at instituting and adjusting policies continually to provide a good quality of life for all citizens, so as to empower people to develop and unfold who they are. This should be undertaken to provide the maximum meaningful positive choices that are personally and socially beneficial in a continually changing world. In traditional economic terms, this means investing in people and their development. The research to do this properly involves advising on what services and regulations are, and are not, required, and how to undertake and revise them as needed. This means ending programs that are no longer useful, beginning new efforts where required, and adjusting to changing needs and conditions. This also means allowing individuals and private organizations to do for themselves and each other whatever they are able to do well, and, when appropriate, empowering them with well constituted incentives (e.g., tax deductions for charitable contributions, and tax credits for investing in solar panels to generate electricity). It means, as discussed in the politics chapter concerning "reinventing government," deciding when it is better for a public service to be carried out by government organizations, and when it is best to contract out the work of achieving public ends. This also encompasses deciding when regulation is best undertaken directly setting and enforcing standards, and when it is more effective and beneficial to regulate indirectly through an incentive system, to make the regulation process as economically efficient as possible (such as reducing global warming producing carbon dioxide pollution through a carbon trading program, if properly undertaken, as discussed in the next chapter on the environment). Consequently, ongoing research is needed to continually reinvent government, debureaucratizing it as much as possible, making it as effective and efficient as practicable in terms of attaining its objectives, while minimizing costs and keeping the administrative process as participatory as possible.[28] Just as participatory businesses find it increases their effectiveness to use as many relevant qualitative and quantitative measures of their operation and performance as possible, so it is with government.

Some Examples of Appropriate Measures

In order to make good public decisions in a participatory society, and keep all its many dimensions and aspects in balance, a great many qualitative and quantitative measures need to be taken and appropriately analyzed covering every aspect of society. Traditional mainstream economic statistics are relevant for some of the technical aspects of keeping the economy moving appropriately—such as looking at the rates of inflation and employment. However, it is important to put a heavy emphasis on quality of life indicators, which are most directly related to the ends of society, and to realize that those measures are ultimately, and often directly, impacted by all the others—and that interrelationship needs to be kept in mind.

Several organizations in the United States have developed sets of measures that are suggestive of what needs to be undertaken. Measure for America, a Project of the Social Science Research Council, provides "easy-to-use yet methodologically sound tools for understanding well-being and opportunity in America and to stimulate fact-based dialogue about issues we care about: health, education and living standards."[29] *The Measure of America 2013–2014* applies the Human Development Index and other data to produce national, state, and major urban area reports on how people in the US are faring in the three areas.[30]

Similarly, Opportunity Nation tabulates the Opportunity Index, an annual composite measure at the state and county levels of economic, educational and civic factors that foster opportunity and is designed to help identify concrete solutions to lagging conditions for opportunity and economic mobility. From preschool enrollment to internet access, from volunteerism to access to healthy foods, expanding opportunity depends on the intersection of multiple factors.

The Opportunity Index was jointly developed by Opportunity Nation and Measure of America, and measures 16 indicators, scoring all 50 states plus Washington, DC, on a scale of 0–100 each year. In addition, more than 2,600 counties are graded A-F, giving policymakers and leaders a useful tool to identify areas for improvement and to gauge progress over time.[31]

Indicative of some of the many concerns is the *National Index of Violence and Harm* (NIVAH), "developed in 2000 by a team of researchers at Manchester College. The goals of this project are to quantify levels of violence and harm done to people in the United States and identify trends over time. The initial version of the Index, spanning the years 1995–98, was released in December, 2000."[32] NIVAH measures both personal and societal violence and harm relative to the baseline year 1995.

The personal index encompasses measures of both interpersonal and intrapersonal violence and harm. The interpersonal foci are homicide, sexual offenses, battery, robbery, and reckless behavior, and the intrapersonal variables are suicide/self-injury and deaths from substance abuse (smoking, alcohol, and other drugs). The societal index includes institutional and structural indicators. Institutional violence is violence caused by the action of societal institutions and their agents carrying out their institutionally defined roles, in government (by law enforcement and correctional institutions) and by corporations (consisting of air pollution, injuries from products, and occupational injuries), and by the institution of the family (domestic violence and child abuse/

neglect). Structural violence is violence that arises from the structure or hierarchies of United States society. This encompasses several factors:

> Social negligence represents basic human needs which are left unaddressed by society at large. We have defined "basic" needs to include food, housing, health care and education, and have incorporated related measures of unmet need. Infant mortality and life expectancy, while not direct indicators of structural violence, provide general indicators of the quality of life and health care that is provided through the overall organization of society. Hate crimes occur due to prejudice and enmity between various social and ethnic groups. Employment discrimination is a measure of active bias on the part of those with economic/decision-making power against groups with lesser power. Poverty disparity measures imbalances in the poverty levels between different sub-populations such as racial, age, and gender groups. Gang membership is used as a marker for those who are deprived of basic family and community resources (or are otherwise disenfranchised from the mainstream culture) and are thus less likely to benefit from societal improvements in education, employment, health care, economics, etc.[33]

Of particular note is the approach of Abhijit Banerjee and Esther Duflo of M.I.T. and Michael Kremer of Harvard who won the 2019 Memorial Nobel Prize in Economic Sciences for their experimental approach to alleviating poverty. In investigating problems such as deficiencies in child health and education they focused on finding and analyzing evidence indicating what interventions would best bring major improvements in overcoming problems, running tests of such proposed policies before seeking to apply them broadly. Among their successes have been the improving of the academic performance of five million Indian students from effective remedial tutoring, and improvements in wellness from inspiring public investment in preventive health care.

Measures Concerning the Environment and Its Relationship to the Economy

Measures relating to the environmental conditions and related public policy are always important, but have become most essential in the current set of environmental crises (discussed in the next chapter). Dealing with environmental issues involves complex short, medium, and long term questions involving numerous aspects of relations between people and the physical environment. This is especially so concerning human economic activity, from the local to the regional, national, and international levels.

A great deal of data analysis and projection of alternative futures depending on how people and governments respond to environmental problems is already being undertaken by a variety of scientific and policy organizations and networks. Most notable is the international Intergovernmental Panel on Climate Change (IPC), which regularly reports on the extent of global warming induced climate change, its likely progression including its impacts on human beings depending on what action is taken to slow and possibly eventually stop it.[34] This includes statements of targets needing to be attained if global warming is not to reach extremely disastrous levels. Various private and governmental agencies have been applying this, and other scientific data to propose and make environmental policies.

Examples include the US Environmental Protection Agency's fuel economy standards for automobiles,[35] and existing state and proposed US policy for requiring percentages of electricity generation to be by other than global warming increasing burning of fossil fuels.[36] Similar research and science based policy proposal has been taking place on other environmental issues. While some more scientific research related to the environment is desirable, the primary current problem is to develop the political will to act appropriately on available information. This is in the face of resistance by wealthy fossil energy interests seeking to maintain and increase profits, and by other business interests desiring to keep their costs low by having less regulation.[37]

Some further development of measures linking environmental quality and the environment would be quite useful, however. Faced with growing serious environmental degradation stemming from stressing narrowly defined economic development regardless of other costs, China has created a system for linking environmental and economic policy. This may be valuable in itself, and suggests what else might be done about balancing economic development with maintaining environmental quality.

In September 2015 the Chinese government initiated the Circular Economy (CE) policy linking environmental and economic policy.[38] It will be somewhat unclear just what the system actually involves and how appropriate and effective it really is until it has been sufficiently put into effect. At the outset, it includes a multilevel system for accounting of natural resources and environmental ecosystem services, ecological compensation, and market based instruments for environmental management.

CE is intended to function with a new business model in which resource use is optimized through waste prevention, reuse, and recycling. It is to include industrial ecosystems, closed loop supply chains, broad-based recycling, and waste recovery. The idea is to increase resource use efficiency (using less and polluting less) to prevent and reduce urban and industrial waste through requiring and encouraging exchange and reuse networks and behaviors, so that economic activity and growth may continue while reducing environmental degradation and increasing the quality of life. An important element is to shift from quantitative to quality oriented development, reducing consumption and resource use while increasing the quality of living. The plan shifts from an emphasis on degradation or partial reclamation at the end of extraction, manufacturing, and transporting, to a focus on holistic transformation aimed at improving the quality of life, while dealing with environmental issues. The problems of making CE work in practice are complex and challenging, so that as of mid-2016, it remains to be seen how useful and suggestive CE will turn out to be.

Thoughts on the Needed Measures

The specific measures to be used to assist public policy related research need to be chosen to properly fit the particular circumstance and be sufficiently accurate and detailed to provide all the relevant information (while avoiding irrelevant information that tends to cloud comprehension), making appropriate changes as new concerns and conditions develop or are discovered. In improving and otherwise changing measures, care needs to be taken to provide consistent reporting across time so that long term developments and policy impacts are clear. This may mean adding rather than replacing measures in some instances. Among the aspects of having sufficient detail, so that important variations are not missed amid averages or larger groupings, is to be sure to include breakouts of all the relevant populations and subgroupings.

In terms of populations, this means including all the geographical, socio-economic, ethnic, or other categories of people who may need particular consideration. In the United States, for example, American Indians and Alaska Natives are an important set of populations with specific concerns and policy needs. Although the situation is improving, census and other data often has not included Native Americans as a separate category, and at times when it has done so, has not done so consistently over time. In addition, it has been difficult to obtain sufficient and accurate data, particularly relating to people who have been socially marginalized. This needs to be overcome. Similarly, it is important to remember the particularity of place, sufficiently taking into account local as well as regional, national, and transnational conditions both in measuring and making policy in all areas. Finally, it essential to ensure that the measures used, and the data collection process, are impartial, and are not subject to political manipulation.[39]

Qualitative information also needs to be considered, because quantitative indicators may be less fully accurate or considerably in error, and even if they are completely accurate, their meaning may not be clear. Such indicators often show that there is measurable and significant change, but they do not necessarily provide a causal explanation of what is occurring. By themselves, quantitative indicators cannot present a full picture of what they are intended to measure and are subject to interpretation as to their meaning. Especially in a participatory society, all data must simply be one input into a discussion with the people concerned regarding real situations, and what needs to be undertaken.[40]

All of the above, and the many other indicators are simply information, which then needs to be subject to analysis and problem solving debate as to what the causes are, and what the alternative courses are for improvement with the full range of their costs and benefits over time, including side effects. Such an approach provides a necessary basis for discussing and deciding what the best courses of public and private action are.

Concerning the policies and actions of businesses, including corporations, it needs to be kept in mind that, while they have instrumental goals of bringing in revenue and making reasonable profits, they should be operated with reference to providing public goods and avoiding doing harm. Thus, businesses should be guided by practical ethics, and regulated to the extent necessary and proper for their acting consistently with public purposes.

Rethinking "Development"

All of the above relates to rethinking "development" as not being ever increasing economic growth, with the goals of endlessly increasing income and jobs. Rather, it is a process of human and community enhancement aimed at improving the quality of life efficiently— minimizing costs in terms of money, resources, the environment, and people. To achieve human development, income and jobs are a necessary means, but they are not the ends. Similarly, this approach includes moving away from an emphasis on people obtaining more and more new things, to maintaining and advancing the quality of life, which in an age of rapid technological advancement encompasses updating and acquiring items that improve the quality of work, and life more broadly.

Among those advocating a human and community enhancement approach to development is Nobel Laureate in Economics Amartya Sen. Sen proposes that development should be evaluated according to the opportunities and capabilities of the people concerned, rather than according to output measures such as Gross National Product (GNP) per capita. "In Sen's view, development is not just an economic process, but is a political one too, and to succeed requires democratization of political communities to give citizens a voice in the important decisions made for the community."[41]

Examples of undertaking development as personal and community development quite successfully are to be found among quite a number of American Indian tribes, an instance of which is discussed below. This largely involves the application of traditional values, though the long history of physical and cultural genocide have, to varying degrees, reduced the extent of their being followed in different communities. Because most Native nations were first denied the right to govern themselves, and then were limited to having inappropriate forms of representative government, many Indian nations have been struggling to return to more traditional, participatory decision making. Their development efforts, though generally quite good, have not been carried out in as democratic a manner as was traditional, nor are they appropriate for a contemporary participatory society.[42]

An important point is that once colonization occurred, American Indian economic development was not very successful until Native nations gained sufficient self-determination to have at least a major say, if not control, of the development process.[43] Imposed development, however well intended, generally failed to take account of tribal values, culture, and local conditions. Not deeply understanding the people and conditions in question, and not involving the concerned population in the development process, has been a general failing of much of Western development policy. Often there has not been sufficient understanding that good general principles need to be applied according to the specifics of each place, and that different situations and locations require different approaches.

Narrow Attempts at Development

An illustrative example, involves US foreign aid to Afghanistan, shortly after World War II.[44] At the beginning of the Cold War, the US government decided that the world would shortly become bipolar, with all nations allying either with the US or the USSR. On the basis of this miscalculation, it was decided that it was important for the United States to try to win over all non-aligned nations, including Afghanistan. The foreign aid question was whether to pave the streets of the Afghani capital or build a dam in the back country that few would see, but which would provide flood control, irrigation for agriculture, and electricity for eventual economic development. Only US economists were asked for advice, and no discussions on the details of the alternative proposals or the local conditions were undertaken with Afghanis. The economists correctly pointed out that Afghanistan had little motorized traffic that would benefit from paving the streets, and that once paved, the streets would be costly to maintain, as this would require new capital investment. Therefore, the economists advised building the dam as a step toward long-term economic development, and the US constructed the dam. The Russians then paved the streets of the capital. Since the Afghani government could now say they were becoming a modern nation, as everyone could see that the streets of Kabul were paved, the Russians won whatever prestige or benefit was to be gained in the foreign aid competition.

The US then decided that building roads was the way to win influence, and proceeded to construct a series of highways across Afghanistan that did not connect to road systems in any other country, in a land-locked nation, with extremely few motor vehicles. For the second time, the aid providers failed to take into account the wishes or the culture of the recipient people. Where paving the streets of the capital had significant symbolic value, creation of a paved rural road system did not, and there was little benefit to the Afghans from building the roads, which soon would deteriorate if the government did not invest in maintaining them.

Moreover, the decision makers failed to research the history, geology, and geography of the area. Providing irrigation water was useless for the area in question, since earlier irrigation had carried salt into the fields so that agriculture was no longer practical. Furthermore, rivers in the region carry large quantities of silt as they rush down the mountains, which then settles out on the river bottoms when the waters slow as they reach relatively flat valleys. This causes the river bottoms to rise, so that every few years these rivers overflow their banks and shift their course. This happened soon after the dam was built, leaving it with no water behind it!

Another example involved a group of international agricultural experts who were involved in developing a new variety of cotton that was much hardier and produced a greater quantity of cotton than existing varieties. They went to a village in India where they asked the inhabitants if they would like to try the new cotton. The agriculturists explained the plants advantages, but never discussed with the villagers what their agriculture involved or what they used the cotton plants for. Most of the villagers tried the new variety of cotton. However, when the agricultural experts returned five years later, they found that only a small percentage of the cotton grown in the village was the new variety. It was only then that the agriculturalists discussed with the villagers how and why they undertook farming, in the course of which the agriculturalists learned that the villagers grew cotton plants partly for their cotton, and partly for their stalks to use as fuel. The stalks on the new variety did not burn very well.

In any case, but especially in a participatory community, development needs to be undertaken in a participatory manner.

Whether local or outsiders, experts and providers need to act as facilitators and resource providers (whether on information, funding or materials) helping people decide what to do within relevant guidelines, rather than deciding for them.[45] This is not only important for the success of the project itself, but for carrying out its important empowerment function of building and maintaining strong community relations. The best builder and maintainer of good participation, is high quality participation, which in turn is a major element in effective development.

While not fully participatory, the successful American Indian development work has been facilitated and led by tribal leaders, with significant community participation. One of many good examples is that of the Mississippi Choctaw.

Mississippi Choctaw Economic Development in Collaboration with Their Neighbors

The Choctaws who remained in Mississippi after the tribe was removed to Indian territory, now Oklahoma, in the 1830s, had to persist in a difficult struggle for survival as a people and as individuals.[46] With the United States government failing to fulfill its treaty obligation to provide allotments to most of those remaining in Mississippi, many tribal members were reduced to share cropping on what had been their own land, for fifty cents a day.

Thus, amid poverty and harsh living conditions the Nation's population declined to just over 1,200 in 1910. In 1918 the federal government finally acknowledged its responsibility and established the Choctaw Agency with a few minimally funded programs. In 1921 the federal government created a dispersed reservation with the purchase of 17,000 scattered acres. By 2013 the tribe had acquired more land than in the original purchase, expanding the reservation to 35,000 acres, comprising seven communities. In the early days of the reservation, conditions remained so dire that it was not until the 1960s that the birth rate began to exceed the death rate. The new federal policies of, first, the War on Poverty, and then,

Self-Determination, empowered the tribe to begin its own process of holistic development, including building an economic base. Business efforts began with the sale of tribal timber, allowing the tribe to hire one of its members as a business manager.

By the late 1960s the Choctaw had established a construction company, building and renovating homes, and an 80-acre industrial park. By the late 1980s the park contained six manufacturing plants, three of which were owned by the nation. One of these, Chata Greeting Enterprises (now American Greetings), before the end of the '80s became the fourth largest producer of greeting cards in the world, by volume. The plant was financed primarily under a compact with the city of Philadelphia, Mississippi, who passed the first industrial bond issue in the United States used for Indian economic development.

A second Choctaw firm, Chata Enterprises, began supplying General Motors with wire harnesses for automobile instrument panels in 1983. The plant was expanded to become the fourth largest employer in the state with many non-tribal workers, again in collaboration with the city of Philadelphia, passing a bond issue. In 1999 Chata Enterprises opened a plant in Sonora, Mexico.

In 1985, the Choctaw set up a credit union to provide much needed banking services to tribal members. Then three years later the Choctaw Shopping Center was completed, housing a bank, a grocery store, a restaurant, a barber and beauty shop, a gas station, and other businesses. As of 2003, the nation owns and operates a broad portfolio of manufacturing, service, retail, and tourism enterprises throughout Mississippi, the Southeast, and into Mexico, including two casino resorts with hotels, golf courses, a water theme park, and two lake recreation areas. The nation also runs a number of festivals and other events that attract tourists.

The Choctaw, in 1985, provided more than 8,000 permanent, full-time jobs, 65 percent of which were held by non-Indians. With an annual payroll of more than $123.7 million, the Choctaw Nation had become one of the ten largest employers in Mississippi. In addition, tribal revenues had helped the Choctaw to reinvest more than

$210 million in economic development projects in Mississippi. Some tribal enterprises, such as the Choctaw Farmers Market, provided non-economic as well as economic benefits to tribal members, in this instance, enhancing nutrition in the course of increasing tribal farmers' incomes.

By the end of 2013, while the United States, and particularly Mississippi and some of its neighboring states, were still recovering from the Great Recession that began in 2008, the Mississippi Choctaw Nation remained among the ten largest employers in Mississippi, though the number of its employees had dropped to around 6,000. By that time the nation's investment in economic development in the state had exceeded $500 million.

On this economic base, the Choctaw have funded tribal and broader community development in collaboration with surrounding localities and governments for mutual benefit. Before the end of the 1980s, this already included an education program from pre-school through high school and a training and vocational center for adult education. This provided learning in a culturally appropriate manner along with Choctaw culture, which had led to more than sixty tribal members earning college degrees by late in that decade. By 2013 education on the reservation had grown to run the largest unified reservation school system in the United States, with 1,700 to 1,800 students. Newer programs included child care, post-secondary education and all levels of post-secondary education counseling, scholarships, and student support services.

In 2013, the education program included ECCC Integrated Technologies Training Center (ITTC), a partnership between East Central Community College and the Mississippi Band of Choctaw Indians (MBCI). The program featured short-term technical classes, five levels of an Industrial Maintenance Technician Apprenticeship program, capacity to earn Industrial Maintenance Technician Apprenticeship credentials, access to an online technical training library for Industrial Maintenance technicians, and financial assistance options for those interested in these training sessions.

The Nation also operated a museum and offered a variety of Choctaw culture and language programs, to preserve and revitalize the traditional culture and knowledge and to enhance tribal member competence in traditional activities, arts, and crafts. Revitalizing Choctaw culture has been important to tribal members knowing who they are, and feeling good about themselves and the nation. This has provided personal confidence for success, and enhanced tribal solidarity.[47]

The Choctaw Department of Agriculture and Rural Development, in 2013, was operating a number of programs that provide assistance and education to farmers and gardeners, along with education for homemakers. The tribe also was offering agricultural programs in partnership with the Mississippi State University (MSU) Extension Service.

The department's conservation, nature and education programs, in 2013, combined with those of the tribe's Environmental Program Office to manage and protect the reservation environment and provide for sustainable development. The nation received consulting from the US Department of Agriculture Natural Resource Conservation Center (NRCS) on good stewardship of its lands and wild life habitats. The tribe monitored air and water quality and ran its own water treatment plant for drinking water and undertook solid waste treatment. Core tribal government had also become well financed by 2013, with its expansion including a court system, corrections, and a police and fire department.

During the '80s, the health program encompassed a forty-bed hospital with three satellite clinics, a 120-bed nursing home, mental health and substance abuse programs, an ambulance service serving nearby communities as well as the nation, a community nursing and training program, and monitoring of sanitation and water quality. As of 2013, the health center averaged one hundred thousand patient visits per year. The rural clinics averaged approximately three thousand visits per year. The health center has provided full service to tribal members and residents of the reservation, and emergency care to reservation residents and reservation visitors. In 2015, the nation completed construction on a new comprehensive health care center. Health services have been enhanced with a dental clinic, a Diabetes Management Center, dietary and nutrition programs, non-emergency medical transportation, a Women's Health Center, and a WIC (Women, Infants and Children) program.

The Choctaw Housing Authority, by 2013, was providing general maintenance, emergency maintenance, housing placement, resident services, and the holistic Drug Elimination Program. Community Services came to encompass a full range of programs, including Child Welfare Service, Foster Care, Handicapped and Elderly Services, Pathway House, STOP Domestic Violence, food and emergency services, and behavioral health programs.

The nation, in 2013, ran a number of youth programs including Boys and Girls Clubs, 4-H, and Boy, Girl, and Cub Scouts, as well as recreational activity including the Native American Sports Association (NASA). NASA promoted "a standard of excellence in the performance among Native American players and coaches," and enhanced "good sportsmanship, honesty, integrity, sobriety, and a good relationship with Native America." Big Brothers Big Sisters program involved Choctaw high school volunteers providing successful mentoring relationships for children five to fifteen years old wishing to participate, who could benefit from a positive role model in their lives. Mentoring activity included such things as helping a child with school work, teaching Choctaw basket weaving or beadwork, reading together, conversing, playing on the playground, eating lunch together at the school, and playing basketball. The volunteer's main role was to be a friend and a role model.

Over all, the Mississippi Choctaws' business success has allowed the tribe to be more self-reliant (though it continues to receive federal Indian and other funding), and to make significant economic contributions to the surrounding non-Indian communities with whom it enjoys largely collaborative relations. Indeed, the Choctaw undertaking of development as tribal and member development, often in collaboration with neighbors, has improved relations both within the tribe and with surrounding communities. Much of the success of Choctaw enterprises follows directly from its supporting its members with income, education, health, and other services. This has served as a direct empowerment, while enhancing their bond with, and concern for, the community. This is much the same as what has made collaborative enterprises successful, as is further developed in the discussion, below, of the Mondragon federation of worker cooperatives. This begins to give a picture of what a cooperative economy might look like, which is developed in more detail in the case of Mondragon.

Section 2: The Example of the Mondragon Cooperatives

The Mondragon Cooperative Corporation (MCC), a system of worker cooperatives located in the Basque country of Spain, is considered to be one of the most significant models of worker ownership and participatory community economic development in the world. The MCC is a highly complex federation of cooperatives bound together by much more than a formal contract of association. Currently, it is comprised of 257 businesses of which 110 are cooperatives and 147 are subsidiaries. MCC employs 74,060 people.[48]

Today, Mondragon adheres to ten principles: (1) open admission; (2) democratic control; (3) sovereignty of labor; (4) participation in management; (5) instrumental and subordinate nature of capital; (6) wage solidarity; (7) intercooperation; (8) universality; (9) social transformation and (10) education.[49] There is clearly an influence and overlap with the cooperative principles as articulated by the International Cooperative Alliance.[50]

Open admission means that there is no discrimination in hiring for anyone who accepts the cooperative principles. This includes adherence to a principle of ideological neutrality including adherence to a secular identity. In the first fifteen to twenty years, the cooperatives had a strong influence of Catholic social doctrine that informed the leadership. In recent years, a more pragmatic, economic, and secular identity has replaced it.[51]

The cooperatives adhere to a principle of one worker, one vote. There are four types of cooperatives in the Basque country: consumer cooperatives; credit unions; educational cooperatives; and research and development cooperatives. The Mondragon group incorporates elements of these. Eroski, the consumer cooperative, includes two classes of members—consumer and worker—and includes both groups in the governance of the firm. Caja Laboral Popular (the federation's development bank) has worker members but in its governance provides greater control to the borrowing member firms. In the university and educational centers, governance is shared between faculty, staff, and students.[52]

Sovereignty of labor means that workers are the highest authority in the firms through the power of the general assembly. The participation of workers in management provides the means for ensuring systems of participation, transparency, consultation, and negotiation that include the voice of rank and file workers. It recognizes that workers are essential to the profitability of the firms. In turn the cooperative ideally provides opportunities to all its members.[53]

Capital is subordinated to labor through the fifth principle which prioritizes the creation and provision of jobs over the marginal return on investments. Compensation should be just and sufficient to allow for savings and to meet members' needs. The members contribute an initial purchase of a membership share, additional obligatory capital investments as explained below, and other voluntary investments. The cooperatives need to balance compensation of workers against the capital requirements to ensure the ongoing well-being of the firm.[54]

Wage solidarity establishes a ratio of no more than 1:6 times between the lowest and highest paid workers. In the early years, the ratio was 1:3 for lowest to highest paid members. Over time, it was necessary to widen the range in order to attract and retain more highly skilled members.[55]

Intercooperation refers to the principle of working cooperatively with other co-ops. The Mondragon cooperatives recognized the importance of this early on in their history. It is key to their success. It has allowed them to experience greater stability in economic downturns. The firms share the benefits and losses at the level of the groups. In the early years the groups were regional and then later became sectoral groups. As they entered into global markets, the institutional cooperation as MCC gave them the ability to adapt to changing markets.

Universality refers to the value of working with all who are dedicated to promoting economic democracy. Through the investment of resources in Otalora (focusing on education, training and cooperative dissemination), the foundation Mundukide, and the university, the Mondragon cooperatives have served as inspiration and as a resource for the creation of other worker cooperatives.[56]

The ninth principle reflects the commitment of the co-ops to support and invest in social change. The social change priorities have been: the promotion and preservation of Basque language and culture and the revitalization of the Basque language as a national language; community development; the promotion of a cooperative system of solidarity and responsibility; and the advancement of the Basque working class.[57]

Last, the tenth principle reflects a commitment to transmit the cooperative experience and its values to its members, especially those in elected positions; and, to provide professional education especially for those on the boards of directors to ensure that they understand their responsibility for and accountability to the workers. The education principle also reflects a commitment to provide education for new generations of cooperators starting with social formation of the children.[58]

The adherence to these values served the cooperatives well by guiding them in rebuilding after the civil war and continue to do so.

STEPHEN M. SACHS

A Brief History of the Mondragon Cooperative Experience: Setting the Stage

The Mondragon story actually begins not with the industrial cooperatives but with a dedicated group of young men and a young priest committed to building a better community out of the ashes of the Spanish Civil War. The Basques are an ethnically and linguistically separate people located on the French and Spanish border on the Cantabrian coast of Spain. In this first phase, it was the local and national environment which dominated in the structuring of the first cooperatives. The postwar period left Mondragon with shortages of food and fuel. According to José María Ormaetxea, one of the founders of the Mondragon cooperatives, the Basque region suffered for the role it had played in the Civil War because it sided with the Republican government in opposition to Franco. The valley of Alto Deva was a battle field from September 1936 to April 1937. Military installations in Mondragon were bombed as were other parts of the Basque region. Many basic goods such as wheat, cooking oil, and coal were rationed. Indigence and tuberculosis were serious problems.[59]

Heiberg in *The Making of the Basque Nation* (1989: 92), describes this as a period of political and cultural humiliation for the Basques, due to their alliance with the Republic in the Civil War. Vizcaya and Guipuzcoa were declared traitorous provinces after the war. This resulted in the revoking of their fiscal autonomy, which had been assured under the foral regime, local laws, and customs dating back to the thirteenth and fourteenth centuries.[60] Most important of these laws were the *fueros*, which were guarantees of exemption from state imposed taxation and Spanish custom duties. The *fueros* continued to be honored by the Franco government in Navarra and Alava, the two other Basque provinces, because of their allegiance to Franco during the war.

Drawing inspiration from the Catholic Action Movement, and having researched guild socialism and the cooperative movement (discussed in chapter 3, section 6), Don José María Arizmendiarrieta, a twenty-six-year-old priest and journalist, began in 1941 to form study circles with youth from the community of Mondragon to identify local problems that they could work on to resolve. Catholic Action was a social movement that originated in Belgium, was dedicated to social reform, and guided by Christian social doctrine. Franco sought through the repression of Basque culture, and especially the language, *Euskera*, to remove the Basques as an organized threat to the Spanish government. This external source of repression only served to strengthen and focus the efforts of the founders of the Mondragon group to develop the cooperatives.

Basque culture was historically based on bonds of universal nobility and egalitarianism and formalized in the *fueros* for Vizcaya in 1526 and Guipuzcoa in 1610.[61] Heiberg's understanding of these values are documented in the work of Manuel de Larramendi, a Jesuit priest in his *Corografía de Guipuzcoa*:

> The traditional *baserritar* cultivating the land and governed
> by the rural values of austerity, social harmony and egalitar-
> ianism in social relations was for Larramendi, the original
> Basque in a state of grace.[62]

According to Heiberg,[63] these are *baserri* values. She found them expressed by nationalists in her anthropological study of Elgeta, a village outside of Mondragon as the dignity of work, religion, honesty, egalitarianism, and individual autonomy. Nuñez, in his book, *Clases sociales en Euskadi* further reinforces this connection:

> the philosophy of the Mondragon cooperatives is imbued
> with the values of the farmers and above all the workers and
> artisans of the industrialized rural and semi-urban zones
> of Guipuzcoa and Vizcaya (excluding the capitals). There it
> nurtured and grew dynamically and creatively, with initia-
> tive and entrepreneurship, aligned with work, valuing the
> organization and discipline, a spirit of saving and in opposi-
> tion to all wastefulness, with a collective feeling of love of

the Basques, and appreciation of work well done, skeptical of a top down Socialism.[64]

The Mondragon group had strong local labor roots, a democratic internal ideology but without a confrontational approach to capitalism and the terms of market economies. Nuñez observed that:

They are mindful of the efficient functioning of the cooperative enterprises and the welfare of the workers relies on their ability to function within the norms of the market economy.[65]

These values were key to the social form of entrepreneurship that emerged in the Mondragon cooperatives.

The Launching of the Cooperatives

The Mondragon Cooperative Corporation founded its first enterprise, Ulgor (Fagor Electrodomesticos) in 1956, as a maker of portable cook stoves. It was soon joined by three other cooperatives in a growing federation supported by a bank (Caja Laboral Popular), a set of consumer and housing cooperatives, educational institutions, and a research and development cooperative. Several aspects of the federation contributed to its success, demonstrated in its rapid expansion from one cooperative of four members in 1956, to 123 cooperatives in 1978, and 170 in 1986 employing more than 20,000 members. Meanwhile, Ulgor grew to become Spain's leading manufacturer of stoves, refrigerators, and other household appliances.[66]

Caja Laboral played a central role as an investment bank and business incubator for the cooperatives. It gained capital as a result of the economic system of the cooperatives. With some similarity to employee stock ownership plans (ESOPs) in the United States, if a worker cooperative made money, a share would go into each of its workers' accounts in the bank, on which a small amount of interest was paid. These were essentially retirement accounts, as in most cases money could only be withdrawn from them by the worker when the member left the cooperatives. This gave members a financial stake in their co-ops and an economic incentive to be good workers. As in the early days when the membership was mostly young, capital collected quickly since few members left. The accounts also provided some financial insurance to the cooperatives, for if they lost money, funds would be withdrawn proportionally from the accounts of workers of that co-op to help cover the downturn. As the cooperatives were very successful for many years, little money went out and capital grew for investment, including in starting new cooperatives and expanding existing ones.

A key aspect of the bank was that it researched carefully before making an investment in a new cooperative enterprise, and then incubated it via a group of advisors, called the god fathers, until it was decided the new venture was ready to go on its own. The bank also would help cooperatives in difficult times with low interest loans and technical assistance. After 1987, the incubator section of the bank, which also assisted cooperatives experiencing difficulties, became a separate consulting cooperative, LKS.

The Mondragon cooperatives also, early on, launched educational cooperatives—including Mondragon University and training entities—a research and development division, and a number of service and consumer cooperatives. The latter included establishing housing cooperatives, as there was not enough housing in Mondragon to meet the needs of the rapidly expanding worker cooperatives. Later, constructing housing for members became no longer necessary, and this effort ended. Similarly, later on, with free Spanish educational institutions available, many of the educational functions were discontinued by the federation. The research and development cooperative has remained an important asset, providing crucial research that the individual cooperatives could not afford to undertake on their own. For example, as manufacturing developed early on, the research cooperative was able to design robots to keep fabrication comparatively productive and efficient. In addition to serving the worker cooperatives, the federation also supported the wider community, including through its consumer cooperatives and in supporting Basque culture and language activities.

Largely because of their somewhat participatory worker ownership, though other factors including Basque pride and solidarity also played a role, the cooperatives were highly successful, at least in the early years returning about 25 percent more return on investment than conventional businesses in Spain. Moreover, no co-op failed, at least through the 1980s, which is remarkable, especially for new businesses.[67]

Moreover, the democratic and financial structure of the federation made it quite innovative and flexible in meeting changing circumstances. This was especially evident when the serious recession of the late 1970s—1980s hit Spain and the rest of Europe. Some businesses, particularly Ulgor, met the loss of domestic business by shifting 25 percent of their sales to the international market, especially in Latin America. Meanwhile, a combination of low interest loans from the bank (some of which were not repaid), money to help cover losses from worker accounts at the bank, some reduction of pay, switching workers from cooperatives that did not momentarily need them to those that did, and sending unneeded workers back to school largely for work related training, kept the cooperatives functioning without layoffs until economic conditions improved.

The Mondragon federation also learned from experience. For example, a rapidly growing Ulgor after a few years developed strained labor relations which broke into the only strike the federation experienced in the early period. Two changes came out of the experience which sought to ensure good cooperative relations and satisfied members.

The first was the decision that Ulgor had become too large for good community communications, and no cooperative would henceforth be allowed to exceed three hundred members. If an enterprise was still expanding when it reached that size, rather than let it continue to grow in members, a new co-op would be started. The second was the establishment of a member elected

Social Council. Operating in each cooperative, a council served some of the functions of a union, giving members ongoing input into enterprise decision making and providing a vehicle for raising concerns. As in the 1980s and 1990s the Social Council was not always very active in many cooperatives. A number of cooperatives were experimenting with various forms of employee involvement. While what is best will vary with the circumstances, cooperative organizations only function well if they operate fully inclusively, with all members views and concerns heard, and their interests represented. To achieve this, in most instances an appropriate form of team process is necessary, as discussed in the proceeding chapter, "Applying American Indian Principles of Harmony and Balance to Renew the Politics of the Twenty-First Century."

The Developing Structure of the Federation

Thus the Mondragon group has grown significantly since its initiation and been economically able to adapt and respond to the development of the global marketplace. The formal organizational structure of the inter-cooperative relationship has also grown more complex over time in response to external factors. The basic building blocks of the system have not changed dramatically since the inception of the first cooperatives, but the superstructure of the group has.

One of the adaptations was to take geography into account as the cooperatives spread to new places. The first group of four cooperatives was created in and around Mondragon in 1965. The period 1975–85 was one of profound economic crisis in Spain. The Mondragon group expanded with new cooperatives across the Basque country. Faced with a major economic crisis in Spain, between 1974 and 1985, the cooperatives decided to develop regional cooperative groups which would provide some security against market downturns through solidarity in their allocation of labor's earnings, as well as add an element of local control. Between 1978 and 1986, thirteen additional regional groups were created.

The further spread of the federation around Spain and internationally brought new inter-cooperative communication issues, particularly for scattered enterprises in the same field. Thus, in 1991 a congress of the cooperatives moved to replace the regional cooperative groups with sectoral groups of cooperatives in related economic activities. It was also decided to further integrate federation operations in the creation of the Mondragon Cooperative Corporation.

The structure of the federation developed in stages, over time. In the beginning inter-cooperative relations were either informal, in piecemeal agreements, or centered on ties to the bank as early as 1982 when the Mondragon group had begun to explore and develop plans for greater intergroup solidarity. A cooperative congress was soon after convened in 1984 for the purpose of developing the elements of a constitutional superstructure for the cooperatives. The cooperative congress was convened again in 1987. At this second congress, the group established policies governing basic principles, compensation of managers, norms for social capital, and the establishment of an Intercooperative Solidarity Fund designed to help cooperatives in crisis.

The Governing Structure of Mondragon

Today, the group operates as a large multinational with both worker members and worker nonmembers. The superstructure is formalized through a cooperative congress which is the equivalent of a general assembly in the base cooperatives. The assembly has 650 representatives. Each cooperative is entitled to one representative per ten co-op members and the remaining seats are allocated with a maximum of two per cooperative. There is also a delegate for each of the divisions (financial area; twelve industrial sectors; distribution; education and research). The cooperative congress meets annually to address issues of cooperative norms and oversees the central operational departments such as budgeting, admission of new cooperatives, and the division structure.[68]

The permanent commission has delegated authority from the cooperative congress. It meets during the period when the congress is not in session. It is comprised of elected representatives designated by the ruling board of the divisions, who must be members of a cooperative to serve. The industrial area has fourteen seats and twelve votes. Distribution has four seats and four votes. Finance has two votes and two seats. Education and Research has one seat and one vote.[69]

The third managerial unit is the general council which serves as the board of directors for the cooperatives. It is comprised of a president, eight vice-presidents from the various divisions, two directors from the central offices, and the secretary general of the group who has a voice but not a vote. The congress president may also attend and speak but has no vote. This body provides strategic oversight for purposes of coordination and control. This body provides institutional leadership in promotion of new innovations and in the advancement of political priorities of the group. In instances where intervention is needed into an individual cooperative as in the case of the failure of Fagor Electronica, the general council determines the nature of the intervention to be taken.[70]

Contrast this with the structure prior to their global investments. In 1982, the system was comprised of one hundred and seventy cooperatives with a common historical experience, cultural identity, and social and economic goals. Instead of divisions by business sector, the cooperatives were organized by locations. The regional divisions shared profits and losses to support one another during economic downturns. Ninety percent of all workers in the cooperative group were worker members. New applicants were eligible to become worker members within three to six months after a probationary period.[71]

As of 2016, each cooperative has a governance model in which workers vote to elect the governing council, the social council, and the audit committee. The governing council in turn hires the CEO. The CEO handles the administration of the cooperative. The organizational structure is summarized in the figure below:

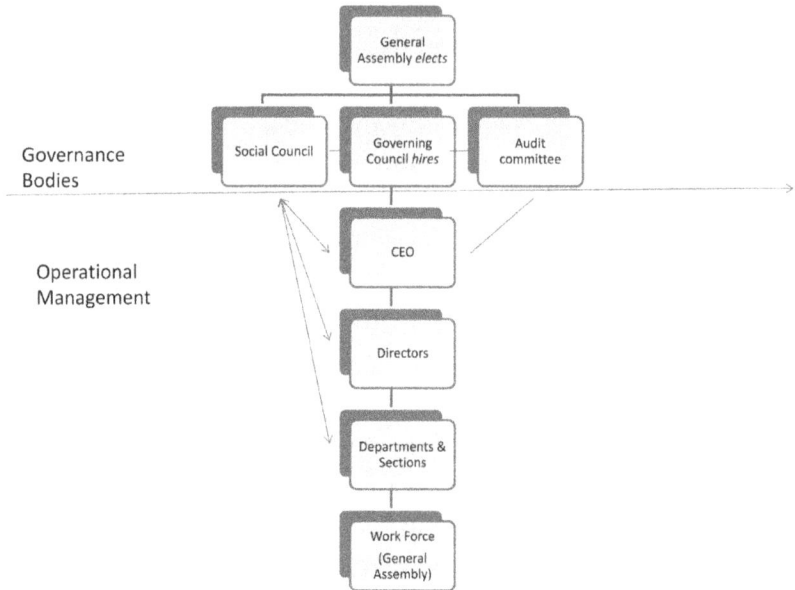

Cooperative law allows for a maximum of 20 percent nonmember workers. There is not necessarily the same common bond felt by all workers, since one in five may not be members of the cooperatives. The cooperative structure was intended to ensure that ultimate authority would always remain in the hands of the members of each individual cooperative while the creation of the superstructure intended to provide them the benefits that can be realized by the economies of scale of larger firms. When the cooperatives entered global markets, the acquisition and joint ventures did not incorporate cooperative ownership and principles, usually because of local law or practice, or the structure or wishes of the partner firm. Had Mondragon been dealing with other cooperative firms in its joint ventures—as would be the case within a fully cooperative society—the cooperative principles would have been maintained. Mondragon subsidiaries account for the rest of the nonmember employees. As of 2008 only about one-third of their workforce were members of the cooperative.[72]

The system of cooperatives has become more complex, the skills and training requirements of managers has increased, and the strong local ties while still present have taken on lesser roles in the operation of the cooperatives. The superstructure gives the cooperatives a stronger presence in global markets through Mondragon International. Mondragon does not have to take all business decisions at the level of the individual cooperatives, as much is decide at the federation level. This is critical to their ability to work effectively in a global business environment. On the downside, it has resulted in greater distance of strategic governance and decision makers from the members of the base cooperatives.

The Sovereignty of Labor Principle and the Challenges in Practice

One of the core principles of Mondragon is a belief in the sovereignty of labor. One of the policies that reflects this principle is the commitment to limits on pay differentials. There is a pay differential restriction that limits the pay of a manager to no more than six times the salary of any worker in the co-op and no more than 38 percent greater between the highest and lowest paid within the entire group of cooperatives, according to Josu Ugarte, the president of Mondragon International.[73]

Early on the co-op members realized that they could not commit to 100 percent worker ownership and remain sustainable in a market economy. In the early years, they maintained no more than 10 percent nonmember worker employment.[74] They also had a strong commitment to create employment in the Basque country for the Basque people out of ethnic pride. They were concerned that extending a share of ownership to workers employed outside of the Basque country could dilute this control or result in plants seceding from the group.

Given the significant role of various industrial cooperatives in the automotive industry, Mondragon had to go where business opportunities took them. As they grew and expanded outside of the Basque country, this led them to consider how to address the place of non-Basques workers in the cooperatives. Overseas, all workers are managed based on the norms of the country where the plant is located. Workers and managers in the overseas firms are typically not membership track employees of the MCC. This has been the source of one of the most enduring conflicts of values and practice for the group. For instance, Copreci, a manufacturer of components for household appliances has had a factory in Mexico for many years. They developed a program to bring workers from the Mexican plant to work and shadow cooperative members in the cooperative as a way to socialize them into the cooperative work culture.

The MCC's goals of local control and ownership of resources coupled with a commitment to the cooperative principles resonate with the desire to create greater democracy in the workplace and better quality jobs that would not disappear when the corporation sought cheaper labor pools elsewhere. The conflict of values led Mondragon to develop plans to incorporate greater numbers of workers into cooperative ownership. This policy ground to a halt with the Great Recession of 2008. MCC reports the following data regarding the current number of members and nonmember employees:

> By the end of 2008, the average number of employees at MONDRAGON was 92,773. 39.7% of these employees work in the Basque Country, 44.2% in other parts of Spain and 16.1% work abroad.

> As a result of the rapid growth experienced over the last few years…only somewhat less than a third of the Corporation's workers are cooperative members at present. The non-members mainly work in the distribution sector outside the Basque Country and at the industrial plants that are also based outside the Basque Country, either in other parts of Spain or abroad.

> This percentage of worker-members will have substantially increased…when Eroski has completed its cooperativisation

process for all its non-member employees, who work mainly outside the Basque Country and Navarra. When this process is complete, the percentage of cooperative members in the Corporation as a whole could be over 75%.[75]

The Cooperative Approach to the Great Recession

The Great Recession of 2008, which was especially debilitating in Spain, was difficult for the Mondragon group as well. But they have a history of setting aside reserves in good times for weathering tough times. In the machine tool sector, they had two years of reserves going into the recession and weathered the recession well. Most affected were the firms involved in consumer durables and retail operations, in particular Fagor Electronica and Eroski.[76] By 2011, with the Spanish economy still in tatters, Fagor Electronica, the largest and first of the cooperatives along with two other smaller firms, Ortza and Egurko, failed. Eroski which is a retail cooperative with stores throughout Spain is now the largest of the cooperatives. It had bad years in 2014 and 2015.

In 2011, the oldest and largest of the cooperatives, Fagor Electrodomesticos, declared bankruptcy. The co-op made a strategically bad decision when it purchased a French firm, Brandt. The severity of the 2008 recession halted all new housing construction in Spain which was Fagor's strongest market. As the losses increased, the co-op continued to pay its members instead of implementing cuts in compensation. The co-op continued to produce products till they simply ran out of funds and materials. The group did invest funds in an effort to save Fagor and concluded a second bailout would not resolve the problem. There have been other failures in the past but none on the scale of Fagor.

The failure of Fagor illustrates both the role of solidarity in the group and the challenges to sustain a democratic ownership culture in larger firms. The other co-ops attempted to save Fagor with a bailout. There were individuals who also made voluntary investments in the firm. Some were retirees and others were individuals with other co-ops. Workers in Fagor did not cut their anticipated earnings at the same rate that workers in other firms were accepting to contribute to the bailout of Fagor. All those funds could not be recouped with the bankruptcy and the workers who lost their jobs received two years of benefits which ran out in October 2015. Other cooperatives absorbed workers from Fagor as they were able. For example, the bank, Laboral Kutxa, hired 150 of the Fagor workers. As of June 2015, there were 150 workers who were still unemployed. They were typically older workers with limited education and physical limitations or mental health issues. An outside firm bought some parts of Fagor that were profitable and hired some of the Fagor workers. Those with greater education and higher skill levels had a much easier time in securing new positions.

Moving into the Future

As of 2016, *baserri* values are not as strong as they once were. The communitarian orientation has been displaced by an increasingly individualized orientation as people have become more integrated into mass culture. Had Mondragon existed in a collaborative economy and society, this almost surely would not have occurred. Forerunners often become diluted by the problems of the society they are attempting to overcome. The years of prosperity have also led workers to be less willing to accept austerity and to make sacrifices, according to one MCC representative. There is much reflection and discussion occurring within the Mondragon cooperative group as they attempt to move forward after the failure of Fagor Electrodomesticos. The cooperatives are considering how they can best proceed strategically.

They see three options: They can proceed as they have without policy changes. They can adopt greater centralization and integration to allow for intervention and more oversight of capital requests. Or they can increase the autonomy of individual co-ops and with this reduce the cooperative's centralized role.

Regardless of which strategic option the cooperatives choose, the group sees its future not in sunset industries, but in new technologies and knowledge based sectors. Staying at the forefront of innovation is their strategy for maintaining jobs in the Basque country. Blue collar work was the focus of their efforts in job creation when they began in 1955. Today, they see the need to develop a highly educated workforce that can lead in fields such as alternative energy, mass transit, tourism, and knowledge sectors of the economy. Ten percent of Mondragon's investments now are in new cooperatives, new investments and greater internationalization; 8 percent is in research and development; and 21.4 percent is in sales in the industrial area for new products and services that did not even exist five years ago.

The Importance of the Mondragon Model

Why is Mondragon still an important model? Mondragon's cooperatives' ability to work together is key to their strength. The co-ops contribute 10 percent of net profits to the Central Fund for Intercooperation, and Laboral Kutxa contributes up to 20 percent.[77] They also treat labor as a fixed cost. This is only feasible because of their intercooperative agreements. The co-ops are able to do this due to three policies: the recycling of workers between co-ops that are countercyclical; the commitment to preserve good jobs in the Basque country while emphasizing engineering innovation; and their social insurance program which is funded based on a 2 percent contribution from workers' earnings. This social insurance program gives workers economic security in hard times.

The intercooperative agreement provides another layer of security. When workers need to be furloughed, there are three avenues for them. Blue collar workers are given the option of working in another co-op or attending community college or university. Public universities are free (€1200 fees). If workers are furloughed, they can receive compensation but will be asked to make up the hours at a later time. If workers are laid off, they receive 80 percent of their wages. Unemployment benefits are paid by Lagun Aro, the social insurance program which is funded by 2 percent of workers earnings in 146 of the cooperatives. This covers 30,000 workers in the group. The fund contribution was raised from 1 percent in 2010 due to the higher costs during the recession. When workers are transferred to another firm, they receive a differential if their job in the other plant would be paid at a lower rate than they were paid in their home co-op. The social insurance also pays the cost of any retraining.[78]

Although it is not perfect, Mondragon continues to serve as an impressive example of successful cooperative and community development for a number of key elements. To begin with, it was developed in a hostile political environment and without government subsidies in the early years. More important, it has been a good, if not complete example of participatory organization extending from the individual workplace to the federation of businesses, serving the community, not only by providing jobs and generating income, but through providing services to the community (though not as extensively as in the case of the Mississippi Choctaw).

The cooperatives and the federation have attempted to operate inclusively and democratically internally, with the exception of foreign and joint ventures where they have been constrained by local law and business practice. They have worked to adopt that democracy to changing geographical, business, and economic circumstances. The model could be improved upon, particularly by a higher degree of participation in workplaces, including the utilization of appropriate forms of full team process as exemplified by such firms as Gore & Associates, discussed in the proceeding chapter.

Particularly notable is that, largely because of its collaborative process and staying consistent with the usually high performance of participatory workplaces, the Mondragon cooperatives have been strikingly successful economically. They produce a significantly higher return on capital than conventional businesses in Spain. With the assistance of their development bank they have been able to grow rapidly, adopt to new conditions easily, and weather harsh economic times, usually without layoffs and without business failures. It was exceptional that in the extremely deep Great Recession, they were forced to close three enterprises and layoff some workers with benefits. It is notable too that during the period after the 2008 recession, the Basque region has had a rate of unemployment consistently below that of the rest of Spain. Youth unemployment while high was also significantly less than the rest of Spain for the period 2008 to 2010.[79] Overall, the extent of success, and the dearth of failures has been phenomenal.

Significantly, with the Mondragon cooperatives, the Basque country continues to be a region dominated by locally owned and controlled businesses with a strong cooperative ownership of the firms, thus providing benefits for the local community with which it has collaborative relations. Moreover, the federation is a good example of how more democratically and organizationally effective small enterprises can have the economies of scale of large organizations, but with more flexibility and democracy than is usually possible in those bigger entities. For these reasons, it has had tremendous appeal as a model for building local economies, and as a basis for large scale participatory economies.

Implementing the Cooperative Federation Model

Just how the Mondragon model improved by making itself fully participatory from the shop floor to the center of the federation can apply elsewhere as well, though would vary according to the circumstances. Indeed, one of the strengths of Mondragon has been its flexibility in adapting to new conditions. Applications would involve the following principles to the specific conditions at hand, as they exist at the outset, and take into account projected needs for future developments.

First, and most important, as discussed in chapter 5, individual enterprises or organizations and their sub units need to be structured as flat, equalitarian, team process entities with full participation decision making from the shop floor, office, sales, or service unit to the center. Decisions also need be made by those who are impacted by them. Thus, issues involving a single unit or team would be decided by its members. Issues involving two or more units or teams would be jointly decided by them, or by an inter unit team or committee, with input from the members of the concerned teams who would have the opportunity to review and check, and perhaps to approve, the final decision. Issues involving an entire division, or the whole organization would be decided at those levels in a similar fashion.

Therefore, an organization would operate as a network of participatory teams. In turn, individual organizations would network participatively with each other, and, where appropriate, be parts of highly democratic federations. As appropriate, an enterprise could also be involved in multiple networks and possibly more than one federation, for different purposes, so long as the basic principles of participatory economy were preserved in balance. For example, a firm making computers might be part of a local business federation or network; an industry network or collaborative organization for research and development, and perhaps political representation; and possibly separate networks or cooperative organizations for purchasing supplies, obtaining certain services, and marketing.

Also, as appropriate, it might be advisable to mix organization member participation with customer or community input; for example, in consumer cooperatives that have employee participation. The simplicity or complexity of organization and participation structures should depend on circumstances, and change with them, consistent with the basic principles of participatory organizations in participatory society.

Second, the system of incentives or rewards needs to be appropriate to engage members meaningfully as owners while enhancing the goals of the organization and wider public goods.[80] Participation in decision making, when it is genuine and of good quality, is rewarding. It provides a feeling of ownership and solidarity with the unit, the organization and fellow workers, and tends to promote good organizational behavior. Collaborative education, good respectful and collaborative standards of behavior and treatment, and other moral incentives may also have an important role. This can include awards or statements of praise for good work or behavior, and penalties or reprimands for inappropriate or inadequate actions. But like other incentives, to promote solidarity with the group and organization, they need to function in a fashion that team members consider fair and appropriate. Otherwise they create dissention, even if they attain some of the intended behavior.

Also important are concrete rewards which can be in money, services and/or material commodities (e.g. food, housing, use of vehicles or equipment) sufficient to make members be and feel fairly treated by the organization. These need to be structured so as to promote good work as a team member, and member of the organization as a whole. Thus, team awards for productivity increases, cost savings, organization profit, or income sharing are generally appropriate. But individual piecework payments are not, except in limited amounts for special purposes, as they tend to promote competition rather than collaboration among team members.

It may also be desirable to have financial rewards that are either, or both, immediate incentives and/or promote long term concern for the organization. As immediate feedback often makes incentives more effective, rewards for productivity increases or profit sharing over short periods, for example over the month or quarter, may be advisable. At the same time long term commitment to the organization can be promoted by practices like payments into retirement accounts such as the workers accounts at Mondragon, or into US 401k and employee stock ownership plans (ESOPS) retirement accounts.

Another consideration in structuring incentives is to give team members a sense of reasonable security. This can be accomplished by having a sufficiently high basic wage, with other variable rewards or compensation above that. The ultimate key is to have the appropriate balance of rewards and incentives which fit the circumstances. To promote solidarity and organizational commitment in a cooperative organization, this means limiting the earnings differential between the highest and lowest compensated team, organization, or federation member, as has been done at Mondragon. Also, as discussed above, for a participatory society, it is important to have a reasonably equal distribution of wealth, which can be accomplished through a limited range of compensation or income and/or a progressive tax structure that is sufficiently steep at its high end.

Third, to properly mix the needs of small individual enterprises and other organizations with economies of scale and adequate provision of member and organization needs, a number of services need to be provided by the cooperative federation itself; by external organizations including other federations; or by government, as illustrated by the case of Mondragon. One of the strengths of the federation has been having its own bank and business incubation. Similarly, the federation has been indebted to having its own research and development cooperatives, while it created housing and educational cooperatives, until sufficient housing was otherwise available and the Spanish government provided much of the needed free university education.

It is important to note that cooperatives are a flexible form, and that all kinds of cooperatives are possible, including adapting them to new and changing conditions. In addition to what we have already discussed, are producer cooperatives, as have been used by artists, artisans, and small farmers to market their products.[81] For example, the internet has spawned platform cooperatives in which individual producers market through websites.[82] Services can be cooperatively provided over the internet with apps, along the lines of taxi and limousine service as carried out by firms such as Uber, linking drivers to rides. In the cooperative version of such services, the drivers or other service providers would own the cooperative, as is the case with Union Cab in Madison, Wisconsin.[83]

Finally, as the goal of a collaborative economy is to provide a well working society for all its citizens, it is important that individual participatory enterprises and cooperative federations have good collaborative relations with the larger communities of which they are a part. This has been achieved, in part, at Mondragon not only by providing needed employment and income in the community, but in such actions as launching consumer cooperative stores and restaurants, while also sponsoring Basque clubs and cultural activities. Similarly, in the instance of the Mississippi Choctaw, a considerable amount of economic development was undertaken jointly by the tribe and the nearby municipality, creating employment both for tribal members and citizens of neighboring communities. Meanwhile, among other things, the tribe has provided ambulance service both for its members and people in the surrounding community. This is all part of the aim of a collaborative society with a participatory economy to honor and enjoy the benefits of diversity in the context of a fully integrated society of friendly relations and mutual support, living harmoniously with its neighbors and the physical environment.

Section 3: Transnational Economic Relations

The relationship of communities to each other, as we have seen, is extremely important for their wellbeing. It has been shown, in the Mississippi Choctaw case, that collaborative relations between communities within a nation are extremely beneficial to the concerned communities, though even in the best of relationships there are always conflicts. However, it was also shown in the discussion on restorative justice in the preceding chapter, it is beneficial for everyone involved for the parties to see a conflict as an opportunity to undertake collaborative problem solving for mutual advancement. This is equally true internationally.

For the purpose of this discussion, there are two areas of the very complex field of transnational economics where it is important for nations to maintain as much balance as is practicable: in having appropriate tariffs and regulations on imports, and in moving to equalize wealth and quality of life among nations, so far as possible. For in the contemporary world, what happens anywhere has significant impacts everywhere, and this is more and more the case, as independent actions increasingly impact the international stage.

Maintaining an Appropriate Balance in Trade

Neoclassical economists often assert the great value of tearing down tariffs and international trade barriers, and moving to "free trade." Experience shows that just as they like to tell us that "there is no such thing as a free lunch," in pointing out that everything has costs as well as benefits, these economists need to realize "there is no such thing as free trade." One nation or set of interests almost always benefits at the expense of the others under so-called "free trade." Thus for at least one nation it will always be "expensive trade." While different people gain or lose differently in any trade arrangement, over all, beginning with the North American Free Trade Agreement (NAFTA), instituted in 1994, among the United States, Mexico, and Canada "free trade" agreements have been very costly for the United States. Indeed the overall impact of NAFTA was negative for all three countries. The major beneficiaries were a small group of multinational corporations and their stockholders.

Prior to the institution of NAFTA, the agreement's supporters predicted that the US and Canada would gain far more jobs than would be lost from NAFTA's implementation.[84] At least through 2001 the reverse was true, particularly in manufacturing. Analysis shows that, overall, the net impact was a loss of jobs in the United States, and a slowing of economic development in Mexico. Particularly telling in Mexico was the impact upon agriculture, where a few producers, particularly of grains, gained, while many others suffered considerable losses. International food imports into Mexico from the US often sold below Mexican small farmers' production costs, driving them out of business. This was certainly the case with the import into Mexico of US government subsidized corn, which sold in Mexico at lower prices than Indigenous people could produce it. This triggered the Zapatista revolution, leading to increased repression of some Indigenous communities by the government and paramilitary groups.

There are substantial food exports from Mexico to the United States, but predominantly by large farmers, most especially by multinational corporations.[85] This tends to concentrate wealth, as most of the income to the business goes to owners and upper level managers, and less to the lower level laborers who are by far the largest part of these workforces. One of the difficulties is that free market arrangements such as NAFTA tend to drive wages (and hence living standards) down in the developed world, when what needs to be done is to focus on bringing wages and living standards up in the underdeveloped world, an issue to be discussed below.

NAFTA and the other essentially similar free trade agreements are only part of much larger economic problems across and between nations caused by neoliberal approaches to the globalization that is sweeping the world. These problems need to be overcome by a broader approach which aims at creating and maintaining balance in various dimensions, as discussed below. The larger free trade problem indicated by the agricultural problems that arose from NAFTA in Mexico is shown more fully by what happened to manufacturing in the United States, and to other aspects of the US economy with the application of neoliberal economics, including free trade, beginning with the Reagan administration in 1980.[86]

Launching with Alexander Hamilton's eleven-point plan in 1791 to build manufacturing in the United States, until the Reagan administration in 1980, US economic policy was to protect and enhance the growth of industry in the country with tariffs. Numerous factors were involved, but this and related assistance to industrial development policy played a major role in the United States becoming, and for some time remaining, the world's largest manufacturing country. In 1980 the US was the world's largest creditor nation, related to the fact that it was the largest importer of raw materials and exporter of manufactured goods. In the 1960s about 37 percent of the US labor force worked in manufacturing.[87] That declined somewhat to about 30 percent by 1980, because of the ongoing combination of improved productivity in industry and heightened demand for services.

Also, foreign competition increased, especially from East Asian nations who worked very actively to build and protect manufacturing, including exports.[88] This has generally continued, but after 1980 became a minor factor, when President Reagan began vetoing tariff legislation and undertook other free trade action. Bill Clinton and later Presidents then expanded the free trade policy with participation in international trade agreements such as the General Agreement on Tariffs and Trade (GATT) and the World Trade Organization (WTO),[89] and with NAFTA and later economic alliances.

Almost entirely, as a result the United States had so much of its manufacturing move oversees that by 2012 it had been transformed into the world's largest debtor, as the balance of trade reversed, and the United States had become the world's largest exporter of raw materials and the world's largest importer of manufactured goods. For a huge number of products made in the United States prior to 1980, it is virtually impossible to find any in stores in 2015 that are US-made. During the 2000–2010 decade alone, 50,000 manufacturing plants closed down in the US at a loss of 5 million jobs. Many of these jobs have been replaced by service jobs, but these generally have been considerably lower paying. Moreover, with the neoliberal reduction in tax rates on higher incomes and reductions in corporate taxes begun under Reagan, since 1980 US wages, which had been rising along with productivity, have essentially remained level. At the same time, productivity, along with top executive compensation and corporate profits largely going to the wealthy and institutions, have continued to increase.[90]

International trade agreements have also increased environmental problems, and have had other negative side effects. For example, firms have often moved to locations where there are fewer environmental, labor, and other regulations. NAFTA was supposed to include environmental protections, but instead only continued the environmental decline. This was particularly so in the free trade zone in Mexico where numerous companies based themselves where environmental enforcement was less than in the United States, and where considerable pollution further degraded the local and sometimes even the world environment.[91]

Mexico's problems from trade agreements have also been related to, and worsened by, other internationally imposed neoliberal policies. This began with Mexico's agreement with the International Monetary Fund (IMF) to restructure its massive foreign debt in 1982, which preceded the creation of NAFTA. This move contributed to the East European post-communist economic and quality of life decline—one piece of the transition to the market program adopted by all nine countries is particularly relevant for this discussion.[92] The combination of rapidly privatizing state owned enterprises, without making any investment to hedge against the ensuing drop in the price of oil, a major Mexican export, left Mexico unable to keep up with foreign debt payments. Subsequently it agreed to a "structural adjustment program" (SAP) with the IMF in order to restructure the debt.

SAP was intended to make Mexico more competitive in the world economy and thus more able to pay its debt by cutting government expenditures and reducing regulations and tariffs, to make Mexico more open to the international market. The result was just the opposite, however. Mexico's ability to pay its foreign debt became weakened as many sectors of the economy were undermined, while under the terms of the agreement with IMF, the government was less able to act to create economic development or to assist those who were suffering from the economic decline. NAFTA exacerbated the situation by further reducing tariffs and the government's ability to regulate.

At the end of NAFTA's first year, Mexico was suffering economic collapse with the peso suddenly losing half its value. In the following year, more than two million people lost their jobs in Mexico, 1.8 million peasants and Indigenous farmers were forced to leave their homes, and the purchasing power of the average wage declined by 54 percent as inflation in 1995 soared 50 percent. One-third of

Mexican businesses declared bankruptcy in the first nine months of that year, and the gross domestic product declined by 7 percent.

East European Problems with Neoliberal Economics and Free Trade

Similar problems with the adoption of neoliberal economic policies were experienced by former Soviet bloc East European countries on their exit from communist economies after 1989. While numerous neoliberal economic policies contributed to the East European post-communist economic and quality of life decline, one piece of the transition to the market program adopted by all nine countries is particularly relevant to this discussion.[93] This was the combination of rapidly privatizing state owned enterprises without making any investment to improve their ability to produce marketable products, while ending subsidies and eliminating tariffs and other import barriers.

Among other ill effects, this led to potentially viable firms being unable to compete with imported products, leading to drops in production, increasing unemployment, and a worsening balance of payments, as sales of imports rose and sales of domestic products declined. A better strategy would have been to invest in the improvement of potentially viable firms prior to privatizing them, and selectively and progressively lowering import duties leading to domestic enterprise productivity and efficiency rising and stimulating continued growth in competitiveness. From 1968 to 1975, Hungary made significant gains with just such a policy for liberalizing its communist economy.[94] Similarly, the economic advancement since World War II achieved by a number of East Asian nations was accomplished by a careful process of incubation in which governments played a major role, in contrast to the neoliberal approach.[95]

However, the very aggressive approach of a number of east Asian nations, doing anything they could get away with to keep foreign competition out of their home markets while taking excessive action to gain market share abroad at almost any cost (often by "dumping", i.e., selling products at a considerable loss, often with government financial support), went too far to the other extreme from free market policies. An appropriately balanced import policy would follow the principles of Hungary's example: for mature industries, setting tariffs and import restrictions just high enough to make up for a foreign nation's lower labor cost, foreign government subsidies, and lower costs because of lack of regulation. This would tend to keep domestic firms competitive, while pressuring them to operate efficiently and effectively.

With developing or transitioning industries, an appropriate policy would be to do just what Hungary did; set tariffs and import regulations (or conversely, provide offsetting levels of subsidies or other incubation assistance) progressively lower to match increases in productivity of developing domestic firms. In addition, foreign firms could be penalized with higher tariffs or import regulations for their own or their nation's improper actions, such as inhumane labor practices or contributing to environmental degradation.[96]

Appropriately achieving such balanced policies is often politically difficult. However, in a sufficiently equalitarian participatory nation, there is likely to be an adequate diffusion of power and balance of interests so that with good participatory problem solving processes, reasonable solutions should be achievable in balancing the interests of industries and their employees through sufficient tariff and regulation protection on one side, with consumer interest in low prices and product availability. Moreover, since finding such a balance is generally in the long term economic interest of most people, there is a common interest in finding a balance that is encouraged to come to the fore by the kinds of good participatory processes discussed in the preceding chapter.

Moving Away from Harmful Neoliberal Globalization toward a Balanced World Economy

The neoliberal globalization which has been in progress in the world through the World Bank, the World Trade Organization and a growing series of treaties, plus the policies of some nations, has caused considerable problems for numerous nations, and generally favored the concentration of wealth in a few individuals and multinational corporations, at the short run expense of most everyone else. Because neoliberal policies tend to cause long range harms, such as the increase of global warming induced climate change, discussed in the next chapter, and other serious instabilities, in the longer term these measures are against everyone's interest. Much of the problem with neoliberal economics is that, with its very narrow focus, it suffers from a serious reductionism, that includes failing to take into account numerous externalities and essential public goods—particularly concerning social costs—as well as failing to include, or properly understand, important factors that are central to its concerns. This is made clearer by considering, briefly, a few more aspects of neoliberal globalization.

Among other problems, neoliberal globalization has encouraged the development of crops for export at the expense of food self-sufficiency. This often involves reducing agricultural diversity (in itself an ecological concern) in order to produce one or a few crops for export. While there are benefits of foreign trade, there are also risks, especially when food self-sufficiency is reduced, because international prices for agricultural produce (and raw materials where economic development focuses upon extracting minerals for export) often fluctuate widely. For example, the Americas Program reported in March 2004 that coffee, which is not indigenous to Mexico, had evolved into a central aspect of economic, social and cultural life with 320,000 growers, 65 percent of whom are Indigenous, mostly on small farms in twelve states, employing more than three million people, in rural areas directly affecting 25 percent of the population economically.[97] Eighty-four percent of Mexico's coffee-growing townships had high or very high levels of poverty, in 2004. Eighty-five percent of Mexico's coffee was exported. International prices paid to producers had dropped severely over the preceding years, with Mexican growers receiving record lows in 2002.

At that time, coffee growers were unable to break even, but the lack of other options kept them trapped in a downward spiral. Producers were left with few defenses in the neoliberal global context. This was largely the result of neoliberal economic policies having brought the Mexican government to dismantle the national production-processing-marketing board (Mexican Coffee Institute-Inmecafe) in 1989. Thus most growers were left to function on their own, without the resources or infrastructure to deal effectively with the buying oligopoly. The same problem occurs with raw materials where economic development focuses upon extracting minerals for export.

Another major difficulty has been the increase of large multinational corporations taking part in a variety of large scale economic projects. These, most often, force local, often Indigenous, people off their land and/or do huge damage to the environment, so it is no longer a viable place for the inhabitants of the surrounding area to live, and frequently causes massive serious health problems.[98] Such projects have included mining and drilling for oil, building dams to produce electric power—sometimes for export, and constructing large farming operations, particularly for palm oil.

While the World Bank and the International Monetary Fund have been funding some of these mass development projects (but have become more conscious of the harm some of them cause), and several aspects of neoliberal economic policies have been facilitating them, the problems of extraction and large scale development extend beyond neoliberal approaches.

Perhaps no nation has done as much damage to its environment and people with its large scale efforts at development as China in its aggressive nationalist economics mode,[99] and other nations whose economic policies are less easily classified, have also undertaken destructive development, failing to realize the need to define it as human and community development, as laid out above

An overview of the problems of neoliberal globalization fostered by the United States government, the World Bank, and the

International Monetary Fund was published in 2002. A global network of more than one thousand nongovernmental organizations (NGOs), the Structural Adjustment Participatory Review International Network (SAPRIN), completed a four-year review in 2002 of the impact of the World Bank's structural adjustments program (imposing austerity measures on governments and encouraging privatization of public services) with the aim of improving national economic performance and reducing external debt.

The report, "The Policy Roots of Economic Crises and Poverty," concluded that structural adjustment measures had significantly increased poverty, inequality, and social exclusion in the ten countries studied. This resulted in loss of domestic productive capacity and jobs; a reduction in small farm agriculture which brought on food insecurity; diminishing real wages, workers' rights and job security; and reduced access to affordable quality services.[100]

Following the imposition of structural adjustment policies, some reduction in the rise of external debt did occur. However, since the economies were weakened by the structural adjustments, those policies cannot be credited with the small reduction in the increase of external debt (and even if they were the entire cause, the cost would hardly be worth the relatively small gain).

A little over a decade later, many of the negative trends noted in the SAPRIN study were found to have significantly worsened, though changes in the politics and policies of some of the nations in that study, particularly in Latin America, had achieved much improved economic and human results. The Organization for Economic Cooperation and Development (OECD) 2014 study, "How Was Life? Global Well-Being Since 1820," used historical data from eight world regions to present "systematic evidence" of trends in areas such as health, education, inequality, the environment, and personal security over the past two hundred years.[101] The report found that great strides had been made in some areas, including literacy, life expectancy, and gender equality, noting that "People's well-being has generally progressed since the early twentieth century across a large part of the world."

However, while income inequality, as measured by pre-tax household income among individuals within a country, fell between the end of the nineteenth century until around 1970, it began to rise markedly at that point, perhaps in response to globalization. The study noted:

The enormous increase of income inequality on a global scale is one of the most significant—and worrying—features of the development of the world economy in the past 200 years. It is hard not to notice the sharp increase in income inequality experienced by the vast majority of countries from the 1980s. There are very few exceptions to this.

OECD secretary-general Angel Gurría, noting the impacts of the still present Great Recession, called on world leaders to:

strengthen our efforts to reduce inequality. The financial and economic crisis has exacerbated rising inequality and fueled a social crisis. In OECD countries the income of the top 10 percent of the population is 9.5 times that of the bottom 10 percent, up by more than 30 percent in 25 years. Anchored poverty has increased by approximately 2 percentage points between 2007 and 2011, with much larger increases in countries that have experienced the deepest and longest downturns. The number of those living in households without any income from work has doubled in Greece, Ireland, and Spain. And worryingly for our future, the youth have now replaced the elderly as the group experiencing the greatest risk of income poverty.

An Overall Approach to Appropriate Globalization

To restore balance and harmony to the world, an approach to international economics is needed that avoids the extremes of neoliberal globalization with its "leave everything to the market" and "free trade approaches" on the one side—which allow almost free rein to extremely wealthy multinational corporations—and on the other of aggressive nationalistic policies found in some East Asian nations.[102] What is needed are policies that respect each nation and all their inhabitants, along with the world environment and all its local ecosystems, while working to bring balance among the nations of the world. This is an Indigenous approach. Since Indigenous people have in many instances been suffering the worst impacts of both neoliberal globalization and national neoliberal policies, and in some cases of aggressive nationalist policies, some of them have been organizing and networking in participatory processes to work toward putting an Indigenous face on golbalization.[103]

The main thrust of such an approach to globalization would involve countries having fair trade levels of tariffs and import regulations just to the point of putting their own businesses on an even playing field with foreign firms, as developed above. In addition, countries would be involved in a respectful system of collaboration and assistance to facilitate less developed nations and communities in raising their living standards to equivalents of those of the more developed world. This would require a transformation of international institutions, including the World Bank and the International Monetary Fund, to function transparently following this approach, focusing on raising everyone up, rather than moving toward equalization by pulling nations down—which is a net effect of many of the current approaches—which are in fact increasing disparities.

This would involve appropriate participatory consulting with all the people involved in a target area in the course of providing funding, appropriate technology transfer, and technical assistance according to the wishes of the receiving people, and within the guidelines of the assistance project. Appropriate transfers of capital and technology are needed, taking into account long run impacts, especially concerning the environment.[104] In the face of the huge dangers, and the already occurring damage from global warming induced climate change, moving technology towards safe renewable energy and other green development, with financial transfers to put them into effect, are essential.

Currently, just as financial disparities are the causes of many tensions within nations, so they are between nations. Thus, steps must be taken, and vehicles put in place, to reduce the disparities appropriately. Where resources, such as water, are in short supply, collaborative transnational problem solving is needed on how best to conserve and share them, taking into account the interest and input of everyone concerned. So far as possible, the world needs to become more participatory and collaborative, selecting policies that in practice are for the long term good of all.

The Participatory Economy and Society Moving toward a Balanced World

We have seen in this chapter on economics and development, and the preceding chapter on politics, that, consistent with traditional Indigenous values, societies have the highest quality of life overall and for each citizen if they function as participatory networks with equalitarian relations among people, and good relations with the environment of which their citizens are a part. Economies are most productive and stable when they function bottom up, as networks of small participatory enterprises with appropriate vehicles for providing economies of scale in a well regulated market economy with wealth and economic power fairly equal.

To attain and maintain good societies with well working economies, governments have a duty to see that their economies are, and remain, well balanced, with equal market power, as well as by empowering citizens to have sufficient and equal opportunities to participate in society and the economy, with a high quality of life. This in turn requires developing and maintaining balanced relations with the physical environment, as well as with other nations, while moving toward balancing wealth, opportunity, and relationships with people and with the environment as a whole.

This can be achieved in part through establishing, and adjusting as necessary, appropriate institutions. But institutions cannot function well unless people understand the complexity of the issues and relationships that they need to be aware of, and to deal with, as developed in the next chapter, "Indigenizing the Greening of the World: Applying an Indigenous Approach to Environmental Issues." This in turn can only be realized with appropriate education, the foundation of a well-functioning society, which is the focus of the final chapter, "Facilitating the Unfolding of the Circle: Indigenizing Education for the Twenty-First Century."

Notes to Chapter 6

1. Reductionism is the narrowing of concern to the specific factors that appear most relevant. This can be a powerful tool, as has been the case in Western science, but often fails to address many factors that may be extremely important, leading to false understandings and actions producing unintended, sometimes quite serious, side effects. As is developed below, this has been a serious shortcoming of much of mainstream Western economics. For a further discussion of reductionism, see the opening of the next chapter, "Indigenizing the Greening of the World: Applying an Indigenous Approach to Environmental Issues."

2. Ladislov Rusmich and Stephen M. Sachs, *Lessons from the Failure of the Communist Economic System* (Lanham, MD: Lexington, 2003). Also that traditional, and some nontraditional, economics too narrowly consider human nature, see Albert O. Hirschman, *The Passions and the Interests: Political Arguments for Capitalism before Its Triumph* (Princeton, NJ: Princeton University Press, 2013); Albert O. Hirschman, *Essays in Trespassing: Economics to Politics and Beyond* (Cambridge: Cambridge University Press, 1981). For a good overview of mainstream economic theory, with discussion of many of the central debated issues, see Ernesto Screpanti and Stefano Zambagni, *An Outline of the History of Economic Thought* (Oxford: Oxford University Press, 1995).

3. The causes of the Arab Spring (and lack of it in some Arab countries) are complex, as shown in the discussion that, after some focus

on the role of media, briefly looks at other causes, among them several important economic factors. See Muzammil M. Hussain and Philip N. Howard, "What Best Explains Successful Protest Cascades? ICTs and the Fuzzy Causes of the Arab Spring," *International Studies Review* 15, no. 1 (2013), http://onlinelibrary.wiley.com/doi/10.1111/misr.12020/full. A similar but somewhat different analysis, also showing economic conditions among the causes, is Filipe R. Campante and Davin Chor, "Why Was the Arab World Poised for Revolution? Schooling, Economic Opportunities, and the Arab Spring," *Journal of Economic Perspectives* 26, no. 2 (2012): 167–87, http://www.jstor.org/stable/41495309.

4. Peter H. Gleick, "Water, Drought, Climate Change, and Conflict in Syria," *Weather, Climate, and Society* 6, no. 3 (2014), http://journals.ametsoc.org/doi/abs/10.1175/WCAS-D-13-00059.1; Francesca De Chantel, "The Role of Drought and Climate Change in the Syrian Uprising Untangling the Triggers of the Revolution," *Middle Eastern Studies* 50, no. 4 (2016).

5. Michel Reich, *A Political Economy of Racism* (Princeton, NJ: Princeton University Press, 1981); Charles W. Mills and Tom Mills, "Racism and the Political Economy of Dominion," *New Left Project*, April 12, 2012, http://www.newleftproject.org/index.php/site/article_comments/racism_and_the_political_economy_of_domination.

6. Andrew Higgins, "Populists' Rise in Europe Vote Shakes Leaders," *New York Times*, May 26, 2014, http://www.nytimes.com/2014/05/27/world/europe/established-parties-rocked-by-anti-europe-vote.html?ref=todayspaper, which states:

An angry eruption of populist insurgency in the elections for the European Parliament rippled across the Continent on Monday, unnerving the political establishment and calling into question the very institutions and assumptions at the heart of Europe's post-World War II order. Four days of balloting across 28 countries elected scores of rebellious outsiders, including a clutch of xenophobes, racists and even neo-Nazis. In Britain, Denmark, France and Greece, insurgent forces from the far right and, in Greece's case, also from the radical left stunned the established political parties. President François Hollande of France, whose Socialist Party finished third, far behind the far-right National Front, addressed his nation on television from the Élysée Palace on Monday evening, giving a mournful review of an election that he said had displayed the public's "distrust of Europe and of government parties." He added: "The European elections have delivered their truth, and it is painful."

7. From an Indigenous point of view, a proper economics is a "sociology," because it is about social relationships, including with the environment and all beings. This is in contrast to most of contemporary mainstream Western economics, which primarily focuses on monetary matters, often in terms of such things as profit and loss, monetary costs and benefits, efficiency and productivity in the use of resources (particularly from a monetary point of view), and so forth. All of these concerns are important in an Indigenous economics, as they affect relationships, but it is the relationships and the condition of the relating parties that is the primary concern.

To say that an Indigenously-oriented economics is a "sociology" is not to say that such an economics, or "sociology," necessarily uses the methods and concepts of any school of past of present Western sociology. It is just to point out its concern is primarily about the full set of relationships among people, and with the environment (encompassing all beings including the Earth), and with the condition of all entities. In this broad sense, the current Western disciplines of anthropology and sociology are both "sociologies," though they each use somewhat different concepts and methods, which has made difficult some attempts to merge them into a single discipline.

For example, see "What Are Sociology and Anthropology?" Gustavus Adolphus College, https://gustavus.edu/soc-anthro/sociologyandanthropology.php; Edward L. Kain, Theodore C. Wagenaar, and Carla B. Howary, "Models and Best Practices for Joint Sociology-Anthropology Departments," American Sociological Association, 2006, http://www.asanet.org/documents/teaching/pdfs/Sociology_and_Anthropology_Joint_Departments.pdf. Some might prefer to say that all the disciplines named above are social sciences. From an Indigenous viewpoint, however, much of contemporary Western economics is an asocial science because it does not sufficiently concern itself with social (and in terms of human beings alone, trans-social) relationships.

For a discussion of an Indigenous view of economics from an Amazonian Native perspective with contemporary application, see

Fernando Santos-Granero, ed., *Images of Public Wealth or the Anatomy of Well-Being in Indigenous Amazonia* (Tucson: University of Arizona Press, 2015).

8. Rusmich and Sachs, *Lessons from the Failure of the Communist Economic System*, 126. That the "invisible hand" of the market fails to have the beneficial effect of aligning private with public interest that laissez-faire economists claim for it, but instead leads to increased concentration of wealth and inequality of wealth while favoring private over public interests and encouraging a low-level of needed research and development activities, see three of John Kenneth Galbraith works: *The Affluent Society* (Boston: Houghton Mifflin, 1958), *The New Industrial State* (Princeton, NJ: Princeton University Press, 1967), and *Economics and Public Purpose* (Boston: Houghton Mifflin, 1973).

9. Rusmich and Sachs, *Lessons of the Failure of the Communist Economic System*, part 2. Galbraith discusses one aspect of keeping economies in balance through countervailing government power in *American Capitalism: The Concept of Countervailing Power* (Boston: Houghton Mifflin, 1952). A discussion of the advantages of having reasonable equality of wealth is Richard Wilkinson and Kate Pickett, *Spirit Level: Why Greater Equality Makes Societies Stronger* (London: Bloomsbury, 2010).

10. In addition to the discussion here and below in relation to the Mondragon Cooperatives, see Barry Stein, *Size, Efficiency, and Community Enterprise* (Cambridge, MA: Center for Community Economic Development, 1974), which provides some interesting consideration about the size of an organization and efficiency relating to its function.

11. Stephen G. Cecchetti and Enisse Kharroubi, "Why Does Financial Sector Growth Crowd Out Real Economic Growth?" BIS Working Papers 490, February 2015, http://www.bis.org/publ/work490.htm. The report is discussed in Gretchen Morgenson, "Smothered By a Boom in Banking," *New York Times*, February 28, 2015, http://www.nytimes.com/2015/03/01/business/economy/smothered-by-a-boom-in-banking.html?ref=todayspaper.

12. Ibid.; Luigi Zingales, *A Capitalism for the People: Recapturing the Lost Genius of American Prosperity* (New York: Basic, 2012). On financial sector wage inequality, see Thomas Philippon and Ariell Reshef, "Wages and Human Capital in the U.S. Financial Industry, 1909–2006," National Bureau of Economic Research, Working Paper 14644, January 2009, http://www.nber.org/papers/w14644. On this and

other major systemic problems in the US economy, and what can be done to correct them, see Joseph E. Stiglitz, *Rewriting the Rules of the American Economy: An Agenda for Growth and Shared Prosperity* (New York: W. W. Norton, 2015).

13. John Kenneth Galbraith, *The Nature of Mass Poverty* (Cambridge, MA: Harvard University Press, 1979); John Kenneth Galbraith, *The Anatomy of Power* (Boston: Houghton Mifflin, 1983).

14. Thom Hartmann, *The Crash of 2016* (New York: Twelve, 2013), chap. 4, particularly 65–66.

15. Landon Thomas Jr., "Europe Fears Bailout of Spain Would Strain Its Resources," *New York Times*, May 30, 2012, http://www.nytimes.com/2012/05/31/business/global/if-spain-is-rescued-who-foots-the-bill.html; Andrew Higgins, "Europe Facing More Pressure to Reconsider Cuts as a Cure," *New York Times*, April 26, 2013, http://www.nytimes.com/2013/04/27/world/europe/eu-is-pressed-to-reconsider-cuts-as-economic-cure.html.

16. Raphael Minder, "Bailout Is Over for Portugal, But Side Effects Will Linger," *New York Times*, May 5, 2014, http://www.nytimes.com/2014/05/06/business/international/bailout-is-over-for-portugal-but-side-effects-will-linger.html.

17. Paul Krugman, "Europe's Greek Test," *New York Times*, January 30, 2015; "The European Debt Crisis: News about European Debt Crisis, Including Commentary and Archival Articles Published in the *New York Times*," *New York Times*, http://topics.nytimes.com/top/reference/timestopics/subjects/e/european_sovereign_debt_crisis/index.html?8qa.

18. "Hitler into Power," Bitsize, BBC, http://www.bbc.co.uk/schools/gcsebitesize/history/mwh/germany/hitlerpowerrev1.shtml, 1.

19. "Timelines of the Great Depression," World History Online, http://www.hyperhistory.com/online_n2/connections_n2/great_depression.html.

20. John Maynard Keynes, *The General Theory of Employment, Interest, and Money* [1936] (London: Macmillan, 2007).

21. Paul Krugman, *The Return of Depression Economics and the Crisis of 2008* (New York: W. W. Norton, 2009); Paul Krugman, "How Much of the World Is in a Liquidity Trap?," *New York Times*, March 17, 2010, http://krugman.blogs.nytimes.com/2010/03/17/how-much-of-the-world-is-in-a-liquidity-trap/?_r=0; Janet L. Yellen, "A Minsky Meltdown: Lessons for Central Bankers," Federal Reserve Bank of San Francisco, April 16, 2009, http://www.frbsf.org/

our-district/press/presidents-speeches/yellen-speeches/2009/april/
yellen-minsky-meltdown-central-bankers/.

22. Hartmann, *The Crash of 2016*, chap. 1; Yellen, "A Minsky Meltdown: Lessons for Central Bankers." A listing, with brief discussions, of depressions and recessions in US history is included in "Economic History of the U.S.," San José State University, Department of Economics, http:// www.sjsu.edu/faculty/watkins/useconhist.htm#DEPRESSIONS.

23. On the savings and loan scandal: "Savings and Loan Scandal," In the 80s, http://www.inthe80s.com/sandl.shtml; T. Curry and L. Shibut, "The Cost of the Savings and Loan Crisis," *FDIC Banking Review* 13, no. 2 (2000): 26–35; G. A. Akerlof and P. M. Romer "Looting: The Economic Underworld of Bankruptcy for Profit," *Brookings Papers on Economic Activity* 2 (1993): 1–73. On the Great Recession: Hartmann, *The Crash of 2016*, chaps. 1, 6; David B. Grubsky, Bruce Western, and Christopher Wimer, eds., *The Great Recession* (New York: Russell Sage, 2011). On bubbles and speculation: Ronald R. King, Vernon L. Smith, Arlington W. Williams, and Mark van Boening, "The Robustness of Bubbles and Crashes in Experimental Stock Markets," in *Nonlinear Dynamics and Evolutionary Economics*, ed. by R. H. Day and P. Chen (New York: Oxford University Press, 1993); Paul Krugman, "Bernanke, Blower of Bubbles?," *New York Times*, May 9, 2013, http://www.nytimes. com/2013/05/10/opinion/krugman-bernanke-blower-of-bubbles. html?src=me&ref=general.

24. US Government Accountability Office, "Report to Congressional Requesters, Poverty in America: Economic Research Shows Adverse Impacts on Health Status and Other Social Conditions as well as the Economic Growth Rate," January 2007, http://www.gao.gov/new. items/d07344.pdf.

25. We emphasize "appropriate" because too often the measures taken do not really measure what is needed to be known, just as too often actions are not "appropriate" because they do not take into account everything significant in the circumstances. Western culture and science often fail to realize the extent of differences in different locations (in time or geography) or circumstances.

26. Congressional Budget Office, https://www.cbo.gov/.

27. US Government Accountability Office, "GAO: Summary of Performance and Financial Information Fiscal Year 2014," GAO-15-2SP, February 17, 2015, http://www.gao.gov/products/ GAO-15-2SP.

28. Osborne and Gaebler, *Reinventing Government*.

29. Measure for America of the Social Science Research Council, http://www.measureofamerica.org.
30. "The Measure of America 2013–2014," Measure of America, June 19, 2013, http://www.measureofamerica.org/measure_of_america2013-2014/.
31. Opportunity Nation, http://opportunitynation.org/opportunity-index/.
32. Manchester College Peace Studies Institute and the Bentley Alliance for Ethics and Social Responsibility, *The 2007 National Index of Violence and Harm*, December 17, 2007.
33. On the application of the personal index to structural violence, see ibid. On the experimental economic work of Banerjee, Duflo, and Kremer, see Jeanna Smialek, "Nobel Economics Prize Goes to Pioneers in Reducing Poverty: Three Professors, Abhijit Banerjee and Esther Duflo, both of M.I.T., and Michael Kremer of Harvard, were honored," *New York Times*, October 14, 2019, https://www.nytimes.com/2019/10/14/business/nobel-economics.html.
34. Intergovernmental Panel on Climate Change, http://ipcc.ch.
35. "Fuel Economy," US Environmental Protection Agency, https://www.epa.gov/fueleconomy.
36. "Renewable Energy Standards," SEIA: Solar Industries Association, http://www.seia.org/policy/renewable-energy-deployment/renewable-energy-standards.
37. Nika Knight, "New Report Details Big Oil's $500 Million Annual Climate Obstructionism," *Common Dreams*, April 7, 2016, http://www.commondreams.org/news/2016/04/07/new-report-details-big-oils-500-million-annual-climate-obstructionism, which reported:

While the world came together in Paris to embrace climate action in 2015, Exxon was doubling down with Big Tobacco tactics and obstruction.

The dark channels through which corporations influence legislation are notoriously hard to trace, but a new detailed report estimates that the world's largest fossil fuel companies are spending upwards of $500 million per year to obstruct climate laws.

Published Thursday by the UK-based nonprofit InfluenceMap, the report (pdf) looked at two fossil fuel giants (ExxonMobil and Royal Dutch Shell) and three trade lobbying groups, discovering that all together the five companies spend $114 million a year to defeat climate change legislation.

More significantly, InfluenceMap says: "Extrapolated over the entire fossil fuel and other industrial sectors beyond, it is not hard to consider that this obstructive climate policy lobbying spending may be in the order of $500m annually."

"It's remarkably useful to see exactly how much Exxon and its brethren are still spending to bend the climate debate," responded (pdf) Bill McKibben of 350.org in a statement. "There's a shamelessness here that hopefully will be harder to maintain in the full light of day."

The group drew particular attention to the sinister lobbying group American Petroleum Institute (API), "one of the best funded and most consistently obstructive lobbying forces for climate policy in the United States," as InfluenceMap notes:

With a budget in excess of $200m, we estimate, through a forensic analysis of its IRS filings and careful study of its lobbying, PR, media and advertising activities, that around $65m of this is highly obstructive lobbying against ambitious climate policy. We estimate that ExxonMobil and Shell contribute $6m and $3m respectively to API's obstructive spending of $65m. Its CEO Jack Gerard received annual compensation of just over $14m in 2013, probably one of the world's highest paid lobbyists. In the run up to COP21 last year, he dismissed the Paris process as a "narrow political ideology."

InfluenceMap created the report to help concerned investors see how fossil fuel corporations were obstructing legislation to combat climate change. Since the #ExxonKnew scandal broke last year, such tactics have been under increased scrutiny from shareholders. "So far in 2016 alone," the nonprofit said, "there have been over 15 shareholder resolutions filed by investors in the US with fossil fuel companies on the issue of influence over climate policy."

In addition, the "sheer fuzziness of corporate influence prompted the project," wrote *Bloomberg.* "Nations hold companies to different standards—or none at all—for disclosures of how they are trying to influence public policy and what it costs."

Bloomberg explained the study's methodology:

To come up with its numbers, Influence Map first had to define what "influence" actually means. The researchers adopted a framework spelled out in a 2013 UN report written to help companies align their climate change policies with their lobbying and communications strategies. It's a broad approach to understanding influence that includes not only direct lobbying, but also advertising, marketing, public relations, political contributions, regulatory contacts, and trade associations.

Unfortunately, though, because of poor regulatory standards the "new report excludes so-called dark money, or money spent on think tanks and institutes, as identified by Drexel University sociologist Robert Brulle in 2013," *Bloomberg* said, because "the researchers were unable to determine how these groups are funded."

"We now know that Exxon knew about climate change impacts for decades, and kept the public in the dark while they lobbied to prevent meaningful action," Vermont Gov. Peter Shumlin pointed out. "This report shows that while the world came together in Paris to embrace climate action in 2015, Exxon was doubling down with Big Tobacco tactics and obstruction. We cannot change this corporation by engaging with it, we must instead bring change from the outside by using economic pressure and divesting from Exxon."

On conservative opposition to environmental regulation, see Judith A. Layzer, *Open for Business: Conservatives' Opposition to Environmental Regulation* (Cambridge, MA: MIT Press, 2014), which presents a detailed analysis of the policy effects of conservatives' decades-long effort to dismantle the federal regulatory framework for environmental protection.

38. Yong Geng, Joseph Sarkis, and Sergio Ulgiati, "Sustainability, Wellbeing, and the Circular Economy in China and World Wide," in *Pushing the Boundaries of Scientific Research: 120 Years of Addressing*

Global Issues [supplement to *Science*] (Washington, DC: American Association for the Advancement of Science, 2016), 73–76.

39. The problem of having adequate data, including sufficient consistency across time, is illuminated by the case of American Indians and Alaska Natives as discussed in LaDonna Harris, Stephen M. Sachs, and Barbara Morris, *Re-Creating the Circle: The Renewal of American Indian Self Determination* (Albuquerque: University of New Mexico Press, 2011), chap. 2. Similarly, this has been a sufficient problem for Indigenous peoples worldwide that the issue has been discussed repeatedly by the UN Permanent Forum on Indigenous Issues (UNPFII), including at a session devoted to the topic at the annual forum in April–May 2015, including at the 8th and 9th meetings (April 24, 2015), "Representatives of Indigenous Peoples Detail Challenges in Protecting Lands, Rights, as First Week of Permanent Forum Concludes," UN Economic and Social Council, http://www.un.org/press/en/2015/hr5247.doc.htm. This is also reported in the discussion of the UNPFII 2015 session in "International Developments," in *Indigenous Policy* 27, no. 1 (2015).

One set of examples of the problem of politics interfering with making correct data and information available for the discussion of public issues has occurred in several states in the United States that are controlled by Republicans. They have not allowed scientific reporting of dangers to health and well-being related to carbon energy production, because of lobbying by extracting and energy producing industries. This is discussed in Marcia McNutt, "Integrity: Not Just a Federal Issue," *Science* 347, no. 6229 (2015).

40. There is some useful discussion on measures and indicators, including the problems involved in working with them, in "Equal Access Participatory Monitoring and Evaluation Toolkit," BetterEvaluation, http://betterevaluation.org/sites/default/files/EA_PM%26E_toolkit_module_2_objectives%26indicators_for_publication.pdf; Garry M. Klass, *Just Plain Data Analysis: Finding, Presenting, and Interpreting Social Science Data* (Lanham, MD: Roman & Littlefield, 2008). The issue of quantitative versus qualitative research is considered, to an extent, in "Quantitative and Qualitative Research," Explorable, https://explorable.com/quantitative-and-qualitative-research.

41. On Amartya Sen's approach to development, see Charles W. L. Hill, *International Business* (New York: McGraw-Hill Irwin, 2004), 29. A partial, but fairly extensive, sampling of successful tribal development by

a number of Indian nations is in the economic development section of Harris, Sachs, and Morris, *Re-Creating the Circle*, chap. 5, sec. 1.

42. Ibid., especially chap. 2, giving an overview of continuing impacts of physical and cultural genocide (continued in each following section on an area of renewal work) and chap. 4, "Harmony Through Wisdom of the People: Applying Traditional Principles to Develop Appropriate and Effective Indian Tribal Governance."

43. Ibid., chap. 5, pt. 1.

44. This Afghani case was discussed in Professor Morton Kaplan's introduction to an international politics class at the University of Chicago in the spring of 1961. Also confirmed and elaborated on in a discussion with an Afghani who had lived near the dam site and Stephen Sachs.

45. Harris, Sachs, and Morris, *Re-Creating the Circle*, chap. 6.

46. Ibid., chap. 5, pt. 1, which also develops additional examples of American Indian economic development as tribal and member development; Sharon O'Brien, *American Indian Tribal Governments* (Norman: University of Oklahoma Press, 1989), chap. 1. For updates on Choctaw tribal affairs, including economic development, go to the tribe's website: http://www.choctaw.org (used in this report). Also see Mississippi Band of Choctaw Indians, *Choctaw Industrial Park* (Philadelphia, MS: Mississippi Band of Choctaw Indians, 1982); John H. Peterson Jr., "Three Efforts at Development Among the Choctaws of Mississippi," in *Southeastern Indians since the Removal Era*, ed. Walter L. Williams (Athens: University of Georgia Press, 1979); "Indian and Indigenous Developments: U.S. Developments; Economic Developments," *Indigenous Policy* 14, no. 2 (2003).

47. Stephen M. Sachs, "Renewing the Circle: Thoughts on Preserving Indigenous Traditional Knowledge," *Indigenous Policy* 27, no. 2 (2015).

48. Mondragon Cooperative Corporation, http://www.mondragon-corporation.com. Note that the background to the writing of the Mondragon section of this chapter is that its principal author, Christina Clamp, has been a longtime researcher of the Mondragon cooperatives, has made numerous visits to Mondragon, and interviewed many of its members. Stephen Sachs, who contributed to this section, visited the cooperatives at Mondragon for ten days in 1984 on a group-study tour of worker cooperatives in Europe and has spoken with a number of researchers of Mondragon over the years about its development.

It should be noted that as of July 2017, a group of collaborating organizations in Boston were working along similar lines to the Mississippi Choctaw and the Mondragon Federation to create more equalitarian economic development in lower-income neighborhoods. The US Solidarity Economy Network (USSN) was functioning on the basis of solidarity, democracy, sustainability, and equity in race, class, and gender. It was planning projects according to the needs and conditions of the communities where they were to unfold. This has included developing worker-owned businesses, such as Cooperative Energy, Recycling, and Organics, which collects and composts waste food and selling the soil to farmers. Also included have been projects such as the Greater Boston Land Trust Network, a set of community-owned locations providing affordable housing, services, and urban farming to their neighborhoods. One USSN effort is the Boston Ejima Project, a democratically-controlled investment fund to assist development in low-income areas. Half of the fund's capital was raised from small donations, averaging a little more than $50, and the rest from a small group of nonprofit organizations working to further the solidarity economy (Chris Merriam, "Turning Capital Against Capitalism," *In These Times*, July 2017).

49. Larraitz Altuna Gabilondo, ed., *La Experiencia Cooperative de Mondragon* (Eskoriatza, Spain: Lanki, 2008), 265–88.

50. The principles that overlap with the International Cooperative Alliance are open membership, democratic control, intercooperation, education, and a concern for community which is embedded in the social transformation principle ("Co-operative Identity, Values, and Principles," International Cooperative Alliance, http://ica. coop/en/whats-co-op/co-operative-identity-values-principles).

51. Gabilondo, ed., *La Experiencia Cooperative de Mondragon*, 267.

52. Ibid., 270.

53. Ibid., 271.

54. Ibid., 273.

55. Ibid., 278.

56. Ibid., 284–85.

57. Ibid., 282–83.

58. Ibid., 265–88.

59. José María Ormaetxea, *The Mondragon Cooperative Experience* (Mondragon, Spain: Mondragon Corporacion Cooperativa, 1993), 31–32. In the early years of published work, Ormaetxea used the Castilian spelling of his name (Ormaechea) but later shifted to the

Basque spelling. I have used the Basque spelling in deference to how his work is cited in Gabilondo's book.

60. Marianne Heiberg, *The Making of the Basque Nation* (New York: Cambridge University Press), 20–23.

61. Ibid., 26.

62. Ibid., 33.

63. Ibid., 185.

64. Luis Nuñez, *Clases Sociales en Euskadi* (San Sebastian, Spain: Ed. Txertoa, 1977), 124.

65. Ibid., 125.

66. Lucas Marín, unpublished paper, 1988; Henk Thomas and Chris Logan, *Mondragon: An Economic Analysis* (London: George Allen and Unwin, 1982). On the earlier periods of the Mondragon cooperatives, also see Alastair Campbell, et al., *Worker Ownership: The Mondragon Achievement* (London: Anglo-German Foundation for the Study of Society, 1977); Terry Mollner, *Mondragon: A Third Way* (Shutesbury, MA: Trustee Institute, 1984); A. Gutierrez-Johnson and William Foote Whyte, "The Mondragon System of Worker Production Cooperatives," *Industrial and Labor Relations Review* 31, no. 1 (1977): 18–30; A. Gutierrez-Johnson, "Compensation, Equity, and Industrial Democracy in the Mondragon Cooperatives," *Economic Analysis and Workers' Self-Management* 12 (1977): 267–89; Robert Oakeshott, "Mondragon: Spain's Oasis of Democracy," in *Self-Management: The Economic Liberation of Man*, ed. Jaroslav Vanek (Baltimore, MD: Penguin, 1975), 290–96; Germal Medanie, "Mondragon: Your Add Is About to Run Out," *Grassroots Economic Organizing Newsletter* 10 (September/October 1983).

67. No cooperative at Mondragon failed, at least through the end of the 1980s, once it had completed incubation. One conventional farm business facing shutdown because of financial problems applied to become a co-op at Mondragon during this period, and was incubated long enough to determine if it could be resurrected. When the godfathers determined that it could not become viable, it was allowed to shut down. Also during this period, a fishing business became a Mondragon cooperative, but was spun off, despite its financial viability, because it refused to follow cooperative principles and rules.

68. Gabilondo, ed., *La Experiencia Cooperative de Mondragon*, 214–15.

69. Ibid., 217.

70. Ibid., 217–18.

71. Ulgor Sociedad Cooperativa Industrial, *Estatutos Sociales* (Mondragon, Spain: Author, 1975), 5.

72. Mondragon Cooperative Corporation, http://www.mondragon-corporation.com.

73. Sam Pizzigati, ed., "Too Much: A Commentary on Excess and Inequality," Institute for Policy Studies, https://toomuchonline.org/.

74. Christina A. Clamp, "Managing Cooperation at Mondragon" (PhD diss., Boston College Sociology Department, 1986), 157.

75. Mondragon Cooperative Corporation.

76. Material for this discussion of the recession is based on interviews with leaders in the Mondragon cooperatives in June and July of 2015.

77. Gabilondo, ed., *La Experiencia Cooperative de Mondragon*, 219.

78. Information on the intercooperative agreement and the social insurance program is based on a presentation by the Lagun Aro staff in Mondragon on May 19, 2011.

79. Maite Martínez-Granado, Patxi Greño, and Mercedes Oleaga, "The Basque Country, Spain: Self-Evaluation Report," OECD Reviews of Higher Education in Regional and City Development, 2012.

80. The structure of incentives is briefly discussed in chap. 5. For a more detailed consideration, see Paul Bernstein, *Workplace Democratization: Its Internal Dynamics* (New Brunswick, NJ: Transaction, 1980), especially chap. 5; Alen S. Blinder, ed., *Paying for Productivity: A Look at the Evidence* (Washington, DC: Brookings Institution, 1990); Edward E. Lawler III, Susan Albers Mohrman, and Gerald E. Ledford Jr., *Employee Involvement and Total Quality Management: Practices and Results in Fortune 1000 Companies* (San Francisco: Jossey-Bass, 1992).

81. "Producer Cooperatives," Grassroots Economic Organizing, http://www.geo.coop/taxonomy/term/139; "Types of Cooperatives," Nebraska Cooperative Development Center, http://ncdc.unl.edu/typescooperatives.shtml; Producer Cooperative Association, http://producerscooperative.com.

82. Tom Ladendorf, "Worker Co-ops? There's an App for That," *In These Times*, April 2016.

83. Union Cab Coop: A Worker Cooperative, http://unioncab.com.

84. Sarah Anderson, John Cavanaugh, and David Ranney, *NAFTA's First Two Years: The Myths and Realities* (Washington, DC: Institute for Policy Studies, 1996); Timothy A. Wise and Kevin P. Gallagher, "NAFTA: A Cautionary Tale," *Foreign Policy in Focus*, October 24, 2002.

85. Wise and Gallagher, "NAFTA: A Cautionary Tale," 40–41; Ginger Thompson, "NAFTA To Open Floodgates, Engulfing Rural Mexico," *New York Times*, December 19, 2002.

86. Hartmann, *The Crash of 2016*, 82–91. Except where otherwise indicated, the sources and references for information discussed below concerning the shift in US trade policy and its results are from Hartmann.

87. Louis D. Johnston, "History Lessons: Understanding the Decline in Manufacturing," *MinnPost*, February 2, 2012, http://www.minnpost.com/macro-micro-minnesota/2012/02/history-lessons-understanding-decline-manufacturing#sourcenote. This piece, while making a very important point about long-term trends in shifts from manufacturing to service in the US economy, is a good example of the reductionism of neoliberal economics, particularly in regard to free trade. It focuses almost entirely on one pair of factors (increasing productivity and rising demand for services) while briefly mentioning another (rising competition from China and Japan). It fails to mention the slowness of much of American manufacturing to meet foreign competition (particularly in automobiles) and to shift sufficiently and quickly enough to meet it in terms of improving quality, productivity, and meeting consumer wants. Most important, it says nothing of the major factor discussed below, the impact of neoliberal free trade policies. Indeed, with no examination of them, the article simply dismisses trade policy as not relevant: "New ideas for reviving American manufacturing seem to appear every day. Many of these notions have merit, but most are built on a flawed premise: that the decline in U.S. factory jobs is a recent occurrence, one that can be reversed through tax cuts or trade policy."

88. "On the Government Role in Guiding Business Development in Asian Economies," in *Economic Development in East Asia* (Washington, DC: Saylor Foundation, 2013); James Fallows, *Looking at the Sun: The Rise of a New East Asian Economic and Political System* (New York: Vintage, 1995). Concerning barriers to imports by Asian governments (while promoting exports), "3. Barriers to Trade," China.org.cn, Foreign Market Access Report, Japan, 2006, http://www.china.org.cn/english/features/fmar/168390.htm, which lists a variety of Japanese barriers to imports reported by Chinese companies. Also see Glen S. Fukushima, "Removing Japan's Barriers to Trade and Investment," East Asia Forum, November 17, 2012, http://www.eastasiaforum.org/2012/11/17/removing-japans-barriers-to-trade-and-investment/; Jae Wan Chung,

The Political Economy of International Trade: U.S. Trade Laws, Policy, and Social Cost (Lanham: Lexington Books, 2006).

89. "GATT and the Goods Council," World Trade Organization, https://www.wto.org/english/tratop_e/gatt_e/gatt_e.htm.

90. Hartmann, *The Crash of 2016*, 77–87. Note that the neoliberal economics begun by Reagan in the United States, but accelerated by Clinton, also brought about reductions in investment in human capital, including cuts in support for education and training and reductions in the safety net, along with moves to privatize as much of government as possible (22, 43, 51).

91. Sarah Anderson, John Cavanaugh, and David Ranney, *NAFTA's First Two Years* (Washington, DC: Institute for Policy Studies, 1996), 1; Elliot Spagat, "Power Sites in Mexico Under Fire: Critics' Suit Claims Plants at Border That Sell Power to West Coast Avert U.S. Controls," *Indianapolis Star,* June 15, 2003, D1.

92. Anderson, Cavanaugh, and Ranney, *NAFTA's First Two Years.*

93. For an analysis of the transition to the market programs in East Europe, see Rusmich and Sachs, *Lessons from the Failure*, pt. 3, particularly chap. 11. The first part of the book illuminates the economic problems under communism that negatively affected the economic condition of the Soviet bloc nations. Part 3 discusses how the neoliberal economic approach taken in those countries after the end of communism worsened their economic situations.

94. Rusmich and Sachs, *Lessons from the Failure*, 264 n. 42.

95. Ibid., 300–301; John B. Judis, "World Bunk: Japanese Officials Think Western Austerity Measures Are the Wrong Medicine for Eastern Europe," *In These Times*, December 13, 1993, 14–15.

96. See Stephen M. Sachs, "We Need International Pressure on Climate Change," *Indigenous Policy* 25, no. 3 (2015), which argues that higher tariffs and/or other penalties ought to be assessed against nations that refuse to do their share in lowering emissions that cause global warming in the pursuit of economic development as an incentive to undertake development responsibly (i.e., sufficiently penalizing them to remove the economic incentive to pollute destructively).

97. Americas Program, http://www.americaspolicy.org/citizen-action/voices/2004/0402coffee.html (unfortunately this webpage no longer works).

98. The problem of large projects that are destructive to people and the environment are discussed in the "Environmental Activities,"

"International Activities," "Environmental Developments," and "International Developments" sections of every issue of *Indigenous Policy*, at least since 2008, at www.indigenouspolicy.org. The problems of extractions impacting Indigenous Peoples have been discussed at every annual session of the United Nations Forum on Indigenous Issues, with reports of the meetings and access to forum reports, including on extraction, available at https://www.un.org/development/desa/indigenouspeoples/.

99. China has been suffering from a variety of serious environmental problems as a result of undertaking a series of very large projects (including a number of dams) and from engaging in a rapid industrialization program involving building and utilizing a large number of coal power plants. Among the many reports on the resulting problems are: Edward Wong, "Cost of Environmental Damage in China Growing Rapidly Amid Industrialization," *New York Times*, March 29, 2013, http://www.nytimes.com/2013/03/30/world/asia/cost-of-environmental-degradation-in-china-is-growing.html; Beina Xu, "China's Environmental Crisis," Council on Foreign Relations, April 25, 2014, http://www.cfr.org/china/chinas-environmental-crisis/p12608; V. Smil, *Environmental Degradation in China* (Armonk, NY: Zed, 1984); Mara Hvistendahl, "China's Three Gorges Dam: An Environmental Catastrophe? Even the Chinese Government Suspects the Massive Dam May Cause Significant Environmental Damage," *Scientific American*, March 25, 2008, http://www.scientificamerican.com/article/chinas-three-gorges-dam-disaster/. It should be noted that in more recent years, China has become increasingly concerned about the environmental degradation that its policies have been causing, and has slowly been taking steps to enact and enforce environmental regulation ("Environmental Developments," *Nonviolent Change* 30, no. 2 [2015]).

100. See Chris Strohm, "Deaf Ears: No Thanks, World Bank Says to Critical Study," *In These Times*, June 24, 2002, 5–6. The countries studied included Bangladesh, Ecuador, Hungary, Mexico, and Ghana. Also worth looking at is the UN Conference on Trade and Development, *Trade and Development Report 2003* (New York: United Nations, 2003), which in October found unequivocally that neoliberal economic policies of globalization, leaving development to the market (with minimal government services and regulation) for two decades has left sub-Saharan Africa an economic wasteland, while declining shares of manufacturing output and employment ("deindustrialization") have

accompanied rapid liberalization in many Latin American nations. Under neoliberal economic policies, "enclaves" of industrialization linked to international production chains have dotted this landscape. In most cases this has not translated into more broad-based investment, value added, or productivity growth. The study reports an urgent need for global economic institutions and governments to rethink policies and to return to carefully designed, vigorous government intervention in order to provide necessary economic stimulus and guidance, and to create and preserve an appropriate climate for development. The report concludes that the policies pursued to eliminate inflation and downsize the public sector have often undermined growth and hampered technological progress. As a result, "the current economic landscape in the developing world has an uncanny resemblance to conditions prevailing in the early 1980s," when many countries slipped into deep crisis. The target level of investment for catch-up growth— estimated by the report to be in the range of 20–25 percent of GDP— has eluded most countries undergoing rapid market reforms. By contrast, active state participation in the economy in East Asia after the debt crisis produced a strong investment performance, growing manufacturing value added, and a rising share of manufacturing exports and employment, while productivity and technology gaps with leading industrial countries rapidly closed. Elsewhere, the report finds a less encouraging record, with industrial progress halted in much of the developing world as only 8 of 26 selected countries succeeded in raising the share of manufacturing value added in GDP between 1980 and the 1990s while enjoying a rising share of investment. In economies with lagging industrialization and a declining share of investment, the share of manufactures in total exports has also been stagnant or falling, while exchange rate depreciation and wage restraint have been the basis for bolstering trade performance. The production structure in much of Latin America and Africa has seen a notable shift away from sectors with the greatest potential for productivity growth towards those producing and processing raw materials. Where trade and investment have risen in the context of international production networks, the tendency has been toward an apparent increase in the technology content of exports without a similar increase in domestic value added. Similarly, a study released in January 2004 found that, when taken as a group, all of the less-developed countries that depend on exporting oil have seen living standards drop—and drop dramatically, "World Developments," *Nonviolent Change* 28, no. 2 (2004).

101. Deirdre Fulton, "Global Inequality Reaches Levels Not Seen in Nearly 200 Years: Growing Wealth Gap 'One of the Most Significant—and Worrying—Features of the Development of the World Economy' since Early 19th Century, OECD Says," *CommonDreams*, October 2, 2014, http://www.commondreams.org/news/2014/10/02/global-inequality-reaches-levels-not-seen-nearly-200-years.

102. There are numerous cases where this aggressive nationalism has involved internal imperialism and conflict. For example, China has been carrying out an internal imperialism against non-Han Chinese groups, exemplified by its Tibetan and Uighurs policies, which have led to demonstrations by the ethnic population and then Chinese government repression which moves into ongoing conflict. Overviews of China-Tibetan relations can be found at: "Tibet Profile: A Chronology of Key Events," BBC News, November 13, 2014, http://www.bbc.com/news/world-asia-pacific-17046222; "Chronology of Tibetan-Chinese Relations, 1979 to 2013," International Campaign for Tibet, 2015, http://www.savetibet.org/policy-center/chronology-of-tibetan-chinese-relations-1979-to-2013/. An example of the conflict with the Uighurs in the Chinese province of Xinjiang is Michael Forsyth, "Suicide Bomber Kills Up to 8 in Xinjiang, Radio Free Asia Reports," *New York Times*, February 17, 2015, http://www.nytimes.com/2015/02/18/world/asia/suicide-bomber-kills-up-to-8-in-xinjiang-radio-free-asia-reports.html?ref=todayspaper. The government of Myanmar is currently involved in similar conflict with a number of ethnic groups. For example, it was reported that fighting erupted between the Army of Myanmar and an ethnic Kokang force, the Myanmar National Democratic Alliance Army, on February 9, 2015, near the Chinese border. By February 17 fighting had left at least 47 government troops and 26 Kokang soldiers dead, as the president of Myanmar declared a three-month period of martial law in the area (Reuters, "Myanmar: Martial Law Imposed in Area Near China," *New York Times*, February 17, 2015, http://www.nytimes.com/2015/02/18/world/asia/myanmar-martial-law-imposed-in-area-near-china.html?ref=todayspaper). And there are other examples.

103. Stephen M. Sachs, "Circling the Circles: Indigenous Movements Towards An Alternative, Appropriate Globalization," *Indigenous Policy* 15, no. 2 (2004). One of these organizations is Advancement of Global Indigeneity (AGI), founded by Americans for Indian

Opportunity (AIO) and Advancement of Maori Opportunity (AMO), http://aio.org/projects/redistribution-2/; Harris, Sachs, and Morris, *Re-Creating the Circle*, chap. 6, sec. 1.

104. Much of the less-developed world has been rushing to develop, causing huge pollution problems for people and the environment at home, and beyond, including increasing global warming and climate change. To a significant extent, these nations have refused to heed calls from the West to cut back on fossil fuels, especially coal, which has been fueling their development. A number of analysts are calling for a different approach to curbing global warming, while allowing for development in poorer nations and regions. They call for international investment in solar panels and nuclear energy, with increased safety in developing nations, asserting that poorer countries will not stop development and cease using coal and natural gas unless they are given a viable alternative. The proponents argue that carbon-free methods do not require much land, much of which is needed for food production, and that with international investment solar and nuclear power present a viable alternative to increasing carbon-fueled power production. For a discussion of these environmental proposals, see Eduardo Porter, "A Call to Look Past Sustainable Development," *New York Times*, April 14, 2015, http://www.nytimes.com/2015/04/15/business/an-environmental-ist-call-to-look-past-sustainable-development.html?ref=todayspaper, which reported:

The average citizen of Nepal consumes about 100 kilowatt-hours of electricity in a year. Cambodians make do with 160. Bangladeshis are better off, consuming, on average, 260.

Then there is the fridge in your kitchen. A typical 20-cubic-foot refrigerator—Energy Star–certified, to fit our environmentally conscious times—runs through 300 to 600 kilowatt-hours a year.

American diplomats are upset that dozens of countries—including Nepal, Cambodia and Bangladesh—have flocked to join China's new infrastructure investment bank, a potential rival to the World Bank and other financial institutions backed by the United States.

The primary reason for this is the West's development-limiting environmental policies. While the authors of this book do not favor expansion of nuclear power (because of its extreme dangers), we find assisting development through clean energy and low-power technology an important policy approach.

INDEX TO VOLUME III

W

Wake County, North Carolina 88
wealth, distribution of 39,
115, 132, 189, 243, 247
Welch, James 14
Wendot 67, 72, 122
Western Social Science
Association Meeting 52
White House 99, 159
WIC program (Women, Infants and
Children); WIC program (Women,
Infants and Children 208
Wiley, Rennie 7, 40
Williams, Roger 27

Working Group on American
Indian and Alaska Natives 99
World Bank 240, 242, 264
World Trade Organization
(WTO); World Trade
Organization (WTO 234, 237

Y

yoga 11, 35, 55
Yugoslavia 72, 86, 152, 184

Z

Zapatista revolution 232

www.ingramcontent.com/pod-product-compliance
Lightning Source LLC
Chambersburg PA
CBHW031426270326
41930CB00007B/588